WHEN THE THIN BLUE LINE BEGINS TO BLUR

Memoirs of an Atlanta Police Commander's struggle to maintain accountability within the APD

KHALFANI B. YABUKU

Published by Khalfani B. Yabuku

Editor: Afiya A. Yabuku Editorial Services

Cover design/illustration by: Bakari K. Yabuku Designs

ISBN: 13: 978-0692406052

CONTENTS

DEDICATION

This book is dedicated to those men and women in blue who honestly and sincerely strive to uphold the honorable nature and noble calling of law enforcement. Those officers who provide the highest quality of service to the communities they serve; but whose hands are often tied by the systemic mentality of "us against them." A mentality furthered by quota systems, unethical practices, or institutionalized unconstitutional policies.

I also dedicate this book to every modern day "Frank Serpico" who exists in every Law Enforcement Agency across this great nation; those officers who dare to challenge the status quo and stand firm in their conviction to hold the Thin Blue Line accountable. Fortunately, their numbers increase daily.

I also dedicate this book to my Mother, Ruth Yabuku and to the memory of my dear father, Mamadou Yabuku (rest in peace), who are both my true heroes. I credit them for instilling in me an equal portion of fairness, compassion and courageousness in everything I do.

Finally and most importantly my beloved children, Tynisha, Ronnell, Tanyka (may she rest in peace), Khalfani-II, Afiya, Italia, Bakari and Trinity inspire me to always strive to act in an honorable and moral fashion in all aspects of life

ACKNOWLEDGEMENTS

I would like to acknowledge Mr. Randall Morrow and Mr. Freddie Miller for their dedicated support and advocacy. This book would not exist today were it not for their relentless insistence, over a two year period, that this story was one which needed to be told.

FOREWORD

In police work, the lines between right and wrong are often blurred. In his memoir, Khalfani Yabuku found this particular struggle to be true. It cost him his career to do what was right. Police work is one of the most demanding jobs on this planet. You must work in situations that are deplorable at times. You primarily police the high crime areas because that is where the work is. There is no real need to do heavy street enforcement in the affluent areas. So we police the poor, as if we were an occupying army. We spend most of our time there with the drug dealers, pimps, prostitutes, hustlers, armed robbers, murderers, drug addicts and the socioeconomically disenfranchised. I know because I spent thirty years in police work. I have known the author longer than that. I clearly understand and have personally witnessed his struggle to do the right thing. As you will see in the first few pages of this man's career, reality hit him right between the eyes. No police academy can prepare you for working the streets; especially if you have to police other police officers. This is a dirty secret that crawls along the gutters of police work. As Khalfani found out, once you cross over and say something to a police officer who is engaged in unethical or criminal behavior, you will find yourself standing alone. You will become ostracized. People begin to wonder and look at you in a different light. Does he for work Internal Affairs, or is he just a plant trying to see what we are doing? Once you take this step to oversee the dirty deeds in police work, you are never looked at the same.

I too have been at this point in my long career, and it can be rough. Back then, I had to deal with racist police officers who clearly did not like me from the jump. In some kind of weird way, they really don't see you at all. They will use racist comments towards citizens just to see if they can get a rise out of you. They will forget that you are sitting there and use racist comments and then look at you with amazement and shock, replying "I didn't really mean that." But with all this craziness, you soldier on; trying to convince yourself this stuff won't last forever. I will become the best police officer I can be and improve the way people are policed in my community. As you will see in the pages ahead, officers like Khalfani will have more problems with their co-workers than the people they come into contact with on the street. As time passes, you get promoted. Now you feel "I can make a difference as a sergeant." You try, and are shot down by the so-called chain of command. You clearly are trying to do some good, but if your reports don't reflect what command wants and likes, it will be coming back to you for corrective action. I hate to say it, but this situation is next to impossible to change. Fortunately, there is a small core of officers out there who are motivated by the aspect of impossibility, and face head on the challenge of holding themselves and their peers to a higher standard of accountability. As you read this book, please try and look at what the author is conveying to you. He is going to take you on patrol. He is going to take you to the dark places and bring you back into the light. He will introduce you to his partners, and at times, I think you will be able to feel the radio crackle to life as he takes you on patrol in one of the biggest cities in America. You will get a firsthand look at what a police career entails. There will be good times and bad; but he never leaves you hanging out there. I applaud Khalfani for coming forward and giving an honest portrayal of his experience as a police commander.

This is a memoir worth reading. So, roll call is over now... get your gear and prepare for the street. Because this may be your first call: “14-10 Grand River and Ohio... man with a gun... shots fired... one down!”

James R. Barren, PhD

Chief of Police, retired

Detroit Police Department, Detroit, Michigan USA

INTRODUCTION

As I sat down to write this book, I did so with the notion that I had an inherent responsibility to give voice to the many law enforcement officers that put at risk their careers and very lives to bring accountability to what has become known as the, "Thin Blue Line." In today's society, as a result of situations such as those facing Ferguson, Missouri; Sanford, Florida; Cleveland, Ohio; and New York City (to name a few), there is a continuously widening gap between law enforcement agencies and the communities they are sworn to serve. General information sources and variant modes of media tend to serve only to widen the chasm between the police and the community. There is a long held belief on the part of the average American citizen of color that there are only 2 categories of cops in this country: (1) the minority, which are basically criminals with badges, and (2) the vast majority, which are honorable men and women of valor, but are just as responsible for the misdeeds of the bad cops because they tend not to hold the unethical cops accountable.

Unfortunately, I found in my career that this perception of the components of law enforcement has a tremendous amount of merit. Most officers are, in fact, content with simply not participating in unethical behavior. For many, it's enough just having a clear conscience that they go to work every day to honestly and sincerely help and serve the citizens of their communities. They tend to look the other way when faced with the unethical or corrupt behavior of their coworkers. They tend to adopt the attitude of going along, just to get along. This attitude is not completely without justification. What officer wants to be in a life or death situation, and help is slow to arrive because he or she made the mistake of becoming labeled a "snitch?" Or, what hard working officer enjoys being passed over for promotions or ideal assignments because he or she earned the reputation of not being a "team" player? As you will find in this book, even the threat of life or limb is very real in law enforcement agencies across the nation.

The purpose of this book is to shed light on and give voice to a third type of officer who exists on each and every police department in this country. I truly believe that each and every honest and conscientious Peace Officer is a true hero in every sense of the word. However, I hold a special place of honor for the unknown and unsung superheroes of law enforcement. Those who make it their responsibility, and forsake everything to take on the extra burden of policing the police. Those who dare to hold the Thin Blue Line accountable when it begins to blur.

I hope to accomplish three basic things with this penning. First, I hope to motivate and influence the average rank and file officer to be steadfast in demanding the highest level of integrity for themselves as well as those who work alongside them. In this regard we are all very much our brother's keeper.

Second, I present examples of my own experiences revealing how agency commanding officers and executive staff can better engage their employees to improve working conditions for their officers while promoting improved community relations.

Last, and most importantly, I hope to convey to the average citizen that in spite of the images of an impending "police state," widespread corruption, racism, and other issues that serve only to widen the distance of distrust and disrespect between the police and the public; there is indeed a faction of officers on every department who stand against the status quo and dare to cross or even break the Thin Blue Line when it begins to blur.

My ultimate desire is to restore the faith of the general public in the idea that this faction of officers is growing exponentially daily. In time, it will become commonplace for departments across the nation to put aside their political agendas and their focus on revenues generation, and get back to the founding ideas of Law Enforcement – To Serve and Protect!!!

While I cannot claim 100% accuracy regarding conversations I've had spanning 28 years of service, my intentions are to be as accurate as possible. I have tried not to distort the truth. There has been no effort on my part to give the impression that my approach to law enforcement was without fault or error. There are a lot of things I would do differently if I had the opportunity to relive certain situations. However, I have absolutely no regrets for approaching every situation with the sincere intention of offering the best possible service to the community I took an oath to protect, and to the brave men and women who I had the responsibility and honor to lead.

Here is my story, and I hope readers will benefit from it.

CHAPTER – 1

ESPRIT DE CORPS

"Why are you still sitting here? Did you not hear the radio, rook???" All I could muster up was a confused look of bewilderment. The Evening Watch (3:00 p.m. – 11:00 p.m. shift) sergeant is clearly addressing me. But for the life of me, I couldn't figure out why. "Yes sir, I did." I managed to spit out. I'd heard the police radio, I saw all the officers in the precinct scrambling to gear up and rush to their vehicles, and I definitely heard the radio dispatcher advise there was a signal 63 (officer needs help) at the business located at Lucky and Spring Street. However, I couldn't figure out what all this had to do with me. I was reporting for my first day of work at the Zone 5 precinct as a newly sworn officer assigned to Morning Watch (11:00 p.m. – 7:00 a.m. shift). I was reporting for my shift an hour early. I had no assigned vehicle, no assigned partner, I had not even met my Morning Watch supervisors yet, and this was clearly an Evening Watch issue unfolding before me. As exciting as this all this was, it was clearly an Evening Watch issue, and I was reporting for my first day of Morning Watch. I remember the next words I uttered, only because the sergeants response to them are indelibly etched in my mind. "I'm reporting for Morning Watch, sarge." I guess my point was to bring to the attention of this supervisor who clearly had at least a couple decades on the job under his belt, that I'm not one of the officers he's been supervising five days a week for probably the last 5 to 15 years. As if there was some sort of mistaken identity on his part or something. "Stand up, rook! Look at that patch on your sleeve" he said. I carefully examined my shoulder patch bearing the city seal depicting a Phoenix emerging from the ashes of the civil war and the dates 1847 & 1865, marking the city's first charter and the beginning of its reconstruction, respectively. Being fresh out of the academy, at this point I'm amazed that I would still be answering pop quizzes about the city's history. That assumption was short lived as his next words stuck with me throughout my entire career with the Atlanta Police Department (APD). "Where on that patch does it say Morning Watch???!!!" the sergeant quipped. This was pre-Thin Blue Line days, but after having spent 3 years of active duty in the US Army/Military Police, I was crystal clear on the sergeant's message. The philosophy of "esprit de corps" was one that I was not only familiar with, but also happy to be a part of in my new civilian vocation with the APD. "Come on! You're riding with me, rook." I jumped in the patrol car with the sergeant and we sped off. Literally 5 minutes on my first assignment and I'm headed headlong into the most serious call an officer will ever face in his or her career. The second most serious call is a signal 59RA (additional units needed right away). This signal is given by an officer or dispatcher when an officer needs immediate assistance with a situation in order to prevent it from escalating into a signal 63 (officer needs help). Signal 63 is issued by an officer or dispatch when an officer is literally fighting for his or her life and facing imminent serious bodily harm or death. For instance, if an officer's last radio transmission was that he or she was about to engage in physical combat or a gunfight with a suspect and dispatch was unable to contact the officer within a reasonable amount of time, the dispatcher would announce a signal 63 citywide. Any officer within reasonable distance will respond to the location until the officer is located and confirmed safe or otherwise. At any rate, the signal 63 can only be cancelled by a supervisor actually on the scene of the incident. The location was a mere few blocks from the precinct, so it took no time at all to arrive on the scene. Once there, the sergeant confirmed that the officer was alright; aside from facial, arm, and leg abrasions, a ripped and tattered uniform, and an obviously bruised ego. The officer had clearly been in a fight for his life. He later related the offender's attempts to disarm him of his service revolver. All in all, the officer did a heck of a job just holding on and staying alive in that situation. Even though he was war torn, I felt proud of and for him. Especially after seeing the size and physique of the suspect who was now sitting handcuffed in the back seat of one of the responding patrol cars awaiting the arrival of the paddy wagon. After checking on the injured officer, the sergeant and I proceeded to the patrol car to examine the suspect. He was a little sweaty, but otherwise, he was in pristine physical condition. I mean, not a scratch on him. The sergeant's next actions would set precedent for the type of misconduct and unethical behavior I would spend the following 28 years fighting against. "Who were the first 3 officers to arrive on the scene?" the sergeant bellowed. The first three officers to arrive on the scene scurried to the sergeant with a look of fear and anticipation. "I'm going to ride around the block for about 4 or 5 minutes. When I get back, this god---n perp (perpetrator) had better look worse than my god---n officer." We drove off to cruise the immediate neighborhood of several blocks with very little spoken between us. After 5 minutes of driving around the downtown area we arrived back at the scene. The perp was no longer unscathed and very much met with the sergeant's approval. He admonished and lectured the 3 officers on the whole "band of brothers" and "us against them" ideology for several minutes. He cautioned them to never repeat the mistake of letting him arrive on a scene again and the perp looks better than his officer. The officers acknowledged they understood, and we headed back to the precinct. I made it back just in time for Morning Watch roll call, thus beginning my first day as a NOT SO PROUD

Atlanta Police Officer. It was clear that this was going to be more of an "infiltration" than it was to be an occupation.

This was the second indication of what I would be facing since I started employment with the APD. The first glimpse into my future happened while I was still in the police academy.

Halfway into my training in 1984, there was a news article that made front page of the Atlanta Journal and Constitution newspaper. I didn't need to read the article. The implications were clear based on a front page layout consisting of a photo array of 12 or more APD officers recently arrested or indicted for a myriad of serious and petty crimes.

This was a clear indication that there would be as much work to do inside of the precinct as there was to do on the streets. Two things were clear in my mind from this very day. First, I was definitely going to make a career of this job. Not only was policing the only thing I ever wanted to do since childhood, but it was glaringly evident to me in that moment that even if I had to stand alone and by myself for 30 years, I was determined to give the citizens of Atlanta at least one cop that was truly serving and protecting them from all threats. Even if that threat happened to wear the same shoulder patch as I did. Second, only at the level of chief of this organization would I be able to affect the degree of change needed to eradicate the systemic mentality, conduct, and practice of "us against them." I reaffirmed the commitment I'd made to myself and God when I accepted the job. I committed that I would not fall into the vices and traps of arrogance, egoism, superiority, and plain ole' bully-ism which I observed in most cops growing up in Detroit and in the Military Police Corps. In fact, my military career (which I will explore in an upcoming book) wasn't very much dissimilar to the test I knew I would face with APD. So for me, it was basically business as usual. Different uniform, same struggle!!!

CHAPTER - 2

ENOUGH IS ENOUGH

It wasn't a typical spring night on the Morning Watch. Instead of the steady ripping and running from one call to the next, there was nothing necessarily remarkable about this particular night. Unusually slow radio traffic didn't offer anything more exciting than the occasional signal 29 (fight call) at one of the local night spots in the Bluff area. The Bluff, on its outskirts, included the Herndon Homes housing projects and Willies Tavern. Officers took turns pulling out of service on a signal 27 (meal break) at a hotel downtown or an 11G (maintenance shop or gas pumps) to refuel their vehicles while they had a chance. Everyone knew that at any given moment, all heck could break loose for the remainder of the shift. In that regard, this particular night did not disappoint. Out of the dead silence of the 3:00 a.m. lull came the heart stopping sound of the radio keying up to the blaring sound of a police siren. Attempting to communicate over the piercing sound of the siren, one of the only 2 female officers on the road that night could be heard. Her voice was 2 octaves higher than her usual pitch... "Radio!!! I have one refusing to stop." She gives out the description of the fleeing vehicle and her best approximation of how many occupants were in the evasive Firebird. She advised dispatch radio that she had a visual on the car, but was having trouble keeping up with it. Dispatch advised all units in the area to start (proceed) for her location as the officer continued to call out street names as they whizzed by at ungodly speeds. Fortunately, it was a slow night with very little vehicular or pedestrian traffic on the roads. Fortunately for me, she was darn good at keeping herself composed and advising with pinpoint accuracy, every twist and turn the suspect took through the streets of SW Atlanta. Had she not done such a good job of transmitting her ever changing location, I'd have been totally lost. I had not the slightest idea where all this was unfolding before me on my police radio. I knew that I was glad I paid attention during the road map reading class while in the academy. Since I was new to the city, I was assigned the paddy wagon and given a map book of the city. This would allow me time to learn the geography of the Zone (precinct) as I spent my first few months developing as a rookie police officer. In most cases, the wagon wasn't needed until several minutes after the officer arrived on a scene. The responding officer had to arrive, assess the situation, take whatever action was required, and then reassess if they even needed the support of a paddy wagon. Since it was my first week on the job and the beginning my 6 months probation period, I felt that I had better be at the location when the chase ended. I came onto the department at a time when the vast majority of new officers were transplants from other cities and states. I was no different. Coming from Detroit, I had never visited Atlanta in my entire life. That's NOT so typical, considering the fact that both of my parents are from the Atlanta area. They're both originally from the Henry County area, south of the city.

My mom's family migrated slightly north to the city, while my dad's folks remained in the McDonough area. After marriage, and 4 children later, my father found it necessary to relocate his family to Michigan around 1948. They later settled in Detroit, where I was born some 10 years later. My father was always clear and made no excuses for the events that led to his premature sojourn to the north.

He related the story of working with the cement crew during the building of the Henry Thomas Homes housing projects. In those days, there was no sharing of the water facilities/sprockets between the races. My father, being my father, helped himself to the only functioning water sprocket when the one designated for him and other workers of color was found to be broken. After having worked himself into a state of near dehydration, my father bent down to refresh himself at the only working water tap on that sweltering summer afternoon. The White crew leader thought it wise to make an example of him and proceeded to kick my father in his hind parts as he bent over. Without even thinking, my father beat the foreman senseless. Several of the white crew members scrambled to rush the crew leader to Grady Memorial Hospital. Simultaneously, several of the black crew members rushed my father toward his home in McDonough. True to form, my grandmother was later paid a visit and advised that her 3rd youngest son, my father, was soon to be deceased. Within days, my father found himself rolling into the Motor City with his wife and children to seek work with the blossoming "Big 3" automobile plants. He would land a job and later retire from Chevrolet body plant.

When I announced in 1984 that I was relocating my family to Atlanta... Let's just say it wasn't the brightest moment in my father's life. He even opined that I should "go to Atlanta on a trial basis but leave my grandchildren in Detroit out of harm's way." He reminded me that it wasn't the force of that kick which made him take the action he took but rather, the indignity of another human being putting the bottom of his foot on him as though he was less than a man.

I knew it hadn't been an easy decision for my father to leave his home in McDonough, Georgia. He was by no means the type of man to back down from adversity. He was the most humble man you ever wanted to meet. My father would give his last dime to a stranger, but he feared no man. The subject of ghosts came up one day. I asked for his take on people fearing ghosts. He looked at me and simply stated, "Sonny boy, I don't consider myself a tough man. Nor do I consider myself better than any other man. However, I don't fear any living man walking this earth. Why would I fear any dead man?" It was always clear to me that my father's exodus to Detroit wasn't about fear for himself, but rather, the safety of his wife and 4 young children. Lessons I would take into manhood on issues of family values. Nevertheless, he seemed to have come around to accepting the reality of my situation as he beamed proudly from the audience during my graduation ceremony. After speaking with my instructors and classmates following the graduation, he appeared to exhibit a degree of relief as they all assured him I was in the capable hands of the Atlanta Police Department. Although he was happy for my accomplishment, he always made it clear to me that he would never consider living in the south again.

"Radio!!! I finally have him stopped in the Ms. Winners parking lot at North Ave & I-75!" the officer exclaimed. "Great," I thought. According to my map, I was only a few blocks away. I should be there within 3 or 4 minutes. "Unit 1501 to radio dispatch, I'm with her" exclaimed the first officer to arrive on the scene to assist the female officer. "1502, I'm also with her" reported the next officer. "1503, show me 26 (arrived on the scene) with her" stated a third unit. "1525, coming up 26 also" the senior patrol officer advised. "1591, I'm 26" the shift lieutenant announced. "You can code 4 (cancel) anymore units. We have enough. Go ahead and start the paddy wagon if he's not already en route" said the lieutenant. "Unit 1515 to radio. I'm en route. About 4 away" I advised. As I pulled into the parking lot of the

Ms. Winners fast food restaurant, feelings reminiscent of my first day on the job resurfaced. I was appalled at what I was witnessing in the darkness of the unlit and recessed area of the parking lot. After 8 years in the military, at that time, I was definitely no virgin to practices of "attitude adjustments." However, it was quite disappointing to see this mob of officers kicking and punching this lone driver for the offense of "running from the Po-leece." In my mind, my options were few. I could leave the scene and turn in my badge. Or, I could leave the scene and report them all to Internal Affairs. My other option was to remain on the scene, keep my mouth shut, and toe the Thin Blue Line as was expected of a rookie officer. None of these options appealed to me in that moment. Before I knew it I was out of my vehicle hustling toward the pile on. As I approached, I saw the senior patrol officer (SPO) remove his nightstick and draw back to take a swing at the pummeled suspect. I was able to catch the SPO mid swing and easily disarmed him of his baton. As I placed the nightstick back in its holster, I peered at him through what I'm sure he thought were crazy eyes and calmly stated... "I don't think you need that. I'm ready to transport the prisoner." The shift lieutenant, who had been standing there verbally encouraging the disgraceful action (contributing an occasional kick or two of his own), was now looking at me with the concern of a child caught with his hand in the cookie jar. "Ok, get him up and into the wagon so he can be transported" he stated to the seemingly disappointed posse. Clearly, some of them hadn't gotten in all the licks built up from the frustration of this unusually slow Morning watch.

Traffic was extra slow at the city jail intake. It took me the remainder of the shift to deposit the suspect in what would be his new home for at least the night. I arrived back at the precinct just in time for shift change. At that time, portable radios had to be returned to the radio room to be issued to the next shift coming on duty. As I turned in my radio I could hear the SPO, whose baton I holstered, speaking to the entire squad room filled with both Morning Watch and Day Watch officers. He stated in a highly irritated tone "these rookie officers have lost their god---n minds." "I don't know what they're turning out of the academy these days, but it's pretty d--n pathetic" he continued. I ignored his rant because what he didn't realize was that my actions were more about me than him. My actions that night served as some sort of recompense for the action I failed to take during the incident I witnessed on my first day with the Evening Watch sergeant. At the very least, I could have let the sergeant know that I disapproved of his actions. Instead, I just resolved within myself that I would never participate in such atrocities. Besides, who was I to arrive on this job with 5 minutes of experience and dictate how the job should be done? I had beaten myself up every day since that first day over my inaction. I was absolutely disgusted with myself. By the time the incident of this night unfolded before me, it occurred to me... who am I to NOT take a stand for what's right and just? I'm either my father's son, or I'm not!!!

As I was walking out the precinct door, the SPO was still taking shots at me with the precision of a well-trained sniper. Growing up in a gang infested environment in Detroit, I was familiar with the idea of "domain establishment." That wasn't anything new to me. It was, however, somewhat disappointing that I would have to start my new career being victimized by such a sophomoric and puerile display. Sometimes the only way to shut a bully down is to out-bully him. And along those lines, "enough is enough" I thought to myself. "SPO!" I yelled across the squad room. "If you have a problem with me or anything I've done, I would hope you would address me personally instead of posturing across the precinct. I gave you the courtesy of not going upside your head with your own nightstick, so I would hope you would give me the respect of a private conversation. If that's too much of a problem, I'm not opposed to handling things in the parking lot since we're both about to leave out anyway." "You see what I mean?" the FPO yelled across the squad room as he walked past me out the front door. "These rookies have no respect for seniority. I'll see ya'll tonight" he stated as he left the building. "I'll take that as an invitation declined" I thought to myself as I gave him a few minutes to clear the parking lot. After I was sure he was gone, I too left to go home to get a well-needed rest.

That incident left everyone thinking that I was either a "plant", or at the very least, I had the potential to be a "rat." If I was some sort of "plant," who was I working for or with? Internal Affairs? Maybe some outside agency such as GBI or FBI? Apparently no one wanted to roll the dice to find out because for the next 28 years, officers took extra precautions to avoid doing anything outside the lines of legality or ethics within my view. Of course there would be times when I would get word of things or times when I would happen upon things. When this would occur, the moment it was recognized that I was in the area, all illicit activities would cease and desist. I'm sure this was all intended to be a sort of ostracism or a message that I wasn't trusted. BINGO!! MISSION ACCOMPLISHED!!! What they failed to realize was that I became an officer to protect and serve the citizens of the city of Atlanta. I didn't take an oath to serve, protect and cover the immoral and illegal shenanigans of my fellow officers. The apprehension on the part of my co-workers as to my loyalty to the backroom antics, which were systemic to the department, was exactly what I wanted. I would enjoy a long, and somewhat prosperous career, nestled in that comfortable designation. My entire life, I was always the bashful loner type; so this was quite a comfortable and familiar existence for me anyway.

CHAPTER - 3

ESTABLISHING PARAMETERS

The next year or so on the job proved to be as exciting and rewarding as I could have hoped for. After a few short months, I was assigned a permanent beat car. The goal of most officers was to land a permanent assignment. Otherwise, you would be considered a "roustabout" and would work whatever beat was available on a daily basis. You would also fill in as the paddy wagon driver on the days the regular wagon driver was off. Having your own beat gave you a sense of responsibility. It also afforded you the opportunity to create crime reduction plans that you could personally see through to fruition. It was definitely the better of the two worlds; at least for me it was. It didn't bother me at all that my new beat would be the infamous "Bluff" which is popular in Atlanta artists' hip hop and rap music these days. This area also consisted of the dreaded Herndon Homes housing projects. Frankly, I was quite comfortable with the fact that this beat was not at all dissimilar to the areas in which I had grown up in Detroit. In fact, the Bluff was pretty tame in comparison. After all, this was just one square mile of impoverishment and its resulting crime. I had come from an environment where 3/4 of the entire city was impoverished and crime riddled.

I knew from my time in the Military Police that my first plan of action was to make a grandiose gesture to the community that I was the new beat officer. I would be fair but have no tolerance for violent crime on my beat such as shootings, stabbings, robberies and rapes. I also needed to establish that I would have a very low tolerance for property crimes such as burglaries, auto thefts, and other larceny types of crimes. I honestly cared less about victimless crimes such as drinking and gambling, but I would have to be adamant that this behavior was not to happen in my presence. Until I earned the respect of the community as a man, the uniform was to be respected in the mean time.

My opportunity to establish myself came in the form of a signal 29D (domestic fight). When I arrived at the location in Herndon Homes, the woman explained how her boyfriend had brutally beaten her and took her food stamps, among other personal property. She went on to explain how he struck her with open and closed fists about her face and head. She described how he kicked and stomped her once she was felled. Finally, she concluded that he ransacked the apartment in search of food stamps and other valuables. Consider the fact that neither she, nor the apartment, bore any indications of her allegations. Not so much as a scratch on her half dressed body or a chair out of place at the kitchen table. I inquired as to when this event took place. I was fully prepared to take a report and advise her on the domestic warrant process since this was clearly a very old incident. She looked my square in the eye and with a choked up whisper stated, “Officer, this happened 30 minutes ago.” I was dumbfounded! It didn’t help the situation that this woman had a very light complexion. In fact, I would later learn her nickname, as is common with light skinned people, was “Red.” She went on to bring to my attention that she had reason to believe her boyfriend was at the Superior Lounge. The Superior Lounge was a bar/club that occupied a corner lot adjacent to Herndon Homes. It pretty much sat at the north/east corner of Herndon Homes. Directly across the street on Western Avenue was Willies Tavern. While the Superior Lounge attracted the younger crowd, Willies catered to the more mature demographic. On certain summer nights there seemed to be a battle of the bands of sorts. You could drive through the intersection and here the hip-hop beats of the Superior Lounge competing with the Blues sounds emanating from Willies Tavern.

Once I entered the Superior Lounge (commonly referred to by its street address – 501 Western), there was absolutely no difficulty locating my suspect. His attire and physical makeup had been perfectly described by my victim. I approached the gentleman, advised that I had a complaint against him, and expressed that he needed to accompany me outside to address the issue. He was sitting at the table with a young lady and two other gentlemen. They were all enjoying bottled beer and were obviously having a pretty good time, at least, until I interrupted their party. My suspect stood up with his beer in hand as did the other 2 males at the table. Pretty much everyone in the club instantly began to lend voice to the fact that my suspect had been in the club buying rounds of beer for quite awhile. Therefore, whatever I was accusing him of couldn't have happened within the past few hours. I advised the suspect that it was personal in nature and I needed him to come outside to work it out. His tablemates suggested he shouldn't leave the lounge. They cautioned that once I got him in my squad car he was going to jail – guilty or not. I told the two guys they were just going to have to trust me. I voiced that I didn't know what type of officers they were accustomed to dealing with, but that wasn't the way I did business. As we walked toward the door, I ordered the suspect to toss his beer in the trash on the way out. I informed him that I would buy him another once we got things straightened out. His friends wanted to accompany him to my vehicle, but I advised them to remain in the lounge. Everything I did was calculated for dramatic effect. Remember, I was trying to make a statement and establish a relationship that would benefit me and the community during my tenure as the beat officer.

I could have requested additional units to assist me in the lounge, but that reeks of fear. I could have allowed him to table his drink, but that wouldn't have allowed me the opportunity to make the goodwill gesture of buying him another. I could have allowed his friends to accompany him to the car. It's not like I was planning to kidnap the suspect or anything. But I couldn't afford to allow them to dictate how I handled my business. The entire time, I was 95% certain that as long as he has no outstanding warrants, I was not going to make charges against this man based on the obvious fabrication of his girlfriend's outcry.

Once he was in my back seat, we relocated up the street to the car wash on Simpson Road and Northside Drive. This was done because there was no area for cover in the wide-open parking lot of the lounge. There was no way for me to protect against an ambush, should his friends have a change of heart and decide to become combative with firearms or other weapons. After we parked at the carwash, I explained what the complaint against him was. I asked the suspect what was really going on with him and his girlfriend and what had he done to piss her off. He explained they broke up months ago. Since then she had filed many false reports on him, which he was always locked up for. Cops always took her side of the story; that was why his friends were so adamant about him not going with me. He went on to relate that on this particular night, he was enjoying himself with his "boys" and his new lady. At some point, a female friend of the ex-girlfriend (the caller) came into the lounge and immediately exited when she spotted him there with another woman. He said he was somewhat relieved to see me approach him, as he fully expected his ex to "show up and show out." I assured him that I was satisfied her claims were unsubstantiated and straight out lies. I told him I was going to run a wanted check on him for outstanding warrants. As long as it came back clear, I would return him to his awaiting companions. Radio dispatch advised that the suspect had no outstanding warrants. We subsequently headed back to 501 Western. Once there, I escorted him back into the lounge and advised the owner, Ms. Miller, who was bartending that particular night, that I would pay for any beer of his choice. After receiving the beer, I walked him back to his table where I was met with a look of bewilderment from the other skeptical occupants. I shook his hand, thanked him for his cooperation, and apologized for any inconvenience or embarrassment. His friends followed me out to my car and asked if they could have a moment of my time. One of the men stated he had never seen a "n----r" in that neighborhood go into the back seat of a police car and come back out. They said when they saw me drive out the parking lot with him, they were sure he was headed to jail – as usual. I assured them I had no idea what a "n----r" was. I asserted that I had never seen one in my entire life, and wouldn't know one if I tripped over them. They inquired as to the pronunciation of my last name, which was affixed to my uniform by way of my nameplate. After a brief lesson in the proper pronunciation, they further asked what my initials K.B. stood for. I obliged. They shook my hand for a second time and gave what can only be described as a look and a nod of approval. When I returned to work after my off days, I was met with greetings of "Wassup, officer Khalfani?" or "What's going on, officer Yabuku?"

The officers who occupied the two adjoining beats were stand up guys. Beat 1502 was covered by officer Wayne Williams, and 1503 was manned by officer Miguel Hall. These were two of the hardest working officers I had known in my short period on the department. More importantly, they were "clean" and conscientious officers who took pride in doing the job the right way. These two were, in fact, my immediate lifelines in any volatile situation I would incur. I would hope to never need them under such circumstances, but I was glad they would be my first responders if anything ever did go sideways. It never did. I like to think that was the case because we had an understanding and firm belief that if an officer interacted with his/her community with the same degree of respect and compassion that one would want their own mother to receive, 90% of citizen encounters could be resolved peacefully. That's not accounting for the occasional drunk, drug addict, mentally disturbed, or flat out bada--. Once people understood that we weren't there to "occupy" their community, but rather to assist them in cleaning up the community, the partnership evolved quite naturally and beautifully. The relationship grew to the point that folks would welcome me back from my off days, literally, with handshakes and hugs. They would invite me into their living rooms or engage me in the front yard with exploits of events that occurred during my two-day absence. Information they refused to share with the roustabouts about certain crimes filled my ears at a pace that required me to always have pen and pad available in my breast pocket. Let me be perfectly clear... this was still a time when "snitches got stitches," but it was also a time when there was such a level of civic and communal pride that certain officers, citywide, were afforded the highly revered and ever elusive "ghetto pass." There were very few officers who were given this privilege. Every Zone (precinct) had only a few officers of this distinction who were known throughout the communities and the department. The one common thread with all these officers was their relentless dedication and ministerial-like commitment to improving their respective communities. It required a genuine insistence on taking personal, everything that happened on your beat. Good and bad. There were so few of us that we all pretty much knew and related with one another throughout the entire department. It helped to know that even if you were the only one in your Zone or on your Watch trying to do the right thing, you weren't alone. There were others on the department fighting the same fight in other Zones. I am in no way implying that the vast majority of cops were crooked or amoral. In fact, the vast majority were great cops with outstanding characters. However, the sad reality is that an overwhelming percentage of officers have a need for acceptance and fraternity. They don't want to go against the grain or find themselves out of step with the Thin Blue Line for fear of reprisal. These officers fear ostracism, career sabotage, or slow response and support from other officers in life or death situations (such as in the case of a signal 63). This causes a lot of good officers to look the other way or justify the actions of less scrupulous officers. Very few officers are comfortable with being cast aside for not being a team player. The truth is, we were very much team players. We simply refused to waver on the issue of which team we were playing for.

The unofficial internal penalization of officers carried beyond the parameters of the street. Sometimes it could even creep into the setting of the dispatch/911 call center. One of the worst, and most dangerous things that an officer can suffer is a dispatcher who has it out for them. Such was the case with Officer Debbie Lawson-Joe (Sgt., retired).

Debbie graduated from the academy a year or so after I did. She came to Atlanta via NYC, so there was a definite street savvy to how she carried herself. Not a masculine roughness, but more like a street-smart sophistication. It was very apparent from the start that she lacked the degree of naivety, which was common in a lot of younger officers at that time. Debbie stood about 5′ 2″ tall and couldn't have weighed any more than 110 pounds (soaking wet). She was possibly the most petite officer on the department at that time. She was quickly befriended by Miguel and me. She was also a very attractive bi-racial woman with flowing brownish black hair. Miguel and I knew instantly that this officer wasn't going to develop a large amount of friends, so we took it upon ourselves to befriend her even though we worked in the "A" sector, and she was to be assigned to the "B" sector. Our first real conversation with Debbie confirmed our assumptions. She related that she had indeed had a rough time growing up in NYC. She had been victim to that syndrome which assails most people of bi-racial parentage... not White enough to have White friends and not Black enough to garner the acceptance of Black friends. We also knew her petite frame would gain the envy of a lot of female officers who'd lost their girlish figures to years of subjugation to junk food on the Morning Watch. The only places to eat during those hours were the convenience stores and the Krispy Kreme donut shop. Finally, there would be the basic standoffish treatment for simply being the "new kid on the block."

We cautioned her against attempting to prove anything to the Watch by placing herself in harm's way. Even male officers who are smaller in physical stature sometimes tend to be reluctant to ask for help or assistance on a call because they want to prove they can carry their own weight, so to speak. We cautioned her to just do her job and that would be enough to win the respect of the Watch. No unnecessary gambling with her life was required.

Our assumptions turned out to be right. However, not before an initial period of adoration and heightened attention was given her by the male officers on the Watch. That was common also. I'm sure it's common in most occupations. Law enforcement is no different in this regard. New, attractive, female officers often received unprecedented and unsolicited assistance and attention from their male coworkers. For a good month or so, it seemed that for every call Debbie was dispatched on, nearly every male officer in her sector volunteered to back her up. It was comical. After a few officers' advances were met with rejection, and the word got around that she "wasn't putting out," fewer and fewer folks began to show up on her calls. After a couple months time, she was handling her calls by herself just like the rest of the Watch. It got to a point where she would have to request backup in situations where additional officers would normally volunteer to start with each other. At this point, Miguel and I became somewhat concerned for her safety. To make matters worse, she had inadvertently pissed off our Zones' primary dispatcher.

Dispatching is the most underrated job in the law enforcement paradigm. It is literally the lifeline of policing. Through time, dispatchers have been deservingly credited with saving the lives of officers as well as civilian. Unfortunately, the only time they seem to be acknowledged or even noticed is when they find themselves in error regarding some newsworthy event. As great as the vast majority of dispatchers are, they still are only human. The average person has no inkling of the tremendous stress dispatchers are under every time they don their headsets and earpieces. The safety of every citizen and police officer in their respective Zone or precinct is virtually in their hands. Throughout my career, I had the privilege of being watched over by some of the greatest dispatchers in the world. I can say without reservation the APD communications section is a world-class operation. Most military and civilian police agencies require their recruit officers to spend time in the dispatch center during their training. This gives the officer a firsthand experience of what actually goes on during the course of a tour of duty. The hope is that this smidgen of insight into the dispatcher's daily life will give the officer a degree of empathy and patience when on the street and under a stressful situation. During APD recruit training, we were required to spend 2 weeks in the communications/dispatch center in an observational capacity. In my Military Police training, we were required to spend an entire month in dispatch. 3 weeks of it was spent actually dispatching. I must admit that I gained my greatest respect for dispatchers by having to man the console myself. When I reached the supervisory ranks with APD, my officers knew not to disrespect dispatchers while I was at work. If they did, I would always require them to spend at least a week in communications. Not as punishment; but as a lesson in appreciation for the challenges associated with that job.

Debbie had the misfortune of seeing a dispatcher who was married to an APD officer involved in questionable behavior with another APD officer.

Debbie arrived at the City maintenance shop gas pumps to refill her patrol car. As she pulled into the area where the pumps were, she noticed another patrol car already at the gas pumps. As she got closer she could identify a female dressed in civilian clothing leaning into the driver's window of the unknown patrol car. When she finally pulled all the way up to the gas pump behind theirs, she saw the female's breasts were exposed. The officer seated in the vehicle was engaged in an all out groping session. The female hastened to fix her blouse and cover herself when she saw that Debbie was shockingly stuck in a gaze directly at her. Debbie immediately recognized her as a dispatcher and also knew the officer was definitely not her husband. They all went about their way as if nothing had occurred. Debbie had done fine in maintaining her little secret for a couple weeks until she couldn't hold it in any longer. While engaged in a gossip session, Debbie mentioned the illicit situation to another officer. A short time later, she learned that the officer she shared the information with, blabbed it to yet another officer. The web began to spin. In short fashion, the news got back to the dispatcher that Debbie had been spreading rumors about her. One night, the dispatcher asked Debbie to report to communications so they could have a talk. Debbie had no problem apologizing to the dispatcher and admitted she was wrong to have repeated what she'd witnessed that night. The dispatcher accepted her apology, and the situation was resolved, as far as Debbie was concerned. Apparently, the dispatcher had a different opinion.

Everyone began to notice the dispatcher seemed to be excessively short and curt with Debbie all of a sudden. At this time, Miguel and I had not been told about the gas pump incident. As a result, the sudden change in the dispatcher's attitude toward Debbie seemed weird to us. We figured it was just some of the typical jealousy and envy stuff that we had seen Debbie subjected to over the course of the few months she'd been assigned to the Watch. With more and more frequency, it seemed that dispatch was missing obvious danger signs to calls Debbie would be dispatched on. For instance, she might be dispatched to a domestic fight call where both parties are in possession of butcher knives. Dispatch would seem to forget to relay that very important detail or neglect to start another unit with her to the call. Calls of that nature are always dispatched to more than one unit.

There was a time when Debbie was on a call and requested another unit. She didn't put in a 59RA but you could hear the commotion in the background of her transmission. Typically, a dispatcher would advise the responding units to proceed with at least Code 2 (flashing lights) urgency. This did not occur, so I came over the radio and asked the dispatcher "Radio, did it sound like that officer was involved in a fight? Have the units responding to step it up Code 3 (lights & siren). I'll be starting in that direction from "A" Sector."

After the call was handled and things were back to normal, I asked Debbie what that was all about. She said she had no idea. She said she was going to make sure the dispatcher knew her concerns. The second time it happened, Debbie was singing an all-together different tune.

Not more than a couple weeks later, a similar situation arose. This time, Debbie had responded to a domestic call. The boyfriend was found to have active warrants on him. When Debbie went to place him into custody he put up a serious fight. This guy was easily twice Debbie's size. The female caller/victim even attempted to help Debbie gain control of this guy, but it would have taken 4 more women of their size to be a match for this guy's goliath size and strength. Amongst the struggle, Debbie managed to key her radio microphone and blurt out "Radio! Start me a..." All you could hear was noise and confusion in the background when her microphone keyed. You could also hear that she was almost out of breath and clearly tussling with someone. Radio went silent for a couple seconds. I asked, "Radio, did you copy (acknowledge) that unit was fighting and needs backup?" The dispatcher said all she heard was a microphone Key but nothing more. I then told the dispatcher, "Well, she's clearly fighting someone, so you need to put in a signal 63. Myself, 502 and 503 will be en route from "[illegible]" Sector." All Debbie could do was hold on and continue to fight until help arrived. While in route, Miguel, Wayne and I passed an all night party store on the corner of Auburn Avenue and Hilliard Street. Because I slowed down at the traffic light before entering the intersection, I was able to see into the establishment. Standing at the arcade table playing arcade games was the Umbrella (roving back-up officer) officer for the "B" Sector. His car was parked right in front of the store. Here was an officer fighting for what sounded to be her life, and this clown was a few blocks away contemptuously playing Pac Man. As I pulled through the intersection I radioed to Miguel "1503, did you just see that?" He responded "copy that! I did!" I said "copy that! We'll handle it on a 16G (when we get back to the precinct)."

The suspect was already in custody by the time we arrived, and Debbie was a tattered mess. I had never seen her so mad in the short time I had known her, but I was very impressed with her will and determination to bring the suspect into custody. Most male officers wouldn't have attempted arresting this giant by themselves. If she hadn't proven herself to me by that alone, she completely won me over with her pull-in from the call. It's required to "pull-in" from all calls by advising the dispatcher how the call was handled or resolved. For instance a standard pull-in transmission might be, "Radio, pull me in Code 17 on the call." That translates to "The call was handled by taking a written report." Debbie's pull-in after that call was "Radio, pull me in Codes 17 & 23 (report taken & arrest made). Show me en route to your location (Communications) and start YOURSELF a Signal 4 (ambulance)." Debbie did just that, but was headed off by the supervisor outside of the Headquarters building that housed the 911 dispatch center. It was later on that night when Debbie gave me the back-stories on how she had rejected the Umbrella officer's advances as well as the incident with the dispatcher. Miguel and I pulled the Umbrella officer aside at the end of the Watch. We promised him that if he ever left an officer hanging like that again, we would turn him in to Internal Affairs... after adjusting his attitude.

Debbie became my best friend on the department that night and still remains so, 30 years later.

CHAPTER – 4

REMEMBER WHERE YOU CAME FROM

There was every type of good and bad to be found in Herndon Homes in those days. You had everything from public drunkenness to murder, on the bad side. That was offset with acts of kindness such as folks taking up donations to help a hungry family. Herndon Homes was no different from any other housing development in the country. Whatever happened in Herndon Homes, pretty much stayed in Herndon Homes. However, if you were not a resident, and you thought you were going to import drama into Herndon Homes, you had another thing coming.

It was a sweltering summer's Thursday night on the Morning Watch. I had just returned from my off days. The roll call was advised that for the last couple of nights, Herndon Homes had been plagued with a series of pedestrian robberies, and they were getting more violent with each occurrence. The common theme was the same or similar description of 4 or 5 black males with a sawed off shotgun. The first thing I knew automatically was that these were not residents or acquaintances of Herndon Homes. However, I could expect plenty of additional information on these guys from the residents. The other thing I was certain of was that someone was going to get shot soon if the other 2 amigos (Miguel & Wayne) and I didn't figure this out quickly.

My typical patrol time consisted of several moving parts. I would alternate my time inside of Herndon Homes with time spent in the Bluff. I would just kind of rove back and forth between the two. The rest of the time would be spent on calls for service or backing up Miguel, Wayne, and other officers on their adjoining or neighboring beats. Since the Bluff area consisted of a traditional neighborhood of city streets, it was best patrolled by driving. Never more than 5 mph and always with the windows down – even in the wintertime. Herndon Homes, on the other hand, was best patrolled by foot. I would make a habit of parking my patrol car in the center of the development and flat-footing it for hours at a time. If I had a particular problem going on, I would spend the majority of my shift going from apartment to apartment, availing myself to whatever information awaited my ears. I would spend time in one person's living room just holding general conversation and then off to the next person's front porch to catch up how his son was doing on the high school football team. I would sit on a garbage can, used as a makeshift chair, on the corner of Gray Street and Western Avenue and listen to some of the older children's dreams of what they planned to do with their lives after high school. At times, I would just stand around in a courtyard with a group of mothers watching over their toddlers as they played in the dirt - only a couple of apartments in Herndon Homes actually had grass.

This one such night, as I went about my usual community policing, I had a specific agenda in play. I needed as much information as possible concerning these robbers. Finishing up my conversation on the importance of education with a group of teenagers, I headed back to my squad car parked in the lot at the center of the complex. I noticed a small group of men and it was clear they were somewhat taken aback when they noticed me. I had, in fact, unintentionally snuck up on them because of the darkness of the hour coupled with the absence of my patrol car. From a distance, I looked just like any other dude walking up the street. I noticed that these guys fit the description of the robbers pretty much at the same time they noticed I was in fact the Po-leece. They all had an unmistakable look of "oh crap" on their faces as it became apparent to me that I was initially to be their next random victim. When I saw that one of them had a sawed off shotgun hanging from a sling I immediately drew down on the five suspects with my service revolver. In those days we carried a 6 shot Smith & Wesson, Model 10, .38 caliber, revolver. As far as I was concerned, that left me with one extra bullet, so the situation was under control. At gunpoint, I ordered them all onto the ground. All complied except the 2 on each extreme end of the line. It was clear they were considering the fact that since they were the farthest from me, there was no way I could catch them if they ran. Especially, since I was alone. They were absolutely right. Instinctively, I anticipated their exit strategy and reached to my shoulder for my portable radio. It's time to put in my first 59 Right Away. Just as I keyed my microphone to request additional units, a familiar voice rang out from the darkness between the apartments. "You don't need to do that officer Khalfani... we got you." As he's speaking, no less than 12 or so figures appear from between the apartments. Most of which were carrying at least one drawn firearm. The residents had already put into play a plan of action to rid themselves of these robberies. They had come together to form roving squads of 6 or more guys to patrol the projects during the Evening and Morning Watch hours. I would later learn the actual plan was to send a message to anyone living outside of Herndon Homes by leaving 5 bodies for the Medical Examiner to pick up in the morning. The two suspects on either end of the line quickly aborted their original plan to run and politely joined their constituents in the prone position on the ground. I only had two pairs of handcuffs so I placed them on my two potential "runners" as my residential backup stood by. During this process, because I had keyed my microphone with no actual transmission to follow, radio dispatch inquired if I was ok and if I could advise my location. I advised her I was alright and that she could start a paddy wagon to my location for 5 in custody. The sergeant advised me to repeat my last transmission as if he was certain he misunderstood the message. I advised, "Sarge, I'm gonna have those signal 44 (Robbery) perps in custody in Herndon Homes." Radio went audibly quiet.

After arriving at the precinct to complete the mountain of subsequent paperwork, the sergeant sat with me. He first congratulated me on a job well done. Then, he laid into me on the myriad of procedures, rules, tactics and common sense I had obviously thrown into the wind. From failing to request backup, to exonerating the possession of what were most likely illegal firearms, to plain ole' heading up my very own vigilante posse. Needless to say, he wasn't the least bit happy with my antics, but he relented that 5 bad guys were off the streets before they actually killed anyone. He admonished me to be more careful and to promise to never pull anything like that in the future. I gave him my assurances and he never spoke of it again. On the other hand, Miguel and Wayne would occasionally jokingly remind me of it until the day I was transferred out of patrol assignment.

In my entire career, I never put in a help call. This would turn out to be 1 of the only 2 times I almost put in a help call in almost 35 years of law enforcement service. The second time would be thwarted by a suspect himself. Right at the onset of battle, he realized it might be in his best interest to take the path of least resistance.

The moment we touched hands, it was unmistakably obvious to him that my earlier assurance that he was definitely going to jail was more of a premonition than a threat. My resolve was extremely obvious. I am by no means anyone's tough guy. Quite the contrary. I found that humility and compassion yet firmness and resolve are qualities the most hardened criminal could respect in an officer. You win the respect and support of a community through actions, rather than lip service. When you demonstrate through your actions and conduct how much you care about a community, people tend to respond in like kind. People aren't stupid! People living in housing projects, lower income neighborhoods and impoverished communities are far from the "animals" they're depicted as in mainstream mass media. No matter how many recording artists and other mediums try to glorify ghetto life, the vast majority of people living in these conditions... would rather not be. No matter how many political talking heads try to expound the idea that a certain social or economic class is parasitic and possesses a disposition to feeling entitled... the vast majority would gladly join the ranks of the working middle class if they could find employment that provided a sustainable living wage.

It was never a challenge for me to remain grounded, compassionate and humble. I am a humanist by nature. I never have to remind myself how to treat people. All I ever have to do is simply "remember where I came from."

CHAPTER – 5

PULPITS & SOAPBOXES

Life on the Morning Watch went by at supersonic speed. The axiom that time flies when you're having fun is a true saying. There was a tremendous feeling of satisfaction when I would drag myself into my apartment every day around 9:00 a.m. after a long, challenging shift. There was a lot to be said about the gratification experienced with being able to look myself in the mirror every morning and know for a fact that I had made a positive difference in someone's life. There's no feeling quite like that of knowing you've contributed to the overall quality of life in the community you serve. I don't believe there was any other aspect of the job that was more important to me. To me, the job was more of a religious calling than anything. It was indeed, my "ministry." And as I saw it, my community was my pulpit.

During one particular summer, there came onto the departments' radar a sudden and exaggerated uptick in shooting incidents in the Ashby St. / MLK Jr. Dr. corridor section of the Zone. This area was known for its male prostitution traffic during the late Evening Watch and Morning Watch hours. This was occurring on Miguel's beat, close to the part that met up with Wayne's beat. There had been a blue or green pick-up truck identified as the suspect vehicle. The truck had been responsible for the shooting of a couple of street hustlers over the course of several weeks. There were almost nightly incidents of the truck driving by and shooting at the prostitutes as they walked the streets of this fairly small area. It seemed the goal of the suspects was primarily to scare and terrorize the gay streetwalkers more so than to do actual bodily harm. At some point, we basically concluded that when someone was actually shot, it was most likely by mistake. We based our conclusion on the fact that there were just too many point blank opportunities where the suspects could have easily taken the life of one of their victims but never did. During the times when someone was actually shot, the truck was speeding by without even slowing. This led us to believe that those instances were most likely accidental. The precinct commander devised a plan to increase police presence in the area by the utilization of "extra patrols." Almost every roustabout and any extra personnel that could be spared from discretionary units were assigned to the area during the late Evening Watch and Morning Watch hours. The plan was to saturate the area with uniforms as a deterrent to these guys returning.

During that period, I would call dispatch on the phone and let her or him know that I would be pulling extra patrols on that beat until a call for service came up on my own beat. I didn't transmit that information over the radio because I didn't want my supervisor to hear me pull out of service, thus pretty much leaving my own beat uncovered for that period of time. He would, without question, order me back onto my own beat. As long as dispatch knew where I actually was, my lifeline was still intact. If anything should go south, dispatch knew exactly where to send backup. Both the regular and relief dispatchers knew how personally the 3 of us felt about handling not just our own beats, but each other's beats also. We always had each other's backs.

One particular night I was parked, backed into the driveway of a rooming house on Ashby St. near Parsons St. This was pretty much ground zero of the street hustle activity in this area. It was thus, the epicenter of the shooting spree. I had patrolled the area for a while and was now parked to be able to immediately respond in any direction that we might get a sighting of our suspect vehicle. I had developed a habit of killing time by reading my ever-present Bible. As I was engulfed in my nightly readings, I was approached by a hooker who went by the name of "Kim." Kim was a young man in his mid to late 20's that stood about 6' 2" in his requisite 5-inch heels. His build was that of a football running back, which I understood he played in high school and the short period of time he attended college before dropping out. I can only assume he had a penchant for tight fitting miniskirts, as that is all I ever saw him adorn the entire time I was assigned to that area. He was a pretty cool guy with an extremely high IQ. He was able to converse on issues and subjects of real substance, with clearly established and inarguable positions.

I never questioned his sexual orientation, but I did question his lifestyle and would inquire as to why he didn't pursue a safer and more lucrative occupation.

Kim had already walked past my parked vehicle several times. As he would pass, he would assure me "I'm not working, officer Khalfani! I'm just visiting with my friends." I would look up from my Bible and give him a friendly nod, visually check my 12, 3, 6, and 9 (360 degree surroundings check), and return to my readings. Finally Kim stopped at my vehicle, apologized for interrupting and asked if he could speak to me for a minute. Of course I was happy to oblige. I thought that he was about to share some information that I could relay to Miguel to help him blow this pestering case wide open.

These days in law enforcement nationwide, officers are putting themselves at unnecessary risk to reap the benefits of special privileges, better assignments, increased opportunity for promotions and the sort. They take chances with their safety, and sometimes the safety of fellow officers, just to make a "case" (arrest). Every department in the country will take the official stance that they don't have a "quota system." In most cases, it's just renamed as a performance-based merit system. Most departments won't publicize that they have a "magic number," but its practices are quite clear based on the fact that the officer who brings in the most fish, is rewarded with a bigger boat. The officer who brings in the smallest minnow is counseled and encouraged to do better. There is a looming implication of some sort of punishment if he or she fails to improve on his or her dismal "numbers" (arrests). This often results in some officers going to extreme and elaborate measures to make arrests. They will make arrests that would not have been made, had there not been the pressure to forego their ability to exercise officer discretion. Some even cross the line of criminality to meet their "productivity expectations," as they're cleverly labeled. There have been instances where officers have actually circumvented or backstabbed other officers just to make a "stat" (arrest). This was not the case back in the days of the Morning Watch. In those days, officers went out of their way to make each other look good in the eyes of the "brass" (commanders). If we knew another officer was having an unusually slow production week, we would work together to find quality cases for the officer. It was imperative to us that only actual criminals went to jail. There was no shortage of them between our 3 beats, so there was no need to make an arrest of someone that didn't clearly deserve to have his or her freedom taken from them.

I was hoping that the information that was about to be imparted to me would be of value and give Miguel a really big feather to place in his chat; especially since these attacks were somewhat of a blemish on the reputation of the 3 Amigos.

Instead, Kim wanted to share some information that was unrelated to the shootings, and a little more personal in nature. He started off by thanking me for the job that all the officers were doing in trying to apprehend the shooting suspects. He then stated that Miguel, Wayne, officer Povolitis and I were pretty much the only officers who treated the streetwalkers with respect on a regular basis. He noted that I always had only words of concern and encouragement whenever I interacted with them. Whenever an occasion would arise that one of them had to go to jail, we always allowed the arrestee to maintain his dignity and never humiliated them. He then made note of the fact that I was always reading my bible, and he asked if that had anything to do with my disposition. I closed my Bible, held it up, and said that the bible had about a third of responsibility for my conduct. Another third was based on simply being incapable of seeing another human being as less than a human being. Even when they do things that would suggest otherwise, such as murder and child molestation. I definitely have my opinion as to their judgment or even their character, but I never lose sight of the fact that they are still human beings. "The last third of the equation," I advised him, "exists within the pages of this other book here." I reached over to the front passenger seat and pulled out the Jet magazine from under the police forms strewn on the seat. He had a puzzled look on his face as he waited for me to continue. I opened up the magazine to the page that contained the article concerning the male to female ratio in the country's largest urban cities. The numbers were somewhere around 7 to 1, women to men, respectively. The number of available heterosexual women increased exponentially when you factored in gay men, imprisoned men, unemployed men, and so on. So I broke it down to him. "Look Kim, the bible teaches me to not judge anyone. I have so many of my own faults, that I couldn't judge anyone if I wanted to. The bible also teaches me that all people are created by God, so who am I to find God in error of what is in fact his greatest creation? Secondly, it's just not in me to hate anyone. I would have never taken this job if I didn't have a love great enough to be willing to lay down my life, without hesitation, for a total stranger. Thirdly, based on this Jet magazine article, were I a single man, your sexual orientation would actually increase my percentages to date straight women." I then offered one last bit of commentary. I opined that, "Once I figure what the homophobes apparently already know - as to how your sexual orientation in fact takes food off my table, money out my pockets, or years off my life... I'll too be out here in a pickup truck shooting at you." He let out a hearty laugh and stated, "officer Khalfani, you so crazy" as he continued on his stroll down Ashby Street.

That would be my last conversation with Kim and the other streetwalkers before being transferred to another precinct... Well... At least, kinda, sorta transferred...

CHAPTER – 6

THE BATTLE of QUALITY vs QUANTITY

I was well into my second year on the Morning Watch. I was feeling a sense of accomplishment and self-worth with the services I was providing the citizens in my community, my fellow officers, the APD and the city of Atlanta, overall. It meant everything to able to look myself in the mirror every day after work and know in the deepest depths of my heart that I had done everything possible within my power to fulfill those obligations. Every day, I looked forward to putting on that uniform and doing it again. I didn't see it as a job or an occupation. For me, it was more of a calling or ministry. It's as if I was on a crusade to singlehandedly restore the public faith in the police department. At the same time, I was also on a quest to hold myself and other officers accountable to the oath that we were all sworn. I was less concerned about stats that represented the requisite "quantity" of cases, and more focused on the "quality" of cases. In fact, I put a tremendous amount of effort into crime prevention techniques such as foot patrols and community outreach. One of the highlights of the spring and summer seasons was an ongoing basketball game with the residents of John Hope Homes. Miguel, Wayne and I had a standing challenge for any 3 players on the basketball hoop situated in a parking lot in the rear of the apartments. We would play a game, and then leave to handle some calls and patrol our respective beats. We would come back later and play whoever was next in line to challenge us. This went on all spring and summer. I don't believe we ever lost a single challenge. That's pretty much what made challenging us somewhat eventful for the opponents. We knew that certain residents would love the bragging rights of having toppled our standing. That served as extra motivation for us to win. The other thing we were acutely aware of was that some of our challengers were notorious robbers, burglars and shooters in the communities. But as long as they were engaged in basketball with us, at least for that small period of time, there was a reduction in violent crimes occurring throughout our sector. It also gave these career perps the opportunity to see another side of law enforcement. The human side of cops. Miguel and I would go on to become a part of the APD International Police Basketball League team. That original team would go on to win the International Police Basketball League title for the 2 years in a row that we were on the team. We seemed to have a pretty good plan in place, as the crime on all three beats were experiencing a noticeable decrease on the Morning Watch.

"Yabuku, I need you to stick around for a few minutes after the shift ends. The major wants to meet with you" the sergeant advised. "Sure sarge. No problem" I replied. I didn't know it at the time, but the same message had been relayed to Miguel, Wayne and a couple other officers. Naturally I racked my brain as to what the issue was. One thing that was pretty much status quo was that if you were called to the major's office, it was probably not for a cheese and wine snack. Later on, I was given notice that the meeting had been postponed until later in the week and they'd let me know. But for now, I was told "stand by to stand by." The sergeant felt it only proper to give me a head's up that the meeting would concern my productivity. The major was personally meeting with everyone who had less than stellar stats. He went on to inform me that the lines dividing the Zones were about to be redesigned and that we would be losing a portion of our beats to Zone 1. The portion being parceled off happened to be my beat, along with Wayne and Miguel's. These three beats were to form a new sector in Zone 1. The "C" Sector. Up until that point, all 6 Zones in the city were composed of 2 Sectors, "A" and "B". It was suggested that the lines were being redrawn in anticipation of the upcoming Democratic National Convention (DNC), which was being hosted by the city of Atlanta. The DNC was to take place in the downtown business district of Zone 5. It was speculated that the realignment was an effort to rid Zone 5 of its housing projects to make it more appealing to the visiting businessmen and politicians. The only housing project left within the borders of Zone 5 was, Techwood Homes. It was further speculated that Techwood Homes was given safe haven due to its historical significance of being the first housing project constructed in the United States, in 1936. I personally think it was spared do its geographical location square in the heart of Zone 5. To redistrict Techwood Homes would have required relinquishing 3/4 of the Zone and scavenging it off to the surrounding Zones.

Thanks to the sergeant, I had a few days to gather my personal stats and prepare whatever defense was possible for my productivity. I always knew I was way below the Watch average in regards to overall arrests. However, I also knew I consistently led the Watch in Part 1 (criminal offenses identified by the FBI's Uniform Crime Report (UCR) as being major crimes) and violent crime arrests. I also knew there was a significant crime reduction on my beat since I took it over. I felt I was pretty much on solid ground whenever the inevitable call came to report to the major's office. It did, and I was.

When I entered the major's office, he met me with a warm smile and handshake. He invited me to have a seat in front of his huge desk as his administrative lieutenant was already sitting off to the side. The air of the situation was very familiar to those I had faced during my career in the Army. I had experienced a phase in the military when it seemed that I spent more time in my commander's office than I did in my own barracks; a time when I spent more time struggling for the rights and fair treatment of my fellow soldiers, than I did in the performance of my actual assigned duties. There was a time when I was thought of as a troublemaker and an "angry Black militant" with an axe to grind against the US Army, due to its mistreatment of Black soldiers. Indeed, a time that will be further explored in an upcoming book.

The major asked if I knew why we were having this meeting. I almost burst into laughter, as I could only imagine how many times he had initiated a similar question on every traffic stop that he probably made as a patrol officer. I could almost hear him ask the question, "Do you know why I pulled you over?" Maintaining my composure and a straight face, I responded that I could probably guess but I'd rather he just told me. He obliged. He lectured me on the importance of justifying my work by way of arrests. He assured me that we didn't have a quota system, but the only way to validate our success was through quantitative stats. The major spent at least 15 minutes educating me on the merits of how locking up people is our primary function, and so forth. By this time I'm chomping at the bit to respond to each point as they're being made, but he suggested that I hold my comments until he finished his presentation, so as to maintain order and constructiveness. I digressed... for the moment. He finished up by informing me that if I didn't bring my productivity up to Watch average, I would find myself facing more aggressive supervision, and possibly even disciplinary action. He then relinquished the floor to me.

I thanked the major for having enough concern for my performance to invest the time into counseling me. I assured him that I heard every word and would make every effort to come up to the Watch expectations. I handed him a copy of my written documentation. He asked what it was and I advised him that I too was concerned about my "stats" and productivity on my beat. Therefore, I had been keeping record of my own performance based on stats that are regularly collected by the precinct. "My way of keeping myself accountable to the job that I was sworn to do" I said. I went on to state, "Just like you sir, I too believe that numbers don't lie." I asked him to bring attention to the fact that the documentation showed a drastic decrease in overall crime on my beat. They went on to reflect an even more dramatic decrease in violent Part 1 crimes on my beat. I explained to him how my style of policing was not based on how many people I could lock up, but rather on how many crimes I could prevent from occurring. I further went on to assert my basic logic. The logic being that if there is less crime occurring on my beat, it would stand to reason that there is less opportunity to make arrests. I could see from the flush beginning to rise in his complexion that he wasn't totally appreciating my position. However, I decided that I was in the deep end of the pool and the only way out at this point was to continue to swim. I continued "Sir, with all due respect, this is what I'm basically saying... If I am the victim of a rape, and the police apprehend and successfully prosecute my attacker, I am eternally grateful to the Atlanta Police Department for a job well done and for vindication. How much more grateful do you think I would be, if by enhanced patrols and greater visibility, I was never raped in the first place?" I was met with total silence, so I continued "Sir, the truth of the matter is that the department is much more meaningful and significant to citizens if they are protected from being victims of crime in the first place, rather than vindicated later." Still silence and a blank stare. I was about to continue on with other points, which I don't remember now, when the major lost his composure and yelled, "I don't care what this paper says, I'm giving you a directive to bring in more cases." The attending lieutenant was obviously startled by the major's sudden change in demeanor. I would later learn that the major had always been a pretty even kilter individual. He considered himself a devout Christian and never had a negative thing to say about anyone. He enjoyed a widespread reputation of being a good man. I have no doubt about any of this, and still hold him in high regard to this day. Apparently, in this particular moment, he took my dissertation as an indictment of his character, rather than a detailed defense of my own self.

As tends to be common with me – much to my own disliking – when someone takes it up a notch with me, I take it up a notch with them. Before I realized what I was saying, I blurted out at the top of my lungs "Major, I apologize if I'm not locking up enough n----rs to make you happy, but my number one priority is to keep my community safe, and preventing crime from happening." Dead silence. 3 startled faces including my own. The 5 seconds of silence felt more like 5 hours. Finally... silence broken... the lieutenant, who had not uttered a single word the entire meeting, stated firmly yet awkwardly "Officer, you're dismissed!!!"

I left out of the office to the blank stares and dropped jaws of the officers who'd obviously been within earshot of the major's office. It was evident by my frustrated demeanor that this was not an ideal time to engage me in conversation as to what had just occurred. Rather, it was more like the parting of the Red Sea as everyone stepped out of my way as I exited the front doors of the precinct.

Within a few weeks, the new Zone lines took effect and the three beats were reallocated to Zone 1. Zone 1 was the precinct that consisted of several locations and areas that are still glorified in modern Atlanta Hip Hop culture. A few of the more popular areas were Hollywood Homes apartments, Hollywood Road, Bankhead Highway, and Bankhead Courts apartments. The Zone redistricting resulted in Zone 1 acquiring the new "C" Sector which consisted of Herndon Homes, the Bluff, Eagan Homes apartments, University Homes apartments, and John Hope apartments. Sector "C" also included the Atlanta University Center, which consisted of Morehouse College, Spelman College, Clark College, Atlanta University, and Morris Brown College.

This new addition to Zone 1 made it arguably the most diverse Zone in the city... at least, within the construct of the African American community. I was retained in my beat car, so as to be transferred to Zone 1 by default. Wayne and Miguel would suffer the same fate. Guilt by association, we guessed. However, a bargain would be struck and Miguel, Wayne and I would be assigned to the Day Watch to give the appearance that our transfers were not a form of punishment. After all... you can't punish someone for not upholding a quota system that doesn't exist... Right???

However, I was to face one more hurdle before my transfer was effective.

It was on a New Years Day, at approximately 7:00 in the morning when I heard a faint knocking at my front door. My wife was in the room closest to the door so she answered it. I was in the back room with the children when my wife walked into the room with a concerned look on her face. I immediately sensed that something was wrong and I rushed to her. Behind her was one of my classmates from the police academy. Not just any classmate, but my very best friend from the academy. She had become close with my family during our time in the academy, as I hosted most of the study sessions at my home. She and my wife had grown close over the months. However, we hadn't seen her in a few months due to the fact that we were given different Watch and Zone assignments. My beloved classmate was standing in my living room soaking wet with bare feet, wearing nothing more than a nightgown and housecoat. It had snowed quite a bit that particular New Years Eve and Day. We sat her down and got her situated with something dry and warm to put on. After she was somewhat comfortable, I took her into a private room so she could explain what misfortune had befallen her. I was nowhere near ready for the account that would follow.

She explained to me that I was going to be upset with her. She made me promise to not judge her and to allow her to get out the whole story before berating her. I assured her that my wife and I both loved her and that I would never stand in judgment of anything that she had done. She said that I only felt that way because I hadn't heard the story yet. She continued. She explained how she had been dating a lieutenant on the department for a short period of time. I asked her why I never knew about him considering she and I had been best friends since the academy. She said that she kept the relationship secret from me because she knew I would never understand or approve of her involvement with this particular person. I asked what brought her to that assumption. She said I had specifically forbidden her to even entertain the idea of being attracted to him in an unrelated conversation we had some months back. She went on to say that at the time of that conversation, they had already been dating for quite some time. Since she knew from that moment that I didn't approve of him, she was resolute that she would never tell me about the relationship. At this point, there was no question in my mind who she was talking about. My only question was... how long this had been going on. She said that she started dating him while we were still in the police academy. That only made the situation worse because this lieutenant was assigned to the academy while we were in attendance there. I wasn't sure exactly what rule he had broken by dating a cadet that was under his direct supervision and instruction, but I was sure there was some obvious conflict of interest with the situation. She went on to tell me the story of how she wound up at my front door on this early New Year's morning.

She said that she spent New Year's Eve at the lieutenant's home. She had been preparing a traditional New Year's Day meal of chitterlings, cornbread, collard greens and black-eyed peas, amongst other dishes. She said there were two other couples over to ring in the New Year with her and the lieutenant. She said there was heavy drinking, and they all had a pretty fun time as they celebrated the countdown together. A few hours and a lot of drinks later, one of the couples called it a day and bid their farewells. The remaining couple continued to play cards and enjoy themselves. The female that remained behind asked to be excused from the party and requested to retreat to the master bedroom to lie down for a while. A short time later, the lieutenant felt compelled to go check on the female in the bedroom. When he returned a few seconds later, he asked my friend to accompany him to the bedroom because he had something he wanted to show her. She felt it an awkward request, but complied. She was the only participant sober at this point because she was not, and had never been, a drinker. That was something else that we had in common as friends. Once in the bedroom, the female sat up in the bed as the lieutenant took my friend's hand and placed it into the female's hand. He then whispered into my friend's ear to join him and the female in the bed. My friend snatched back her hand and quickly exited the room. At that point, she chalked up the behavior as a not so funny joke, motivated by intoxication. Though initially bothered, she didn't think much more of it. She went back to prepping the food for later on in the day. She ignored the lieutenant's shouts from the bedroom for her to reconsider. She started to become increasingly annoyed. His persistence made it obvious that this was not a joke, but in fact, something that the man she felt so in love with, actually desired. After a short time passed, the lieutenant emerged from the bedroom and began to drag my friend into the room. He began to shout things to her that revealed a side of him she had never witnessed before. He demanded that she was going to obey him or suffer physical consequences. He continued to drag her into the bedroom, and she continued to escape and run into the front room. He began to punch her in her face and about her body. He demanded her cooperation. All the while, the visiting female was lying in the bed, eagerly awaiting my friend's compliance. The female drunkenly assured her it wasn't as bad as she thought, and she would like it if she tried it. Just adding more taunting to a situation that was already rapidly spiraling out of control. After a few back and forth struggles, my friend was able to get off a good solid kick to the lieutenant's groin. She grabbed her purse and headed for the front door. Even in this injured drunken state, the lieutenant was able to compose himself enough to pull her purse from her hand as she ran out the front door. Fortunately, he couldn't muster up the strength to physically stop her from running out of the door. It was about 3am when she made her way her way to Interstate-20 and flagged down an 18-wheeler. The trucker drove her to the Interstate-285 connection, where he dropped her off on the side of the road. She then flagged down another rig on Interstate-285 that would carry her to the Camp Creek Parkway exit. From there, she walked the remaining two snowy and slushy miles to my apartment on Herschel Road in College Park. I knew there was not much to be done on New Year's Day as far as reporting the incident was concerned. However, I did know that we had to take photographs of her condition and injuries and get her medical attention. After taking photos, I drove her to Grady Hospital, where she was treated for her injuries. Just as important, would be an official medical record of her injuries. She then spent the rest of the day at my apartment. The following day, we stopped by her apartment to freshen up. We then headed directly downtown to the Office of Professional Standards (OPS/Internal Affairs) where she filed an official complaint against the lieutenant. I also gave my statement as her "outcry" witness. Within a few hours of our arrival at OPS, we were summoned by the investigator assigned to the case to jump into the car with him. I asked where we were going, and he said that we were headed to the lieutenant's house with a warrant for the retrieval of departmental property. He told me that OPS was going to use the premise of retrieving my friend's departmental issued service weapon and B & C's (badges & credentials) to search the premises for evidence of any other crime he may have committed.

Once at the lieutenant's home, a soft forced entry was made so as not to destroy the door and to insure that it would be capable of securing once we left. After an hour or so, her weapon and credentials were recovered. There was no evidence of other crimes during the OPS search, but they did confiscate a large photograph and video stash hidden away. It seemed the lieutenant had maintained a catalogue of his sexual exploits with other police recruits and several other officers at various rank levels within the department. There were at least 4 female officers that I personally recognized, photographed in sexually explicit acts. The video and photos were taken into custody to add credence to my friend's story of the incident.

The lieutenant was charged in the Delkab County Superior Court with several charges. The D.A. created their witness list from the officers and other female city employees divulged in the photos and videos. In all, approximately 13 sworn employees were subpoenaed to give testimony on behalf of the prosecution. All of the subpoenaed officers either invoked the 5th amendment, or stood in contempt of court by simply no showing up. In the end, only 1 officer would actually take the stand... ME!

After giving my testimony, the lieutenant made a point of finding me in the hallway during a short recess. He approached me and said I had ruined my career by testifying against him. He also said there would only be rough roads ahead for me while on the department. He was about to say something else when I cut him off. I told him that he could save his breath, and that he wasn't as smart as I had always given him credit for being. I told him that anyone with half a brain could see the obvious. If I was afraid of him, I would have never taken the witness stand against him. Therefore, he could desist with the idle threats. Furthermore, it would be a cold day in he-- before I found myself afraid of any coward that would beat on a woman. He smirked, shook his head and muttered "I always knew you were crazy" as he walked away. He was allowed to plead to a lesser charge (misdemeanor) so he could maintain employment with the department. A felony conviction would have meant mandatory termination, and the evidence was overwhelming.

Still, considering the nature of the charges, the lieutenant could not be allowed to remain an instructor at the academy because he would still be in a position to prey upon unsuspecting recruit officers. So In the department's infinite wisdom, where did they decide to reassign him??? To the one Section that is the most highly populated with female employees. The one Section that is tantamount to putting the proverbial fox into the proverbial henhouse... The Communications section!!! Not to mention that the female in question from the night of the incident was, in fact, a dispatcher. When I read the personnel order, I almost fainted. What genius had come up with this idea? Apparently, it didn't take long for someone to figure out the irony. He was transferred to a Zone assignment a short time later.

My friend didn't last much longer on the department. She caved in to the constant harassment she received for bringing charges against such a highly favored member of the department. She was just supposed to keep her mouth shut and deal with the ramifications of wanting membership into a male dominated profession. She had, in fact, sabotaged her right to stand shoulder to shoulder on the Thin Blue Line. After several threats on her life, she decided to pack it in and go back to teaching elementary school in her hometown.

I would later learn from another female friend of mine that there had been a plot on my life as well. It seemed the male companion at the party that night was also an officer who happened to be the best friend of the lieutenant's. This other officer was actually married, and the female he was accompanying that night was just one of several women that he slept with behind his wife's back. That explained why he had no issues with the female at the party engaging in the intended threesome with the lieutenant and my friend. Sometime after the dust of the trial had settled, he and the lieutenant hatched a plan to have me transferred under the lieutenant's command in the Zone. At some point, I would be set up to be ambushed on a fake 911 call for service. The only thing left was to figure out how they would facilitate me being transferred from the Day Watch to the Evening Watch.

As I said, I came across this information from one of my female friends. My friendship with this young lady was established while I was assigned to the morning watch. She worked the late shift at the fast food restaurant on Miguel's beat. One night, while in conversation, she revealed that she was a member of a local Satanic cult. She shared with me the identities of other APD officers and a supervisor who were also active members. She told me stories of their rituals and practices. She even shared with me the difference between the hard rock groups that were truly devotees to Satan, and those who were simply posturing for theatrical value. Often times, our conversations would carry on most of the night. Between calls, I would head back to be educated on more of her intriguing tales. At a certain point, I felt that she had been placed in my life as a test of my Christian faith. Not so much as a challenge of my faith, but more as a test of the strength and capability of my faith to convert or guide her out of what I perceived as being "darkness." I commenced in my efforts to help her gain her "salvation." If we spent an hour discussing Satanism, we spent 2 or 3 hours discussing Christianity. I invited her to attend church with me as well as bible study. She told me the last time she tried to step foot in a church, she became ill and passed out. I thought she was just making excuses until I was finally able to entice her to attend a church service. She did fine for a few minutes. All of a sudden, she began to complain of feeling lightheaded. I assured her it was only psychological and to maintain her composure. She tried, but to no avail. As her apparent discomfort worsened, I had to rush her out the front door. I still don't know if it was all an act; but I do believe that it was genuine, at least in her head. I do know that once something is fixated on in a person's psyche, the rest of the world's reality doesn't count for squat. For them, in that moment, reality is whatever's occurring inside of their mind. Anyway, if I had indeed just witnessed the control of Satan in this woman, it only made me more determined that I was going to prevail in her conversion and deliverance. From that point, I shifted into high gear. I was relentless in my efforts to save this woman. She eventually left the cult. However, it was not before my wife suspected my involvement with another woman. One day, as I sat in the restaurant sharing scripture with her, my wife pulled up in a cab. I could see her approaching the restaurant as I ran outside to meet her. She did not make a scene or become belligerent. In a calm voice, she said that she just wanted to see for herself why I had been coming home late, and now that she had seen it for herself, it was time that we both returned home together. On the way home, I explained the entire situation to her. She seemed to accept that I was telling the truth. I assured her there had been no intimacy between my friend and I. My wife never brought it up again after that day. Even to this very day.

At some point shortly after the lieutenant's trial, my friend from the restaurant started dating the lieutenant's best friend. One night while in bed engaged in small talk, he sought to impress her with his gangster swag. Out of the blue, he began to brag of how he and his best friend, a lieutenant, were going to F--k up an officer. She asked him for what reason? He said that some lowly patrol officer had the nerve to take the witness stand against the lieutenant in a domestic related case, which was none of his (my) business. He went on to say that by the time they were through with this officer, "he would be just as f----d up as his f----d up name." She asked the natural question, "What's f----d up about his name?" She told me when my name fell from his lips she almost fell out of the bed. She said she was barely able to maintain her composure to get through the rest of the evening. She said that she would be meeting with him the next week and asked if I wanted her to make an effort to elicit more details about the plot. I told her that wouldn't be necessary and assured her that I was in no real danger. I told her there wasn't enough combined brainpower between the two of them to pull off something like that. Besides, I was too busy settling into my new Day Watch assignment to be bothered by the idle threats of irrelevant characters. I never reported it and they never followed through; but I did remain vigilant in keeping an eye out for any suspicious content in dispatched calls.

CHAPTER – 7

YOU'D BETTER NEED ME

Getting adjusted to Day Watch wasn't exactly a piece of cake. Facing the morning rush hour traffic, the seemingly inordinate amount of people stirring about in the city, and the overbearing presence of the command staff, took some getting used to. None of these elements existed during the Morning Watch hours of 10:30 p.m. to 6:30 a.m. No vehicular traffic, no large degree of foot traffic, and best of all... no "brass." The trade off was, of course, being able to interact with the people in my community during daytime hours. I would discover that, for whatever reason, there was an almost totally different set of problems and issues that plagued the community between the two shifts. For instance, the Morning Watch shift consisted of mostly stranger-stranger crimes, such as robberies and shootings. Conversely, Day Watch was comprised of mostly acquaintance issues, including neighbor disputes and domestic concerns.

The supervision in Zone 1 stood in somewhat contrast with that of Zone 5 in one significant way. The supervisors in Zone 5 were pretty much just that... supervision. In fact, there was a phrase that was expounded from the podium during every roll call I attended. Every supervisor would issue the edict as the last thing uttered at the end of every roll call. Right after we were cautioned to "be safe." We would lastly be advised, "If you need me, call me. But if you call me, you had better need me." Only 1 supervisor on the Morning Watch, as best as I can remember, never uttered the phrase. As a result, no matter what situation you found yourself in, you could always count on Sgt. Melvin Denson (Lt., retired) to be there to help guide you through the troubled waters. Don't get me wrong, as was implied during roll call, the other supervisors would respond upon request to whatever issues you had. The difference was that Sgt. Denson didn't have to be requested. He was always out there watching our backs, even when we weren't aware it. There were several times when I would come in at the end of the shift, just to be pulled aside and met with a kind, yet stern, oral reprimand from him. Through the course of the shift, he would have observed from a secluded vantage point, some conduct or action that I had engaged in that was less than safe, or that I should have requested back up on. He was out there being proactive and providing an extra layer of security for a bunch of rookie officers, regardless of how seasoned we may have felt we were after a measly year and a half or two years on the streets. Sgt. Denson would go on to make the rank of lieutenant and hold some of the most significant and critical positions on the department. He would establish himself as a man of honor, integrity, and fearlessness. He was renowned throughout the department as being someone who was always willing to fight the fight that others didn't have the guts to fight. He was truly a supervisor who ALWAYS put his troops before himself. APD suffered a tremendous loss when he was offered a better position with the Dekalb County Police Department. APD refused to match the offer. In retrospect, his departure from the department signaled a new era or transition period within the leadership or supervision within the APD. In fact, it signaled the dawning of the age of extinction of "leadership," which was replaced by "de facto supervision."

Zone 1 Day Watch was different though. The supervisors in the entire precinct on all Watches seemed to be on the same page with Sgt. Denson. It was as if there were two different mindsets between the two Zones. In Zone 1, it seemed that every turn you took throughout the course of the day... you were being met by a supervisor. They were in constant radio contact with us. They would show up on several of our calls. In fact, it started to become somewhat overbearing. So much that I finally requested that the sector supervisor meet me at a location to ask the very pointed question of why Wayne, Miguel, and I were being surveyed so closely by them. I assured him that although this was a new precinct for the three of us, these were still our regular beats, and we had been working them for some time. Lastly, I asserted that the three of us were of the highest integrity, and he didn't have to be concerned about any inappropriate conduct on our part. He sort of chuckled, and asked if I had ever considered the fact that although the three of us may be familiar with the newly structured "C" Sector, he, on the other hand was not. He simply needed to familiarize himself with his new territory. Plus, as a supervisor, he added, it was his responsibility to assess us on calls as new employees and to observe how we handle ourselves interacting with the public. The third factor, he frankly explained, was simply to see for himself, exactly what special kind of "mess ups" we were to have all gotten kicked out of Zone 5. "If it's any consolation, there's a reason why they gave ME this new sector of supposed misfits," he said. In the months to come, it would become extremely evident why sarge was relegated to the assignment of "C" Sector sergeant. If sergeant Denson ever had a clone of leadership styles, it was definitely our new Sector sergeant Claude Richardson (RIP). He was definitely a leader of men. He too was of the variety of leadership that is all but non-existent in law enforcement agencies on every level of government throughout the nation. Sgt. Richardson was the kind of supervisor who always looked out for the troops. He would steer us from the traps of conduct that, regardless of our pure intentions, could land us in front of Internal Affairs. He was always there to provide an extra hand whenever a situation was bigger than the three of us. He was the kindest and most compassionate person you could ever meet. His gentle and compassionate way extended to his officers and the community we served. He was truly a gem. At times, we would sit in amazement and count our blessings that he was not only our leader, but that he was a righteous man. He was one of those people who you were really glad had made the choice to be on this side of the law. By no means was he someone you would relish going up against in an alternate universe kind of situation. No matter what the situation, he could always provide a remedy that would fit comfortably within the borders of legality, departmental procedures, safety and morality. That is, until one day...

Radio dispatched a domestic fight call to University Homes projects on Greensferry Ave. The address is located on beat 113. Miguel's beat. Naturally, I advise dispatch that I'll be heading that way to assist. Wayne was not at work on this particular day, but whoever is covering his beat was en route also. When we all arrived on the scene, Miguel filled us in on the details of what had been going on. Apparently, there was a disgruntled man that had soft barricaded himself inside the house, and he was holding hostage his infant child and the child's mother at knifepoint. He had been in an argument with his child's mother, and she fled the location once he became physically violent toward her. He was holding their child hostage until she returned to the premises, which she did after calling 911. The child's older sister was standing by with Miguel when we 26'd (arrived) on the scene. Miguel was pushing her for whatever additional intelligence she could provide for SWAT, who was required to be requested per protocol (SOP). We advised radio of the hostage situation and requested that a supervisor meet us on the scene. It would be Sgt. Richardson's responsibility, per SOP, to assess the situation and formally request assistance from SWAT. Sarge was obviously already in route, as he appeared on the scene no more than 30 seconds after I requested him. He was briefed on the situation and any additional information the daughter could provide as the circumstances unfolded. The father/suspect was last known to be in the rear bedroom area with the child when the daughter fled the apartment. Within a few minutes of us being there, the suspect would emerge in the front room window. He was demanding that we leave him alone and leave his home, or he would cut the baby's throat. When we questioned the daughter as to the likelihood of the suspect harming his own child, she responded that argument was basically over the legitimacy of the child. In other words, he was highly likely to carry out his threat. Sergeant Richardson requested an estimated time of arrival (ETA) for the SWAT team. Radio advised 30 to 45 minutes. Dispatch asked if he needed additional units to respond, and he advised there was no need for more units to just stand around and wait for SWAT. He pulled Miguel and I off to the side and asked for our assessment of the situation. We advised him that it seemed like our hands were tied by the SWAT SOP. Miguel offered to continue trying to negotiate with the suspect until SWAT arrived. The suspect continued to caution us to leave the scene or he would kill the baby, who he doubted was actually his anyway. Miguel told the guy that there were a lot of possible outcomes to this situation. However, the police leaving was not one of them. Suddenly, the mother began to scream hysterically at the top her lungs from inside the apartment. She yelled "he's about to kill my baby." Sgt. Richardson inquired of radio again, "Radio, can you advise on SWAT's ETA now?" Radio advised "approximately 15 minutes." Radio's last transmission was partially drowned out by the mother's deafening shriek, "he's killing my baby!" With nothing more than a half rage, half tear filled gaze, Miguel and I looked at sarge and beckoned his instructions. Suddenly, sarge gave us a nod and barked "f--k SWAT!!! Let's go save that baby!" I'm sure his intention was for us to quickly form a 3 or 4 man entry team and execute a calculated rapid assault on the apartment. I have no doubt that would have been the prudent thing to do. However, Miguel and I were both fathers, so all we heard were the words "Let's go save that baby."

I took off like a bolt of lightning with Miguel close on my tail. By this time we had been watching each other's backs for so long that we knew each other's thoughts and instincts. We had taken down many a criminal on a daily basis without the necessity of a solitary utterance between the two of us. Sometimes, it didn't even require a look. We just knew. The daughter had advised that the barricade was a soft one, such as a sofa or a couple chairs. Bam!!! I hit the door like a freight train. It offered surprisingly little resistance. So little resistance, that it caused me project across the room almost past the suspect. I was able to decelerate enough to jerk his arm with the knife away from the throat of the baby, who was being held in his left arm. Miguel had enough head steam to make a flying tackle at the suspect's legs and jar the infant loose from his grasp. The child was then handed off to sarge, who had followed us in at the 3rd position. Once taken down, the suspect surrendered without a struggle. Once we ensured there were no further threats at the location, we gathered ourselves and exited the apartment with the suspect in custody. We were met by the offsetting glares of the newly arrived SWAT team as we loaded up the paddy wagon and headed for a better location to complete our paperwork.

We complimented Sergeant Richardson on handling the situation, and we thanked him for allowing us to do our job. That event would set a tone for the level of respect that we would eternally hold for sarge and for the level of trust that he would bestow on us going forward. We would go on to fight a lot a crime together with a confidence that we were a team. We also had confidence that we were all doing things for the right reason and in the right way. There would be many occasions when sarge would be called onto the commander's "carpet" to account for the comparatively low rates of our monthly stats. He would always stand proudly before the lieutenant and major and provide them with documentation of our performance. Sarge reported the fact that we consistently led the Watch in violent, and other major Part 1 crime arrests. We were also leading in crime reduction. He NEVER once warned us to make more cases. He always said, "Keep reducing your victim base and only putting in jail those that truly need to go."

Only after I entered into the leadership ranks of APD, could I truly appreciate his sacrifice in standing up for us.

In the weeks following the incident, sergeant Richardson would later reveal to Miguel and I that as we were departing the scene that day, the old school SWAT commander snapped at him "The next time you call us... you'd better need us."

CHAPTER – 8

AS SALAAM U ALAIKUM???

My time on Day Watch in Zone 1 passed quicker than most assignments I would go on to have over my career with the APD. This was mostly because it was one of the most rewarding and gratifying assignments I worked. The old adage about time flying when you're having fun would be an absolute truism in regards to this phase in my career. I looked forward to the unknown that lied ahead of me each day. I enjoyed the challenge of being faced with the most impossible situations and resolving them in a way which would be a win-win for all parties involved. I was acutely aware that I was in a rare position to play a part in the healing of the void that existed between law enforcement and the communities they served nationwide. I recommitted myself to not squandering this unique opportunity to make an actual difference at the grass roots level. The job was anything but a job to me. I took extreme pride in giving back to a community not at all unlike the one I was reared in. Whenever I would transport a prisoner for myself or another officer, I made a habit of lecturing them all the way to jail intake. Like I said, far be it for me to pass up the opportunity to minister to a literal "captive audience." I had only one objective with these impromptu interventions. That was to instill in my prisoner, a sense of responsibility for their actions. Whenever they would be placed in the back seat, it was always someone else's fault for them being there. It was the arresting officer's fault, or it was their wife's fault for calling the police as he was beating her to a pulp. Sometimes it would be the alcohol or drugs' fault. Probably the reigning excuse that I would face was that it's the system's fault because the system is set up to keep a black man down. My objective was to ensure that by the time we arrived at intake, my passenger had verbalized that they understood how they bore some responsibility in their incarceration by the choices he or she made. That was important to me because I knew the first step in avoiding recidivism was the acknowledgement of the defective behavior.

One time while shopping at the grocery store with my 12 years old son, I noticed a gentleman in another line paying particularly close attention to me. Most officers are aware of one simple fact. Because we may lock up a thousand people in our careers, it's next to impossible to keep a mental catalogue of all the faces. However, for many of our customers, the arrest was the only one or few they've ever experienced. Therefore, it's nearly impossible for them to ever forget how the officer looked, sounded, or even smelled. The guy's face was familiar, but I was totally perplexed as to where I had encountered him. Could it have been in my work environment or at church? Maybe it was the gym? At any rate, this guy would not break visual contact with me. After a while, it seemed he couldn't contain himself any longer. He began to make a bee line for me and my son. When it was clear he was coming straight for me, I situated my son behind me and slid my hand under my shirt onto my pistol handle. He noticed my discomfort and hurriedly, but discreetly stated "Hey, Officer Yabuku... There's no need for you to do that. I just wanted to thank you for saving my life." He said "You probably don't remember me, but you arrested me about 6 months ago." He explained how he had been in and out of jail and rehab and the drugs had taken over his life. He added that he always used his addiction as an excuse to act out and that I was the only person who'd ever been able to make him admit responsibility for his own vicious cycle. He said of course he had admitted it before as a rouse or prerequisite to get out of rehab or get a reduced prison sentence, but he never truly accepted responsibility in his heart of hearts until he found himself in the back seat of my cruiser. He said he had been sober for 6 months, which was his longest sobriety to date. He shook my hand and thanked me again before departing the store with his groceries. The look of admiration in my son's eyes was priceless. I think he and I both experienced a greater appreciation for this magnificent opportunity to impact lives.

APD is no different from most major city departments where the rank and file are understaffed, underequipped, underappreciated and underpaid. To offset the pay deficiency, officers are allowed to work extra jobs (moonlighting). I was a family man, so I was very adamant about not working extra jobs. On occasion, when Miguel was in a bind, I would fill in for him at the McDonalds across the street from the 5 Points MARTA station downtown. On this particular day, he would need me to report to the extra job as soon as I got off of duty. He actually cleared it with the sergeant for me to leave about 30 minutes early so I could arrive at the restaurant by 2:30 p.m. By the time I reached the restaurant, radio dispatch called for the Day Watch early cars to make a 16G (report or return to the precinct). The 16G signals the end of the shift for off going officers. I was relieved when I heard the 16G because I was feeling guilty about leaving early on a day when we were running such a minimal amount of cars. I worked an early car. This meant that my work hours were from 6:30 a.m. – 2:30 p.m. The late cars worked from [illegible] a.m.- 3 p.m. Upon hearing the 16G, I reasoned that I would have been getting off the clock at that time anyway so I hadn't, in effect, left any of my co-workers hanging. The worst thing in the world would have been for a call to come up on my beat between the time I left and the time I was actually supposed to get off, leaving another officer had to handle my call. Due to the tremendous pride I took in handling my beat; that would not have boded well with me. However, the 16G had been sounded, and I was in the clear.

I had just settled in and made my initial rounds inside of the establishment when I heard a signal 63 go out over the radio. An Evening Watch officer was on a taxicab fare dispute call, and he was not answering his radio after putting in a help call. All Watches were running thin that day. We had run a skeleton crew on the Day Watch also. I knew that most of the units were in roll call at the precinct located several miles away. The remaining Day Watch cars were probably in route to the precinct, if not already there. Apparently, the officer had been dispatched on the call in lieu of roll call. This will happen on occasion when the call occurs so close to watch change and dispatch determines that the call will unnecessarily tie up an off going unit, causing them to be held overtime. This also happens if there is some urgency attached to the call. In this case, I believe the issue was that the complainant was afraid the accused might flee the scene if the officer didn't respond right away.

Given that the precinct was miles away, and I was literally just down the street from the call, I responded. The store manager asked where I was going in a concerned tone. This particular restaurant had been victim to several robberies and gang fights, hence the reason for extra security. I replied to the manager that I understood his concern, but I had a fellow officer down, and I believed I was the closest person to him. I apologized to him again and jumped into my personal vehicle. I advised dispatch that I was en route. By this time, dispatch had given out updates that the officer had been shot and the suspect was still in the area. I heard several units 26 with the officer, so I asked dispatch for additional information on the suspect's location. She advised that he was last seen in the rear of an apartment located a couple of buildings from where the shooting occurred, but in the same complex. I advised radio that I was 26 in the rear of the complex with several other officers. We conducted a search of the crawl spaces under the buildings furthest to the rear of the complex. We were halfway through searching the first building when another group of officers came across the suspect at the next building. He was hiding in the small crawl space in the center of the building. We ordered him out of his hiding place, but he refused. He said that he would only surrender to a Muslim officer. A lot of people were under the impression that I was a Muslim based on my name. I would always have to educate them on the fact that my name is Swahili and not Arabic. After explaining this nuance to the Evening Watch sergeant on the scene, he asked if I could attempt to establish negotiations with the suspect anyway. I approached the crawl space with great caution and started to talk with the suspect to build rapport. By this time, dispatch had advised that the suspect was in possession of the officer's service weapon as well as possibly having the officer's backup weapon. Being aware of that fact, I declined when the suspect invited me to come into the crawl space to talk. He was clearly testing the truthfulness of my assurance that I only wanted to talk to him. Naturally, he assumed I was attempting to set him up for execution by the quickly amounting APD officers. From a safe position outside of the hideout, I began negotiations.

I asked what it would take for the suspect to surrender to me peacefully to avoid any further injuries. The suspect responded that it was too late for all that, as he knew he had killed the officer. He stated that he was certain of it, but it was not intentional. He stated over and over again, "I didn't mean to kill that man, officer." He sobbed and was very emotional as he repeated this mantra. I continued to assure him that the officer was still alive, so it wasn't as bad as he believed. I was being less than truthful because, I was hearing radio transmissions that suggested the contrary. There were radio transmissions that the officer was "low sick" (critical), mixed with transmissions that he was possibly signal 48 (deceased). I honestly didn't know what to think. The only thing I was sure of was that I was personally going to bring in this suspect who had viciously shot down one of my fellow officers. He kept pleading for me to not let the other officers shoot him down in cold blood. I was able to convince him to tell me why he shot the officer since he claimed it wasn't intentional.

He stated that he caught a cab home from downtown. He was a street peddler and, ironically, had some sort of goods stand in the same 5 points area that I was responding from. He said he got out of the cab and went into his home to retrieve the fare for the ride. The cab driver suspected he was attempting to beat him for the fare when it took him a considerable amount of time to return. By the time he scrounged up the money, he found himself in a full-blown argument with the taxi driver. He said the officer arrived and spoke with the cab driver first. Apparently the cabbie advised that he wanted to press charges and the officer had made up his mind to oblige him without even hearing the suspect's side of the story. The suspect stated that the officer had his weapon drawn when he approached him at the front door. He said that whenever he attempted to give the officer his side of the story, the officer told him to be quiet and that he was under arrest. The suspect said he asked the officer to start a supervisor to the location, and the officer refused and advised again that he was under arrest. He said the officer became visibly shaken by the suspect's continued demand for a supervisor. He said the officer began to wave the gun somewhat uncontrollably in his face. He stated that he asked the officer to holster his weapon before he accidentally discharged while the suspect's young child was also standing there in the doorway. At this point, there was a growing tension. The officer was insisting that the suspect was to be taken into custody, and the suspect was verbally refusing the officer's demands to put his hands behind his back for cuffing. He told me that he continued going back and forth several times, asking the officer to call his supervisor to the scene and to holster his weapon. After the officer reached a level of agitation, the suspect feared the gun would accidentally discharge. The suspect said he disarmed the officer of his weapon. He said he apologized to the officer and pled with him to call his supervisor to the scene. He told the officer that he would relinquish his weapon to his supervisor, but he would not return it to the officer. He said his concern was that the officer would accidentally shoot him out of fear. He said the officer began to struggle with the suspect for control of the weapon, but he was knocked down. He said the officer began to reach for his backup weapon, and the suspect again pled for the officer to not do that and to just wait for the sergeant to arrive. He said he stated to the officer that he was sorry for disarming him but he didn't want to hurt the officer. He said that his concern was that the officer appeared so fearful of him, and was shaking so much that he thought the officer would accidentally shoot him in front of his son. He told me he didn't think that the officer held any malice toward him, but that he was shaking like a leaf with his gun drawn from his initial contact with him. The suspect said, "He was shaking so badly with that gun that I thought it would go off at any moment. That's why I took it from him." He said that once the officer went for his backup weapon he felt he had no choice other than to shoot the officer. He said he then fled with the officer's gun(s) and ran to this hiding place. At the time he was unclear as to whether he fled with both of the officer's weapons, but I was operating under the assumption that he was in possession of both firearms.

He again asked that I not let the now arrived SWAT team shoot him down like a dog. The suspect assured me over and over again that he didn't mean to hurt the officer. He explained again how he was only attempting to protect his family from a situation that seemed to rapidly spiral from bad to worse. I gave him my assurances that I wouldn't allow an execution as long as I was on the scene. After a few minutes he asked if I was Muslim. I was very much a Christian. But in my efforts to establish rapport, I made the mistake of indicating that I was of the Islamic faith. I had always been a student of world religions and therefore thought I knew enough about all the major religions to get me through the situation. Upon my revelation, he then greeted me with the traditional Islamic salutation of "As Salaam U Alaikum." I responded with "Wa Alaikum As Salaam." "Easy enough" I thought. Then he dropped a bomb. "Since you're a Muslim, I believe that you'll do everything to protect me, so I'm going to come out with you" he said. He continued "however, I know in my heart that those SWAT officers are probably going to shoot me down, even if it means shooting through you to get to me. Therefore, I want you to make Shahaadah (Muslim declaration of faith) with me before I come out there." "Crap!!! The jig is up!!!" I thought. "Look, brother" I said. I'm not actually fully converted to Islam yet, but I am studying to become a Muslim soon." I was desperately trying to salvage what little trust had been earned. Too late! His entire demeanor changed as he backed further into the crawl space and demanded a Muslim officer. He was adamant that he would only surrender to an officer of his faith.

I advised dispatch of the situation and requested any available Muslim officer on duty in the city. After checking, she advised that there were none, but that she would attempt to locate an off duty Muslim sergeant. After several minutes, dispatch advised that she had contacted Sgt. Adil Muwakkil (retired). I was vaguely familiar with the sergeant and advised radio that I would stand by until he arrived. Sensing the urgency of the situation, the sergeant 26'd in what seemed to be no more than 30 minutes. Once he arrived, I stepped off to the side and advised him what I had. He took over negotiations. The Sergeant spent a considerable amount of time talking with the suspect. He wanted to make sure that he had a full grasp of the situation. After what seemed like an eternity, they began their prayers in Arabic. A few minutes later, the sergeant reached into the space and retracted his hand with the officer's weapon(s), followed shortly by the suspect himself.

In relating this account, I am in no way suggesting that the suspect was justified in his acts against the officer. I am merely recounting what the suspect articulated to me (in the actual moment) as being his motivation for taking the course of action he did. Could he have been fabricating, embellishing, or even mistakenly misinterpreting the actions of the officer? Definitely! However, in the heat of an ongoing and still very volatile situation, his outcry to me rang sincere (at least, based on what seemed to be his honest perception of the events). Factor in that the suspect literally had no time to concoct such an elaborate story before speaking to me, and you have the reason that I feel compelled to report the conversation as it actually occurred. That being said... I am not insinuating that the officer was actually scared or any less courageous than any other officer who places him or herself in harm's way on a daily basis, globally. From my personal experience with the officer prior to and following the event, he has no hatred, disdain, or indifference toward people of color. I never worked with him in a capacity that would lend to me being able to observe his level of discomfort or fear of Black or Brown people. I have, however, been privy to this phenomenon throughout my career, both military and civilian, and can attest that it is a very real issue.

Unfortunately, this would not be the only case in my career where there was the suggestion of an officer being afraid of the members of the community that he or she was charged to serve and protect. Often times, this fear is not born out of racism or bigotry, but rather a prejudice that permeates throughout American culture. A prejudice based on stereotypes and handed down misperceptions. The demonization of the African American is something that is taught in our culture from childhood. It's reinforced through everything from the slanted reporting of the nightly news, to misinformation taught in our educational systems. This prejudice is even further perpetuated through word of mouth handed down by generations of biased thinkers and outlandish characterizations in the cinematic community. American citizens are, to a degree, systemically indoctrinated into the perception that people of color are animalistic and predisposed to violence. That's just a sad, but true fact. It's also the result of the very humanistic nature of fearing what one does not totally understand. As much as no one wants to admit it, a dangerous fear of people of color exists on police departments across the nation. Dangerous, because it often results in an officer overreacting to a situation that could have been handled more delicately or less aggressively. Indeed, even more objectively. Again, it's not always a matter of racism or bigotry that causes an officer to respond to a situation heavy-handedly. Some officers are so convinced and indoctrinated in their precepts about the criminality and natural violence of Black and Brown folks that they actually believe they're reacting to a situation reasonably. Thus, in their minds, they're getting the jump on the perceived "thug" before the perceived "thug" gets the jump on them. An even more disturbing aspect to this lunacy is the fact that there are even officers of color who hold these same beliefs and are equally afraid of Black folks.

In my career, I would come into contact with this phenomenon countless times. It would result in me rescuing the citizen from the officer whenever possible. It would get me further labeled and subjected to the opinions of my colleagues. It would even get me accused of being a racist myself at some point (which in my opinion... the oldest trick in the book is to label the person that calls out racism or injustice, as being the racist). Be that as it may, I would continue to combat injustice inside and outside of the precinct walls until my retirement in 2011.

The officer in this case would survive the attack and go on to one day become a sergeant himself. Sgt. Muwakkil would retire from APD some years later, but not before he and I would become good friends. I would actually convert to Islam the following year, and would remain a devout Muslim for [illegible]0 years before leaving the religion.

CHAPTER – 9

THE CALL

There is a practice in policing that I'm certain exists in other professions. Being punished for being a good worker is prevalent in law enforcement. Often times if you're an ideal employee, it can be a direct impediment to career advancement. There are supervising officers that flat out refuse to facilitate the career advancement of an officer simply because they don't want to lose a good worker. While this is intended, in most cases, to be a compliment to the hard working officer, oftentimes, it's the proverbial dagger through the officer's heart and his or her career. It's almost as if you're being punished for your dedication. There are a few commanders who promote excellence in their employees for the employee's benefit. Unfortunately, this number is exasperatingly low. Most times, the commander is simply exploiting the hard work of their employees for that "feather in their cap" to further boost themselves up the command structure. This often creates an environment that is encapsulated in a common military adage, "You have to mess up, to move up." You have to render yourself less than stellar or deficient to almost force your commander's hand in passing you on to someone else. A way of transferring the headaches as opposed to molding or supervising that officer into a productive team member. It often seems that employee development requires too much energy and/or commitment on the part of supervision. "Mess up, to move up" is also the military's way of explaining the seemingly lack of common sense at the upper levels of the rank structure. The same can, and often does, apply to law enforcement. Again, I'm certain that if took a poll of most professions where there is an organizational or paramilitary pecking order, the same can be found. I'm not picking on law enforcement or the military services. I'm just speaking from personal observation spanning over 35 years of total experience in the two fields. In effect, officers are often trapped in their own greatness...

And then there was the exception to the rule...

The word came down that Zone 1 was to receive a new precinct commander. This particular commander had been the precinct commander for Zone 6 for quite some time and had a pretty good reputation as being a fair man. He was known for being gentle in his ways but firm in his convictions. Major Lovett Goss (retired) would be a welcomed addition to the Zone 1 family. However, I was not aware at the time that my stint with him would be drastically short lived.

No more than a couple of months after his arrival, I got a phone call. I was at home enjoying my regular off days. After a couple of years of hard work and leading the watch in Part 1 arrests, I had finally earned weekends off. I was at home enjoying my family when my wife handed me the telephone. She had a concerned look on her face as she whispered "It's your job." Naturally, a million thoughts ran through my head as to what it could be. Had I messed up a report that needed correction? Was there an emergency in the city that required all personnel to be called in to work? Had I accidentally taken home the patrol car keys...again? As it turned out, none of the above was the situation. To my greater shock, it was the major himself on the line. This took me aback because the chain of command on police departments, as in the military, works both ways. That is to say, information is usually passed from one level of supervision to the next.

Information or communication usually doesn't jump 5 ranks, as it did in this case.

Major – "Officer Yabuku?" he asked as I answered the phone.

Me - "Yessir."

Major – "This is Major Goss. How are you doing today?"

Me – "Fine sir, and yourself?"

Major – "I'm doing great, but I'm curious about something. How long have you been assigned to Zone 1 Day Watch?"

Me – "A little more than a couple years, sir."

At this point I was curious as to what rookie mistake I'd made to give cause for the major to call me at home on my off days to chew me out. Whatever it was, it must have been pretty darn fantastical to warrant him jumping 5 command levels to speak to me personally. I was instantly upset with myself. As far I could tell in my couple of months or so of observation, the new major wasn't the type to rattle easily or get bent out of shape over minor issues. Whatever it was I had done, it had to be the dumbest thing I'd been able to muster in my career thus far. My respiration is increasing as the conversation continued...

Major – "Officer Yabuku, have you done anything during this period to piss anyone off, or have you been in trouble with OPS or anything like that?"

Me – "No sir. Not to my knowledge."

Major – "I've been going over all the personnel files in the Zone since I've been here. I haven't been able to locate any adverse action against you since you've been sworn."

My respiration begins to slow a little bit. But what exactly is he getting at? I continued to listen and respond with the customary "yes sir" to indicate that I'm still attentive to and in agreement with his assertions.

Major – "I see you have specialized operations military expertise as well as a counter- terrorism supervisor with your Army unit. You also have the best arrest record in the Precinct. Quite frankly, I'm having trouble figuring out why you're still in the Zone. Have you ever requested to go anywhere else within the Department?"

Me – "No sir."

Major – "Why???"

Me – "Well sir, as you noted, I have spent quite a few years in the military. 3 years active duty, as well as 10 years in the reserves. Since APD is a paramilitary organization, I figured it would be inconsiderate and insulting to the more senior officers on the department to even mention transferring out of the Zone before paying my dues."

Major – "And exactly what do you figure that to be?"

Me – "Well sir, based on military customs, I figure that to be at least 5 years of "grunt" work before I could consider myself as

> *having earned the right to request a transfer. I've only been on the job for 4 years so far."*

> *Major – "Well, that's quite noble of you, but I have a different opinion of the situation. I've seen a lot of officers' careers destroyed because they were not allowed to utilize their full potential. I've also seen the department suffer from the same thing. As far as I'm concerned, your performance record clearly shows that you've earned an opportunity. Don't get me wrong... I would love to keep you and let you continue to make me look good. However, that would be selfish on my part and the department would suffer from not capitalizing on training and experience that the Army has given you... at no cost to the City. I would love to look out for my specific Zone, but I have to think about the bigger picture and the benefit of the department."*

At this point I'm looking at my phone in complete astonishment. The fact that the MAJOR had invested so much thought into the issue was sobering to say the least. I had spent 2 years in Zone 1 and had never laid eyes on my precinct commander. The only time I even glimpsed at my Zone 1 Major, after 2 years, was when he basically kicked me out of his Zone. So much for command interacting with the common folks.

> *Me – "Yes sir, I understand and thank you for your acknowledgement."*

> *Major – "Great! I think you'd be better suited in the Special Operations Section (SOS). I just need to know, where in SOS would you be comfortable?"*

Me – "Well sir, I'm ashamed to ask... but, what units make up the SOS? Like I said, I truly had no plans on even familiarizing myself with other options on the department until after my 5th year."

Major – "SOS is comprised of the Motors (motorcycle unit), SWAT, Mounted Patrol, Air unit and the TAC (tactical) squad. I just need to know where you want to work, so I can call back the SOS commander and let him know. Once I inform him of where you want to go, he will advise me on a reporting location and time. Regardless of where you go, your reporting date will be Monday."

Me – "Sir, you mean the day after tomorrow?"

Major – "Correct. Is that a problem?"

Me – "No sir. When do you need my answer?"

Major – "Before we hang up in the next few seconds."

Me – "Yes sir. In that case I would like to be assigned to the TAC squad, just as break from uniform for a while."

Major – "Great! Either I or Major Holley, the SOS commander, will call you back in a while with the reporting information. Stay near your phone."

Me – Yes sir, and thank you very much for this opportunity. I won't make you regret it."

Major – "I'm sure you won't, son. Good luck on your career."

This would be my only direct contact with Major Goss, as my return call would be from the TAC unit sergeant, Jessie Pitts (retired). He would provide me with my reporting instructions for what would go on to be one of the shortest, yet impressionable and rewarding, assignments I would have over my entire career.

CHAPTER – 10

STICKY FINGERS

The TAC (Tactical) squad was a citywide plain-clothes unit that handled all street crimes. The only crimes we didn't handle were homicides and rapes. Everything else was fair game for enforcement. We ran all robbery decoy and stakeout operations citywide. The squad consisted of about 14 officers. Gender and racial diversity went a long way towards the unit's success. There were 7 Black males, 4 White males, 2 Black females, and 1 White female at the time I entered the squad. We were broken down into 2 person teams for our day-to-day patrols. We would combine teams to whatever size to fit whatever racial or gender profile situations dictated. There wasn't a very big turnover rate in the unit because it was considered a pretty choice assignment. Another reason for the low attrition rate was the nature of the job. Trust wasn't something that came automatic in this assignment. We were given a tremendous amount of leeway to conduct the type of operations that were necessary to yield such remarkable results. Because we were given so much latitude, it was imperative that the unit's members were screened with great scrutiny on issues such as honesty and integrity. Basically, you didn't select the TAC squad, the TAC squad selected you. It was a breath of fresh air to be in the company of a group of like minded individuals... A group of folks who took more pride in locking up the right people and preventing as much havoc in the communities, than in hitting a certain arrest number. The most remarkable and gratifying thing for me was the fact that every single person assigned to the unit was conscientious about doing everything above board. We took a lot of pride in not having to cut corners, deviate from departmental policies, or flat out break the law just to make a solid case. Every soul in the unit displayed the utmost integrity and character. I'm proud and honored to have had the opportunity to work with such a fine group of individuals. For some period of time prior to my arrival in the unit, the TAC squad had been lauded as the most effective unit in the department. I was pleased to see that tradition was still carrying on when I got there. You would be hard pressed to find a group of harder-working and committed professionals anywhere on the department. We tried to give the perception that we were everywhere, and we were quite successful in doing so. We took a great amount of pride in being able to think outside the box in order to bring some pretty significant and newsworthy cases to resolution. Wherever a trend developed within the city, we were dispatched and tasked with bringing it to closure before it could reach full potential. When there was a rash of convenience store robberies, prior to my arrival, the unit formed the "stakeout" detail. The detail was still going on when I got there. There had been a significant reduction in the robberies due to the squad's growing reputation for putting down robbers rather decisively, to say the least. Community concerns began to surmount at the growing prevalence of the police shootings. This facilitated the creation of window signs to give would be robbers fair warning at stakeout locations. The signs stated plainly that you were entering an APD stakeout location and any attempt to rob the store would be at your own risk. The robberies had simmered down enough that the unit could direct its major efforts elsewhere, but still keeping an eye on the robberies. Shortly after my arrival in the squad, convenience store robberies spiked again. Majik Markets and 7 elevens were being hit like they were going out of style. There was no one set of description(s) for the suspect(s). Nor was there any apparent rhyme or reason as to a specific pattern. We amassed all reports city wide and disseminated separate copies to each 2-person team. Using the same color-code system, each team highlighted whatever patterns they saw with a specific color highlighter. Once that was done, we put all the reports together and plotted all the combined patterns on a pin map and, wah-lah!!! We had a clear indication of the most likely location to be robbed next. You had to be there to really appreciate the look on a robber's face when he's staring down the barrel of a shotgun and wondering how in the hell we knew to expect him. We got eerily good at predicting dates, locations, and even times the robberies were most likely to occur. Sometime the robbery would take place just as we were setting up behind the 1 way mirror overlooking the store clerk and register. Seldom did we have to stake out a location more than a week. Even more rarely did we have to sit in hiding more than a few hours. During my stint on the robbery detail, we were able to eradicate the issue without a single shooting. I think that was greatly due to the already established reputation of the detail. When we would present ourselves from the back room, suspects would hurriedly lay down their weapons and assume a prone position on the floor. All the while yelling "don't shoot, officer!"

We resolved trends that received a high volume of media coverage. When there was an emerging trend of rapes occurring in the city's SW quadrant, we were dispatched. When there were a growing number of women being harassed in the downtown area by vagrants, we were dispatched. One of the most memorable assignments was when there was an increasing amount of pedestrian robberies in the downtown area. We identified the targeted victim profile as being touristy-looking, White males. We just happened to have a perfect decoy in the unit... The commander himself. Captain "Cap" Harold B.

Goldhagen was a middle aged, White male with a receding hairline. One of the most unassuming individuals you would ever meet. However, he was not to be taken lightly. Although he had a heart of gold and the demeanor of a rabbi, he had nerves of steel when it came to the job. He also had a very short fuse when it came to protecting his officers... in the streets or "upstairs" in headquarters. He always kept the brass off our backs, and we always went 10 extra miles to bring in career changing cases.

Once we profiled our likely victims, Cap quickly volunteered to take the role as decoy. He made an unusual request. He said that he really wanted to catch this guy dead to right with no chance of the suspect walking away from prosecution on a technicality. Therefore, he wanted us to wait until the suspect actually physically assaulted him in some sort of way before the cover teams would move in to affect the arrest. We begged to differ with Cap's plan of action but acquiesced when he insisted that he wouldn't allow the suspect to bring great harm to him. Reluctantly, we accepted his terms and set out for the detail. I was personally assigned to another detail on the other side of town, so I was not a part of the surveillance/take down team that would be covering the captain. When I did see him in the precinct later on, I was able to see the small laceration to his forehead. The respect and pride that I would feel for Cap in that moment was never earned by another commander for the remainder of my career with the APD.

Then came the changes...

A year or so into the assignment, we lost several personnel to natural attrition. Some officers were promoted to detective, others made supervisor promotions, and some left the department all together for various reasons. The most heartbreaking cause was the one officer who succumbed to his own service weapon because of domestic issues. At any rate, we received a few transfers to the unit to fill the growing void.

One of the transfers was an officer from Zone 3. He was a likable enough guy and was known for his excellent skills behind the keyboard of an organ or piano. He was assigned to ride with me and my partner officer, Delrick "D.O." White. D.O. and I were a perfect mesh. We got along great and had a lot in common. We shared identical beliefs as to our approach to the job and our intentions regarding making a difference in the communities we serviced. We were assigned a new officer to the unit to break in until he could be situated with a regular partner. We had no problem having a temporary addition to our team, but made it very clear to him that we had a particular way of going about our business. For years now, Zone 3 had been steeped in bad press and criminal prosecution of corrupt officers. In fact, the newspaper photo array of arrested and indicted officers mentioned in an earlier chapter, were predominately Zone 3 officers. We told him that we did not want to prejudge him, but that we had ZERO tolerance for corrupt behavior. He acknowledged that he understood. D.O. and I were looking forward to breaking in the new guy.

About a week or two into the new guy's orientation with the unit, the honeymoon was over. This was as normal a Saturday as any, I suppose. The three of us set our agenda for the day, and we agreed that the first thing on the list was a meal break. Most of our planned activities would take place later on in the evening. As we headed to S&S cafeteria on Campbellton Road, on the city's SW side, our new officer advised that he was low on cash. Once we arrived at the restaurant, he reiterated that he was broke. D.O. and I thought he was joking, so we began to laugh amongst ourselves. Frustrated with our dismissal, the officer turns out his pants pockets in an effort to prove his assertions. We stopped laughing and agreed to pay for his meal. He went on to explain how he had left his wallet at home and how he was going to pay us back and so on. We explained that it wasn't a loan, and he owed us nothing. All we asked was that he have our backs when we "accidentally" left our wallets at home. We all had a good laugh and a pleasurable meal. As we were in route to our pre-designated location to meet up with another team, we happened to drive up on some activity that was easily recognizable as drug sales in the Techwood Homes area of Zone 5. The 4 suspects didn't recognize we were the police until we bailed out of our unmarked vehicle. Our badges were in plain sight hanging from lanyards around our necks as we jumped from the car. The suspects took off on foot into a wooded area in the rear of the apartments. Each of us took off after a different suspect. I went straight, D.O. went to the left, and the new guy went to the right. The 4th suspect was home free. We figured 3 out of 4 wouldn't be bad. Besides, we could always get one of the three to give up the fourth suspect during our interrogation after the arrest. Yes, I said interrogation. That was pre "debriefing" days. In those days, if you were a witness or victim, you were "interviewed." If you were a suspect, you were "interrogated." Period! That's not to imply or conjure images of a suspect sitting under a spotlight and being assaulted with a phone book. Those were just the terms used to distinguish which was which for prosecutorial purposes. It clearly indicated if you were being questioned by the police as an accused or otherwise. Semantics of a pre overly politically correct society. Nowadays, "debrief" is the politically accepted term for all investigatory conversations.

I lost my guy, but D.O. caught his. We began to yell for the other officer who was now out of our sight. Great! The last thing we needed was to get this new guy hurt before he'd had an opportunity to be assigned to a regular partner. We began to grow concerned. He was not responding to our calls for his location. We couldn't leave D.O.'s guy unattended at the car, nor could I leave D.O. alone with the guy because we were in plain clothes. Also, to leave him alone would leave too much room for him to be outnumbered and ambushed by the other suspects should they circle back. We couldn't take the suspect back into the shrubbery with us. Just as we decided to cut D.O.'s guy loose and head back in to locate the new guy, out he pops from around the building with a suspect in tow. We asked him why he didn't answer us. He stated that he didn't hear us. We blasted him concerning his tactics and assured him that we would work with him on improving them. However, we commended him on actually catching his suspect.

The entire time, the suspect was asking to talk to either me or D.O. We initially informed him that we would speak with him later after we spoke with the other officer. The suspect waited patiently. When he surmised that we had finished our conversation with the officer, the suspect again requested an audience with either one of us. Assuming that he had information on the other suspects, we told him that he could speak to all three of us.

Neither I, nor D.O. was totally prepared for what the suspect was so pressed to share.

"Well sir. That officer right there (referring to the new guy) took money from me in the woods. That's why he didn't answer when he heard you calling. We both heard you calling very clearly" the suspect said. I'm sure I used a few expletives when I grabbed the suspect up in his collar and cautioned him to be very careful about his accusations. I told him that we were not a bunch of renegade officers such as the type that he was probably used to dealing with. I retorted that we didn't do that sort of thing. D.O. had a few choice words for him as well as we both got all the way up in the suspect's face. I'm sure that to anyone passing by we looked like a couple drill sergeants indoctrinating a new recruit fresh off the bus. However, we were quite serious with our assertions. All the TAC squad members were very careful in our conduct so as not to bring such accusations down on the unit. No one wanted to be that team that gave the unit a bad name. We took a tremendous amount of pride in being an honest squad. Especially in a time when so much was going on throughout the department to bring into question the overall integrity of the police force.

The suspect insisted so much that D.O. and I asked the officer to turn out his pockets in front of the suspect. Our intent was to discredit the suspect's claim and squash any OPS complaint that he may try to file against the officer later. The officer looked at D.O. and me with utter disbelief, disgust, and disappointment. He questioned our loyalty to the badge and the Thin Blue Line. He couldn't believe that we would take the word of a perp over his. While the officer was rebuking us, the suspect went on to inform us that he had a $50 dollar bill, tri- folded, with specific writing on the back. He said the officer had placed it in his right pants pocket.

Faced with our repeated insistence, the officer finally gave in and turned out his right pants pocket. He attempted to palm the folded bill as he removed his hand from his pocket. However, D.O. and I both caught his attempt at slight-of-hand. We confiscated the bill and gave it back to the suspect. The officer began to protest that it was actually his money and we had no right to give it to the suspect. We quickly reminded him that he had turned out the same pocket no more than an hour ago to reveal it was empty at the restaurant. He digressed. We informed the suspect that he had every right to file a complaint with OPS, but that we would rather he allowed us to handle it in house. The suspect indicated that he had no intention of going to OPS, as they would never take his word over a cop's anyway. He said that all he wanted was his money back, and he thanked us for being the first honest cops that he had ever encountered in his life.

We requested transport from the Zone 5 paddy wagon for our two prisoners and then headed back to the precinct to finish up the paperwork. Needless to say, it was a long and arduous ride. We were only a few minutes from the precinct but the silence and thickness of the air made it seem like an eternity. As soon as we arrived at the precinct, I told the officer to stand by and that D.O. and I were going to fill the captain in on what happened. I told him that Cap was probably going to want to speak to him after we were finished meeting with him, so to just sit tight for a few minutes. D.O. and I sat our paperwork down on the table in the squad room and headed straight for the captain's office. We knocked on the door. "Come in!" the captain yelled. We both sat in seats, side by side, directly in front of the captain's desk. "What can I help you with?" he asked. D.O. began first. "Well Cap, we need some advice on the best way to handle a situation that…" D.O. was mid sentence when I cut him off by interjecting "Captain, that motherf----r can't ride with us anymore!!!" The captain's jaw dropped, as it was his first and only time hearing me cuss. In fact, D.O. had the same reaction an hour earlier when he witnessed me cussing for the first time as I jacked up the suspect's collar upon his accusation of the officer's theft. I always prided myself in being able to communicate without the use of such language. For 14 years I had avoided the 3 traps of the Army – alcohol, coffee and cussing. I was determined that I would not fall into those same three vices that were also customary within civilian law enforcement. This day would be an exception to my rule. For me, cussing was never an indication that I had lost my cool or was out of control. In fact, the truth of the matter was quite the contrary. My use of choice words was always very calculated for shock effect or emphasis behind a statement that I felt very strongly about. Whenever used, it was always to drive a point. The captain turned his attention to D.O. and asked what I was talking about. We both went on to explain to him in detail what occurred. We finished by telling the captain that we didn't care what he did with the officer, but he could never ride with us again. We told him that we would be happy to write statements if he desired them. He directed us to go ahead and write the statements, and he would take it from there. That was the last time the officer worked in our unit. We never knew what happened to him, and we never asked. We did later hear that he was eventually fired for misconduct. Imagine that.

CHAPTER – 11

FIF GONE TOO FAR

My time on the TAC squad really flew by. Within a year's time, I learned so much about the job and community relations. The unique opportunity to experience the eclectic and diverse nature of the different Zones was eye-opening. It was as if each Zone was totally autonomous of the other 5. That had also been the impression I developed as a cadet going through the academy's field training program. Field training consisted of 12 weeks of training. Each cadet officer worked two weeks in 5 of the Zones. We partnered with an FTO in each Zone. We spent 2 weeks in each Zone, for a total of 10 weeks of Zone training. Every cadet also spent 2 weeks in communications, assigned to a dispatcher. This resulted in a grand total of 12 weeks of field training. During Zone field training, it was the SPO's responsibility to train you in doing your job. It was a form of on-the-job training that was required before you graduated the academy and was assigned your actual work station/Zone. The primary function of field training was to acquaint the officer with a taste of the actual dynamic and unique nature of each Zone. The intention was to familiarize you with the structure and inner workings of the precinct itself, as well as the idiosyncrasies of the indigenous population of each geographical region/Zone. However, I couldn't truly appreciate the diversity of each Zone until I was completely immersed in the various cultures for the extended period of time spent in the TAC squad. Another glaring differentiation between the Zones was the department's approach to how services were provided for each particular Zone.

After having worked many special details while in the TAC unit, the Street Sweep / Zero Tolerance special detail would be my last. I had worked the abortion clinic demonstrations detail, which eventually led to a bombing of one of the clinics. I had worked Freak Nic, later known as Black College Spring Break details. I had also worked several decoy details for robberies, rapes, and drugs. As I said, if there was a problem anywhere in the city, we were thrown at it. We actually enjoyed the variety in our work and looked forward to the daily surprise of a new challenge.

However... the Street Sweep detail was a horse of a completely different color!

To this day, I have no idea what facilitated the need for the, now infamous, Street Sweep/Zero Tolerance detail. I don't know if there was a drastic surge in crimes in the city's most impoverished areas, or if there was a particular incident that triggered APD's response. For all I knew, some politician, or perhaps the chief himself, just came up with a notion to deal a heavy-handed blow to crime in the city on a citywide scale. I simply did not, and still do not know. The only thing I was sure of then, and now, is that I did not like what I saw, in the least bit.

The detail was established throughout the city in the housing developments and the lower income areas, such as the Bluff. It was focused solely on the south side. It included a collection of officers from every work site within the department. If you weren't assigned to a specific and critical task within the department, you were assigned to the detail. There were somewhere around 80 or so officers assigned to the detail. Possibly as many as 100. When the detail was formed, I thought it was great that the city was finally serious about crime in these communities. "The department is finally committing a substantial amount of resources to actually make an impact on crime," I thought to myself. I took a loose head count of all the officers packed into the roll call room. There were a lot of familiar faces in the once large, but now seemingly small, roll call area. I shared small talk with a few officers I hadn't seen in quite some time, and it was to some degree a pleasant reunion for a lot of us present. I also noticed that because the staffing was done with mostly "non-essential" personnel, some of these folks would definitely be fish out of water in some of the areas that we were to create a presence. I was happy to see that during the assignment phase of the muster, the officers with less experience or exposure were being assigned to officers with more. Each group would have its share of land, sea, and air types. We were to be divided into teams of approximately 10 officers and be deployed to various areas citywide. So far, so good. At this point, the detail seemed to be really thought-out and well-planned. I was feeling more optimistic about the department's desire to clean up the neighborhoods than I had ever felt before.

Then came the marching orders.

The commander who conducted roll call gave a summation of the purpose of the detail. It was to create uniform saturation in the city's highest crime areas and push down the incidents basically by officer presence. Our objective was to challenge everyone on the streets in these areas, thereby discouraging crime. At this point, the sweet taste in my mouth began to sour as I envisioned exactly what that would look like. At first glance, it wasn't a pretty picture. I kept my thoughts to myself as we were dismissed and started to our designated areas. I figured I'd at least see how the first day panned out before I formed an opinion.

The day was spent just as predicted. We would stop each and every person walking through any area that we determined to be a high crime area. I was always big on visibility and other crime prevention measures, so this was right up my alley. I was actually enjoying the opportunity to reconnect with some of the residents in the Bluff area as well as Herndon Homes. It was also enjoyable to establish new relationships in some of the areas that I had never worked before. After all, people are people. This experience would have a shelf life of about 1 week.

Then came new marching orders.

Somewhere around the second week of the detail, someone higher up decided to up the ante a little. We were now being instructed in roll call to continue what we had been doing. There had apparently been a slight decrease in crime stats, but not dramatic enough. Now we were to incorporate a practice of completing an FIF (Field Interview Form) card on anyone we stopped that gave us the least suspicion as to their activities or reasons for being in the area. After roll call, I asked for an audience with the commander. I asked him to explain exactly what constituted "suspicious activity." He instantly grew defensive and asked me how long I had been on the department. I told him I had been on about 5 years. He gave me a stern, and somewhat disgusted, look. He quipped that I should know what's suspicious by now. He began to walk away, but seemed to reconsider. He stopped and turned back to me and snapped "Just break up any groups you see forming out there." I told him that with all due respect, based on the area I grew up in, 3 or 4 Black dudes walking down the street together is not suspicious to me. He said "well, it is to me... So just keep everybody moving!" "Copy that, sir" I said. I left the room to meet up with my team.

Over the next few days, people began to take note that I wasn't filling out any FIF cards. I would explain to them that I was really wrestling with the constitutionality of that practice. Until I could figure a way to square it with my conscience, I would just be out there for backup in the event of any fights or other violence. Another disturbing thing began to occur. Certain officers started to become creative with the FIF forms. They decided to take it upon themselves and show initiative to the command staff. After taking down a person's pertinent information, such as name, birth date, address, nicknames, associates present at the time, visible scars/marks/tattoos, etc., they would then have the person to affix their thumbprint to the back of the card. They would then take it a step further and take a Polariod photograph of the person that they would staple to the back of the card. As the day went on, more and more officers began to pick up this tactic. By the end of the day, the entire detail was rolling with the new process.

What!!!

I don't think I got any sleep that night as I laid awake rehearsing how I would present my case to the command staff in the next day's roll call. I would do as I had done before and wait until roll call broke. I would then approach one of the commanders and make him or her aware of the improper practice that was beginning to take root and allow them the opportunity to squash it before it got out of hand. Good! I'm set for work. Once the roll call was formed, the commander began to give the updates and any additional information we may need before being turned loose to our respective areas of concentration. Just as he was about to release us to go to work, he stated that he had one more thing. It had been brought to his attention that some officers had taken the initiative to evolve the original plan to better suit our efforts on the streets. He went on to actually applaud those "innovative" officers and encouraged everyone else to adopt the new creative tactic.

Again, What!!!

"Sir" I chimed in just as he was about to dismiss us. I'm having a serious problem with the constitutionality of this practice." He asked "what exactly is your problem officer?" His tone was clear. He was not asking what my problem was with the instructions. Rather, his tone suggested that he was questioning what my personal malfunction was. Whether he meant it that way or not, I took it personally. Feeling personally attacked, my father came gushing forth. One of the officers shared with me later that I was noticeably offended. I assured him that I most definitely was. I went on to explain my position to the commander and the entire roll call of 80 or so officers. I said "the idea that a person who is not accused or even suspected of a crime would have an official police file generated on them is reprehensible, illegal and unconstitutional. I would hate to think that just because my son was frequenting a particular area he would find himself in a police department's database as if he were a criminal. Not to mention, the message we're sending to the community and our own collective psyche is that "you may not have committed a crime yet... but you will... you ALL do... and when you do... we already have you in our system." With all due respect sir, I refuse to participate in this unconstitutional action."

By this point, the commander was visibly irritated with me. He glared at me and snapped "does anybody have anything else?" Eerie silence. "Good! Dismissed!" he barked. As I began to walk away, he yelled out to me, "Yabuku, let me speak to you for a minute before you go out. It's clear to me that you've had a problem with this detail from day one. These orders come down from high up, and it's not going anywhere anytime soon. I understand your concern, but THEY want names on cards and a boatload of cases to justify allocating all this manpower. We can expect to be out here for at least the next few weeks, if not months. What do you propose to do? Do you want me to pull you off the detail and send you back to your regular assignment?" "No, sir" I responded. "My partner is working the detail and I wouldn't leave him to have to work with someone else. I'll consider myself extra security for him and the others assigned to my group. I'll make cases where they present themselves and perform all aspects of my sworn duty, but I meant what I said about not participating in anything I feel is unethical" I said. "Yabuku… I appreciate you not bailing on us, and I'm told you're a pretty good cop. Just go out there and do what you always do" he said. "Copy that! Thank you, sir" I said. The detail went on for several more years.

The TAC squad would receive some devastating news midstream of the detail. We were being disbanded!!

Out of nowhere came the news. We were taken totally off guard. There was a newly formed REDDOG (Run Every Drug Dealer Out of Georgia) drug unit. It was created a couple of years earlier, and its mission was to form a direct assault on the street level drug traffic in the city. The officers dressed out in military style battle dress uniforms (BDU's). Their orders were to hit the drug trade hard and relentlessly. They did just that. Some of their hard line tactics brought a lot of media attention and public scrutiny down on the city. The naysayers faded away as the charismatic chief of police began to find favor with the communities and the local media. There could be no denial as to the effectiveness of the unit. The only debate lied within their tactics. Of course, that too became a non-issue because they fared well in the court of public opinion.

There began to circulate a rumor that we were being disbanded to beef up the REDDOG unit. At that time, the TAC squad was bringing in more and bigger drug cases with our 12-person unit, than the 30 or so persons that comprised the REDDOG. The problem was that they were specifically designed to work drugs...solely. The TAC squad never set out to outdo the REDDOG unit with drug arrests. Besides, we worked all crimes. Truthfully, drugs were the crime that I enjoyed working least. Besides, there was already a Narcotics detective unit to work drugs. Now, there was the addition of a tactical arm to the city's war on drugs. We figured that our mission was so divergent from the REDDOG mission that the rumors had to be false.

When the TAC unit dissolution came, there were feelings of resentment. Despite being told that our expertise was needed to benefit the department's shifting priority to fighting street level drugs, we couldn't help the feeling that there was another reason for our demise. We felt the true reason was that we had outperformed the new unit. This, of course, produced a little embarrassment for its creator and benefactor, who was now the chief of police. There was an interview process for REDDOG assignments, soon followed by a written order. Just like that... The TAC squad was no more...

When the personnel order came out, there were a few surprises on the back page. As it turned out, not everyone was REDDOG bound. 8 officers were assigned to REDDOG, including D.O. Two officers were to be sent back to their original Zones where they worked prior to their assignment to the TAC unit. Officer H. Singletary (retired) and I were to be assigned to the SWAT team. We would become SWAT team partners after completing training. Our fairly new commander on the TAC squad, Lieutenant Ronnie Shaw (retired), who replaced the then retired Captain Goldhagen, was to be assigned to SWAT also. One of the TAC unit's sergeants would be transferred to the Fugitive Unit. We were literally dispersed to the 4 corners of the department. It will always be the most memorable assignment of my career. Good times... Great times!

CHAPTER – 12

SWAT: WHAT? HOW? AND WHY?

Being a member of any agency's Special Response Team (SRT) or Special Weapons And Tactics (SWAT) team is not only one of the highest honors to be bestowed on an officer, but it's also one of the greatest responsibilities an officer will face in his or her career. I took both aspects of my new assignment quite seriously. After going through an extremely rigorous basic SWAT training, which was conducted by a handful of select APD SWAT team members, it was mandatory to attend the State's SWAT training at the Georgia Public Safety Training Center (GPSTC) in Forsyth, Georgia. Frankly, the two weeks of training in Forsyth seemed like a walk in the park compared to the challenge of the 6 weeks APD SWAT school. I will refrain from going into detail about the training, for obvious reasons, but suffice it to say that it was the toughest training I have ever endured to date. That's taking into consideration all other training I've experienced, including Army Basic Training, Airborne training, Drill Instructor training and even Expert Infantryman Badge training. Just knowing they too had conquered the monstrous challenge, I had no problem being able to trust the skill set of my fellow SWAT officers.

Still, I couldn't help being curious as to how I had dodged the bullet of being transferred to REDDOG.

To me, REDDOG was one of the most undesirable jobs on the department. This was based solely on the fact that I had no interest in narcotics enforcement. For some reason, it seemed that most departments across the nation weren't serious about the so-called "war on drugs." From my perspective, it all seemed to be just a show. In the mean time, narcotics officers were being killed and seriously injured all over the country for something that amounted to nothing more than a dog and pony show to placate the advocates of this national endeavor. At any rate, I've always held narcotics officers and agents in the highest esteem. I just could never reconcile the loss of a single "narc's" life with the underlying agenda of the so-called "war on drugs."

The SWAT team was solid. There wasn't a weak link within the unit as far as I could tell. There was excellent supervision, coupled with the most talented tactics officers on the department. I was honored to be amongst them and wear the SWAT uniform BDU's. The team was divided into 2 Watches. The Day Watch worked from 10:00 a.m. – 6:00 p.m., with the Evening Watch working from 6:00 p.m. – 2:00 a.m. I was assigned to the Evening Watch. After settling into the assignment and having established myself as a qualified SWAT officer, I took the opportunity to approach one of my supervisors with this burning question. I asked how I had come to avoid the mass transfer to REDDOG. In fact, I thought I had been keeping a pretty low profile since joining the department. I was always the quietest person on any assignment I worked, and I tended to keep to myself or with a select few officers in order to avoid involvement in anything questionable. True enough, there had been a few occasions where I challenged some systemic practices, but surely those incidents were constricted to their specific locales. After nearly 6 years on the job, I still had no idea how much and how fast news traveled around the department. Fortunately for me, pretty much just the good news about me had traveled into the SWAT precinct. The supervisor explained that the commander had kept an eye on me since my academy days. What??? How??? Why???

During the academy, I had been an overachiever. There were awards handed out at graduation for academics, shooting, and physical fitness. My objective, from day 1 was to be the recipient of all three. A clean sweep… My motivation was simple. I wanted to do it just to prove to myself it could be done. I had graduated my Army basic training with honors for the same reason. In fact, my entire life had been nothing more than one continuous marathon of competitions with myself. My goal in high school was to be an honor student and an All American athlete. I have always wanted to be the best at anything I have ever set my sights on. The police academy was no different. Unfortunately, I would fall short in my efforts.

> *As was customary on the first day of the academy, each student was required to introduce him or herself and briefly explain why she or he wanted to be the po-leece. When my turn came around, I simply stated that I wanted to be an officer to save lives; and that I intended to work my way up to the chief's job. At which time, I would be about the business of changing lives. I still maintain that goal today. I lost count of the times during my career that people would tell me this was just a pipe dream. "Yabuku, you're not political enough to ever be chief" they'd say. If I had a nickel for every time I was told that, I would be scribing this book from a billion dollar mansion.*

> *I was pretty consistent with my performance in all areas and phases of my mandated training. My scores were consistently high. I was neck and neck with a couple of other com-*

petitors in all three categories. In spite of my hard work and dedication to achieving my goal, I would ultimately fall shy of the objective. The final tally would determine that I would be edged out for the academics award by .5. Yep! 1/2 of a stinking point... However, I couldn't have fallen to a better man. Vernon Shuffett (retired) was a true gentleman, scholar and officer. He would go on to be the first person of our class to be promoted to supervisor. He would then turn around and give back the promotion, once exposed to the unethical or questionable requirements required of the rank. A true pillar of a man... I would place second in the shooting competition also. Again, by an excruciatingly close margin. Once the final scores were calculated, Gil Fernandez (RIP) had beaten me out by 1 bullet. Gil was a transplant like myself, but he'd previously worked at some police department in Florida. He had an over-the-top, cocky personality and always felt that he was in competition with everyone. He was, by far, the most high-strung cadet in our class. In fact, he was so assured of himself that he regularly tested the nerves of the training staff. They took great pleasure one day in bringing him down a peg or two. It was the first time any of us had seen any human vulnerability in this guy. No matter how hard the staff rode him, he was never revealed to have a chink in his armor. At least not until one fateful morning...

It was around the 6th week of training. We'd only spent a couple of hours of classroom instruction on what I believe was a Wednesday morning. It was our normal break time between 1-hour blocks of instruction. This would have been our second break of the morning. Just as we were about to break, we were ordered by the instructor to remain in our seats. Then, we were told that we were being subjected to a random drug dog search. Our personal vehicles in the parking lot would be searched as well. They went on to instruct us that if anyone left the classroom or attempted to leave, they would be terminated from employment on the spot. I can't begin to describe the looks on our faces. To say that we all felt ambushed would be an understatement. Nevertheless, not a single cadet had a look of fear on their face. I was sure we were all good to go. At least I knew for sure that I was. The dogs came through the classroom and failed to hit on any of us. No surprises, as everyone in the class seemed to be pretty confident of a clean search. We were ordered to go stand by our vehicles. You could almost see everyone's expression change. We all looked at each other almost apologetically for what could possibly happen. I could clearly see that everyone else was thinking the exact thing I was. "I know I don't have any drugs in my car because I don't consume any type of drugs... But I can't vouch for my knucklehead cousin or brother or best friend who borrowed my car a couple days ago." We all had the most defeatist looks on our faces that can be imagined. The dogs methodically went by every car and cadet. No hits. One car left. Gil's car... The dogs went absolutely bat crazy!!! They had to pull Gil away from his own vehicle before the dogs turned their aggression to him. The K-9 handlers got the dogs under control and pulled them off the vehicle. A quick vehicle search yielded a bag of marijuana. Of course, Gil denied any knowledge of the drugs as he was stretched out on the hood of his car to be handcuffed. They sat him to the side and began the interrogation. Gil's usual tanned olive complexion was now stark white.

The grilling went on for what seem like an eternity before they took off the cuffs and announced that it was all an elaborate prank. I believe it was Investigator Darleen Neeley (Major, retired) that made the statement to the entire class. "Let this be a lesson to all of you that it doesn't pay to be an a'hole to the people who are trying to train you to stay alive out there" she said.

Sheesh!!! Point taken!!!

The one award that I would be the recipient of was the physical fitness (PT) trophy. I, apparently, made somewhat of a spectacle of myself in the process.

The final PT test consisted of 5 components: the obstacle course, pull-ups, pushups, sit-ups, and the mile and 1⁄2 run. I was always in pretty good physical condition. I played basketball in high school and was known to be one of few players who could play every second of every game if necessary. I did a tremendous amount of laps around the University of Detroit (U of D) every day of the week, and all year long. On Sundays after church, I would change into my running clothes and hit the run. During the offseason, I would hit the run. After an already exhausting practice, I would sometimes hit the run. This gave me a decisive edge over my teammates and competing schools as far as endurance goes. I ran in the snow, rain, or sun. It just didn't matter to me. In fact, I still maintain a daily running regiment to this day. Going into the military directly upon my graduation from high school made basic training considerably easy for me. Almost everything we did was built on fitness and endurance, which was something I had no shortage of supply. I went from active duty into a reserve unit and was a consistent recipient of the Army's annual fitness award (300 Award). By the time I got to the police academy, I was in the best shape of my life. Because of the camaraderie nature of the academy training, often times the entire class is required to adjust to the pace of the slowest person in the exercise. This is to instill the long held tradition of all occupations of arms – "Never leave a man behind." The only problem was that, over time, this was causing my level of fitness to decline. As a remedy, I would remain behind after class and make an additional run after everyone else had left. After awhile, I began to also incorporate working out in the gym, which was located on the grounds. On certain days, the SWAT team and other officers would show up for their pre or after work workouts. They seemed to be a pretty cool bunch of guys, but I was a recruit and I knew where my "place" was. When sworn officers would come into the gym, I would lower my gaze and not speak unless I was spoken to. I would then gather my things and immediately exit the facilities. This went on until one day SWAT officer Kirk Butler (Sgt, retired) invited me to work out with him. I started to explain to him my recruit status when he interrupted me. "I know what the f--k you are, but I still need a spot. Besides, all your instructors are gone home, so stop being a p---y and spot me up." "Yes, sir" I responded. "That sir" sh-t's not going to work either" he said. "I can go back to being "sir" tomorrow, but right now I'm Kirk or Butler" he said. Neither of us knew at that time that one day we would become the best of friends and SWAT teammates. One day, one of my instructors would show up after duty hours and catch me working out red handed. He asked if I hadn't been PT'd enough during my regular training day. I told him that I had, but I was always kind of crazy when it came to punishing myself and testing my own limits. He said that he could only admire my dedication and gave me his blessings. He warned me to make sure I didn't let news of this get back to the rest of the staff, because it was absolutely against policy. "Copy that, sir" I said, as I went back to exercising.

The final PT test was for the official record. Unlike the other 2 categories where the final score was based on a cumulative scale over the entirety of the academy, the PT award came down to this one day. I had the highest score on the obstacle course. 1 down and 4 events to go... I had the highest score on the pull-ups and sit-ups. So far, so good. Not a cakewalk, but still within my grasp. In the mile and 1/2 run, I came in at 2nd or 3rd place. Not so great, but I was hopeful that I had enough of a cushion in the other events to keep me in a comfortable position. The only event remaining was the pushups. I had to really put out on this event because Gil was only a few points behind me. I knew this because he was beginning to really irritate me by trying to make this a competition between the two of us. I was in my usual zone of competing against myself. I truly just wanted to see how far I could push myself. It was for no other purpose than to feel accomplished in knowing that I had left every ounce of sweat and effort out on that PT course. Gil had another agenda. Some of the other classmates came to me to let me know that Gil was checking with the scorekeeper after every event to inquire what MY score was. He was overheard saying that he was going to deny me the PT trophy the *same way he had denied me the shooting trophy. I didn't know until that moment that he had been in a self imposed competition with me the entire span of our training. I didn't have a clue.*

To this day, I still have no idea why Gil singled me out. I trained hard and was always willing to help my classmates in any way I could. As I stated before, I tended to keep to myself, but I wasn't anti-social by any measure. I had held several study sessions at my home to help others with the academics. I had invited a couple of classmates to stay after hours to assist them with improving their running times. Most importantly, since several of my classmates were younger than me, they tended to seek me out for advice on a multitude of issues. Gil had always been standoffish in a way, but I had no idea how deep the apparent resentment ran.

Everyone else had completed their pushups, and it was now my turn. I wasn't keeping track of anyone else's score, but based on my loose count, no one had done more than 75 pushups. As I got down in to the front leaning rest (pushup) position, I was pretty confident that I would be able to cinch the PT trophy. Since my time in the Army, I had been doing at least 1,000 pushups almost every day. It was a part of my daily exercise regimen. I actually preferred pushups to weight lifting for resistance training. Once in the starting position, the training sergeant would give me the signal to begin as he started the clock. This is an untimed event. The object is to execute as many pushups as possible before experiencing muscle failure. As long as you could maintain the front leaning rest position, you were still in play. You could rest for up to a minute as long as you were able to maintain the proper front leaning rest "up" position. In other words, you couldn't flop or rest on your belly at any point. If so, the clock and the count would end. No problem. Military rules. I was used to that. I began – 1!

I think I was somewhere around the 250 count when the sergeant decided to take his lunch break. He motioned for one of the other instructors to take over the count, and he left. 275, 300, 350... By then, the entire academy staff was in the audience and amazed at the exhibition. People began telephoning other officers nearby on patrol. 375, 400, 450... At this point, people were beginning to cheer me on. "Keep going, keep going" they said. I was totally oblivious to the surmounting crowd because I was all the way into my zone at this time. 500, 550... The sergeant had now returned from his 30-minute break and I was shaken out of my trance by his exclamation "god---n! He's still going?" The sergeant tagged back in to resume the count. 600, 650... Because I was jeered from my zone by the sergeant's return, I was now clearly aware of the crowd that had now amassed. The cheers were no longer inspirational but had digressed into what felt like gawking. The kind of gawking that people do at a carnival, circus, or other freak show. I began to feel more like a spectacle than anything else. My initial intention was to do my usual 1,000, but I could no longer bear what had now grown into an embarrassment. I was never a person who was comfortable with spotlight attention. If I did something exceptional, that was for me. Not for anyone else's praise. Being a devout Christian, I always feared praise and gave honor to God for anything I accomplished. I always steered clear of vanity, egoism and taking credit for anything that God had gifted me to do. I continued to push up as all these things ran through my mind. These thoughts led me to a solution for my dilemma. Since I had inadvertently garnered all this attention to myself, I had to find a way to divert the attention back to the One who had strengthened me to be able to perform this feat. Based on my decision, I now had only 50 more pushups to go. I would stop at the number that would give glory to God and not me. I would stop at the number that represented the most holy and perfect number 7, according to scripture. I would stop at the holy number 700. Up until this point, I had been knocking them out in quantities of 50 at a time. I would do 50, rest in the up position for a minute, and then do 50 more. So when I stopped at 700, everyone was amazed. I hadn't collapsed. I wasn't struggling, and I appeared to still have the strength to continue. 40 minutes after the first pushup... I just stopped. Everyone was astounded. Not by the number, but by the fact that I stopped when I clearly had many more in me. When questioned, I just responded that 700 seemed like a good round number to me. I did offer a more honest explanation to a few classmates who I felt would be more receptive of the real reason I had stopped. Up until this writing, the only 3 people that knew the truth of the matter were recruit Karen Klant (Officer Karen Bounnakhom, retired), recruit Tina Miller (Lieutenant, retired), and of course my best friend, who I spoke of at length in an earlier chapter. The 4 of us had shared many hours of conversation on religion and spiritual issues during our time in the academy. As a result, I knew they could relate to my reasoning.

People still ask me about the pushups, to this day. It always amazes me when I'm faced with the inquisition. The reality is that I'm more proud of, and thankful to the Universe, for my accomplishment in the mile and 1/2 run. Heck, I'm thankful to have even been able to complete the run at all.

> *Just 6 years prior to the police academy, while still on active duty in the Army, I suffered a severe ankle injury as a result of a roller skating accident. I managed to subject myself to a compound displaced fracture of my right Tibia and ankle joint. In those days, I would get around the rink at a pretty high velocity. When I sidestepped to avoid a small child who had steered into my direct path, I stepped foot first into a wall. The sound of the fracture was so loud that it could be heard over the blaring music. I hobbled off the floor and tightened up my shoestrings as I took a seat. The employees of the rink offered to summon an ambulance for me, but I declined. My younger sister Cheryl was there with me. She loaded me up in the car and rushed me to the nearest hospital. When I got to the hospital, they finally lifted my pant leg to examine the break and discovered the protruding and exposed Tibia bone. Once they removed my skate, they discovered that the ankle joint was also displaced. I explained what happened to the hospital staff and was somewhat joking about being a bone head for getting myself in this predicament. Especially since I was at home on leave for only a couple of weeks before I was to ship out to Germany. The doctor looked at me with amazement and asked how I was even conscious considering the amount of pain I must be in. He was even more astounded that I was able to joke about the situation. In the final analysis, the doctor regretted to inform me that I would always walk with a limp (I don't). He said that I would never run again even*

though I was an avid runner (I still run). The last thing he prepared me for was the fact that I would most likely need the assistance of a cane by the age of 40, if not earlier (I don't). At that time, I was at the ripe old age of 20. I nodded my head to indicate that I heard everything he said. I then proceeded to tell him how he was wrong in his prognosis, and I would never surrender to his words of defeat.

When I earned the PT trophy, the run had the most significance to me and was my greatest accomplishment. I was extremely proud of the fact that I hadn't allowed another man to speak HIS reality into MY life. Rather, I had gone about the business of creating my own reality. When I finished the run, it was a very proud and humbling moment in my life. A few years later, I would go on to further defy the doctor's prediction by jumping from perfectly good aircrafts and graduating from the US Army Airborne School at Ft. Benning.

Not only had I secured the PT trophy for my recruit class, but I set an academy record in the process. My record still stands to this day. This is partly due to a revision in the PT testing criteria, which occurred shortly after my performance. As it stands now, all events are timed with a 2-minute time limit, with the exception of the run and obstacle course.

The SWAT supervisor went on to explain to me that the commander had been keeping an eye on me since the day of my PT test. Butler had also given me a glaring recommendation based on our workouts together during my academy days. So when the TAC squad was disbanded, I was one of the commander's natural choices for SWAT.

SWAT turned out to be my longest assignment. It would also be a cumulative 10 years of daily challenges.

CHAPTER – 13

DISCIPLINARY ACTION

My years on SWAT were, by far, the most exciting period in my career. I knew there was a great amount of responsibility attached to the assignment. Nonetheless, there were those in the command level who held the opinion that the Unit was filled with a bunch of prima donna loafers. Their opinion was basically formed by the fact that SWAT was seldom seen in the course of day-to-day work. The assumption was held that whenever an officer was out of sight, he or she was somewhere goofing off. Granted, that's a pretty low opinion for an employer to hold for an employee, but that was the general consensus of some of the executive staff. In reality, SWAT should be maintained out of public view until mobilized. That includes the view of the general public as well as the view of the employing agency.

SWAT, by design, shouldn't be seen or viewed as regular patrol officers for several reasons. First, they should be viewed by the rank and file as something to aspire to. The specialized weapons, tools, and training should not be normalized as a traditional addition to normal or regular police operations. Hence the term "Special." Secondly, SWAT should hold some degree of mystique in the community being serviced.

As a youngster, I can recall when the Detroit SWAT team would be headed to a call. They traveled in a slow 15 or 20 mph, 6 to 8 vehicle procession with flashing blue lights. No sirens. The scene was quite somber. The psychological effect it had was not one of impending death for the person who was to be the subject of whatever action SWAT was about to take. But rather, my mind immediately focused on the thought that someone had been such a challenge or threat to the regular police officers, the situation warranted a response from SWAT. Even at such a young age, my automatic response to adversity was to first seek the causation of the problem. These days, the question that tends to be asked is why the police make such a heavy-handed response to a particular situation. There never seems to be a question as to what action on the suspect's part, facilitated such a heavy response.

I know this country has had its share of death related incidents involving police officers. A fair share of these incidents have involved White officers killing Black men and children. Based on a lot of information that's been revealed by the media, quite a few of the cases have been at best, questionable. Without exception, I'm always sought out for my opinion by non law enforcement family members and friends, as well as cop friends. To date, I have never voiced an opinion one way or the other. The reason? I tend to see such a big picture from both sides of these incidents, that it causes my opinion to be fluid. When people ask your opinion, they're not really seeking your opinion as much as a validation of their own opinion. Since I know more times than not, I can't help them with that, I tend to opt out of the conversation. The truth is that I tend to see cops' actions through the eyes of a special tactics instructor. I tend to see the actions of citizens through the prism of "cause and effect." I also have had the opportunity to work alongside a fair share of White officers, and I have found very few of them to be racist. I'm not saying that I haven't encountered hardcore racist officers, because I have. But they represented a very small population of APD officers. As I stated in an earlier chapter, my conclusion is that there are a portion of White and Black officers who simply fear what they do not understand or cannot relate to. This tends to cause an overreactive response on the part of the officer when they encounter people of color. It seems to be based more on misperception and preconceived notions stemming from a prevalent media (TV, written media, motion pictures, academic text books, etc) bias. I truly believe a great number of people in this country don't even realize their fear of Black people comes from years of social conditioning.

However, to give it the attention and depth that it deserves, that's a subject best left for another text.

During my years in supervision and management at the command level, I had two separate opportunities to recommend an officer for cultural awareness and or cultural sensitivity training. One of the situation[illegible] led to me requesting additional training for the officer at the police academy. This training included criminal procedure, criminal law, cultural awareness, and several other areas of concern. True to form, the executive staff ignored my recommendation and instead, transferred the officer to a different precinct. Within a few months of being assigned to the new zone, he racially profiled a motorist on the morning watch, and [illegible] caused the city to make an $80,000 settlement in the resulting lawsuit. The officer was then immediately fired. The officer apparently profiled a Black gentleman in a luxury car driving through a known high crime area (the Bluff), with his hat turned backwards. The officer never allowed the suspect (suspected of what, I don't know) to explain why he was driving through the Bluff at [illegible]:00 a.m. He basically jacked up the guy and put some legal but lame charge on him. The two problems that arose from the situation were: (1) a legal charge becomes illegal if it is not predicated on probable cause or at least reasonable articulable suspicion for stopping the vehicle in the first place. You know... that whole "fruit of the poisonous tree" thing they taught us all back in the academy; and (2) if the officer had allowed the gentleman the opportunity to explain himself he would have gleaned the obvious. Based on the geographical proximity of the Rice Street (Fulton County) jail, one of the avenues of approach is directly through the Bluff, depending on what direction or side of town you're traveling from. The officer would have also learned that the guy was an attorney on his way to represent a client who had just been transported to the jail.

Another reason SWAT should not be held out for general public consumption is the most important, in my estimation. Simply put... Anytime SWAT is not on an actual call, they should be training. It's plain and simple. If these are supposed to be your cream of the crop tactical experts, they need to be spending every available waking moment honing those skills. When the proverbial manure hits the proverbial fan, the last thing you want showing up on your situation is an ill-prepared or undertrained SRT or SWAT team.

There was a tug of war going on between the SWAT command staff and the executive staff. The execs wanted us to be utilized for every extra detail that came along. We directed traffic at the Braves games and the Falcons games. We worked every annual parade such as the Thanksgiving Day parade and Christmas Tree lighting, the St. Patrick's Day parade, and the Caribbean Day parade, to name a few. We worked every road race. These included the Peachtree Road Race, the Mile and 1/2 Marathon, and the myriad of impromptu corporate races that would pop up all year long. Perhaps, the most notorious of our assignments was the annual Freak Nic (Black College Spring Break) detail. As far as the top brass was concerned, when SWAT wasn't on an actual call, we were to be utilized as a utility squad. It wasn't until my final few years on SWAT that we finally received some more tactically minded commanders in the executive and command staff levels.

Chief Beverly Harvard (retired) was a big proponent of having a properly prepared SWAT team. She allowed us to train more than we had in the past. There, of course were still a few old heads that felt SWAT was better used as utility personnel. They would stick us with a detail when they could, but their time was running out and they were rapidly losing their stronghold with that ideology. Chief Harvard bought into the idea that a well-trained SWAT team equaled less civilian and sworn lives lost on a SWAT call. The philosophy is really commonsensical when you think about it. It was refreshing to have a leader who got it. She would even come out to observe some of our training from time to time. A couple of times, she even participated in the training with the team. The more she observed, the more she understood the serious need for training hours.

We had the opportunity to train on a regular basis with some of the most elite tactical groups in the country and metro area. We trained regularly with tactical units from MARTA police, FBI, ATF, Military Police, Delta Force, German Polizei, Israeli Police and Navy Seals. We also trained with a host of metro area SWAT and Tactical teams.

There was no shortage of adrenalin filled call-outs to respond to during that period, but we never had to take a life to resolve a situation. This was a result of having exhaustive training. It resulted in an unwavering trust in our own training as individuals, as well as a trust in each other. We took tremendous pride in the fact that we were able to end situations without the loss of human life on either side of the equation. For us, it was always about bringing a situation to resolution. We actually took pleasure in the challenge of arriving to a scene that seemed to be impossible to resolve peacefully. We enjoyed coming up with options to affect the contrary. People often think of SWAT as the "dumb jock" type of officers that have a pretty straightforward resolution to every situation. You know the "hut-hut-hut" guys, as usually depicted on TV and in the movies. Our team took tremendous pride in being thinkers. Reason and logical deduction were our greatest tools.

During my years on the team, we were involved in many situations that gained national and international attention. Some of the more well known cases were the Other Side Lounge bombing and the case where two police officers, John Sowa and Patricia Cocciolone, were ambushed by a deranged gunman in the city's Buckhead section. Officer Sowa died on the scene, and officer Cocciolone was in grave condition when she arrived at the hospital. She survived, but was left with serious and extensive disabilities. I was the lead counter-sniper on that situation and had the suspect in my crosshairs the entire time the negotiators worked on him. After a significant amount of time passed, he finally agreed to surrender to the SWAT officers. When certain people found out I had the perp in my crosshairs the whole time, there were some officers of the opinion that I should have basically executed the guy. Of course, I understood their anger in the way these two fine officers were brutally cut down without warning. I also understood the fact that the same could happen to anyone of us at any time. I would explain to them how I did not have legal justification in taking the suspect's life and just leave it at that. As they were talking, I would think to myself "that's why I'm a counter-sniper and you're not."

Another case we were involved in was when a militia extremist held himself hostage in front of a Jewish Synagogue in the city's Midtown area. He taped a sawed off shotgun to his own head and threatened to kill himself if certain demands weren't met. The several hours standoff was ended when the team assaulted the vehicle with a "flash-bang" grenade and took the guy into custody, unharmed. The news footage of the actual assault was later used in the opening segment montage on the, still popular, COPS reality television show.

We faced many other incidents that failed to reach the national or international prevue, but were equally challenging, if not more.

Some of my personal challenges came in a more ideological or conscientious form.

There were two times when I was written up for undesirable conduct or unsatisfactory performance while on the SWAT team. Both times involved special detail assignments.

The first time revolved around a Falcon's game traffic detail. It was during a period when all SWAT team officers had off days of either Saturday/Sunday or Sunday/Monday. In either case, the common off day for SWAT was Sunday. SWAT had been traditionally working a traffic detail for Sunday football long before I was even considered to be a part of the team. This practice had gone on for what seemed like millennia, and we all just accepted it as a customary part of our job. All of Special Operations was one big family, and we had no problem helping out in areas of personnel shortages in the other units. Unfortunately, one day I discovered that the presumed personnel shortage was a result of supervisory scheduling. It turned out that the Motors unit wasn't short staffed due to a lack of officers assigned to the unit. Rather, they were short staffed because the Motorcycle unit supervisors were allowing regular assigned officers to take the day off in order to work extra (moonlight) jobs around the event. Now these were officers who were regularly scheduled to work on Sundays. So basically, SWAT had to give up our off days to cover for some officers who were allowed to be off on their regular workdays. This meant that I had to give up one my off days that should have been spent with my family, to cover for someone else so they can make some extra money to spend on their families. The situation was compounded by the fact that this was during a high volume SWAT call in period. It was not uncommon to get called in to a SWAT call in the middle of the night, work the call for upwards of 12 hours and get called right back to the precinct to handle another call before you could even get back home from the first call. There were countless times when I had to call my wife to pick up the children from a restaurant or other location because I needed to respond to a SWAT call, and it would have taken too much time to go back home first. Not to mention times when I would have to sit perched on some rooftop or hillside, looking down my riflescope in inclement weather for 24 or more hours at a time... At any rate, it seemed unreasonable for SWAT to continue to handle the Falcons detail in light of this new information.

That next Saturday we were advised by the sergeant in roll call that we were to be working the Falcons detail the next day. Business as usual... When given the opportunity for comments, I explained to sarge and the other officers standing in roll call what I had discovered about the Motors officers. Everyone agreed that it was not a fair situation, but because we had been doing it for so long, they doubted the practice would ever change. I continued to challenge the validity of the assignment as the sergeant and several of the officers continued to point out the futility of my argument. The sergeant became somewhat irritated with my persistence - mostly because I was after all, still relatively new to the Unit in comparison to the seniority of the majority of my teammates. It reached a point of his voice escalating at me as he pointedly exclaimed "Ya[illegible]uku! That's just the way it's always been!!"

It's as if he summoned my father by name. Per usual, when he raised his voice at me, I responded in like turn. Instantaneously, I found myself yelling back at him "that doesn't make it right, sarge. Based on that logic, your people would still have my people in physical chains!!! You could have heard a pin drop in the room. I'm sure it was just my imagination, but I could have sworn everyone else took one step backward leaving me alone on the line. After roll call, the sergeant approached me and apologized for raising his voice at me. He contended that he respected my position, but he maintained that I was fighting a losing battle. I too apologized for losing decorum and calmly explained to him that I intended to stand by my convictions, so I would not be at work the following day to work the game. I told him that I fully understood what he had to do as far as disciplinary action, and I accepted whatever I received. He suggested that I just call in sick to avoid penalty. I explained that, first of all, it would be ridiculous to call in sick on my regular off day. Besides that, I was standing on a conviction, and a compromised conviction is nothing more than a ploy. I wasn't trying to get out of working! I was trying to change an unfair practice.

As promised, I didn't show up for the game. That Monday morning, I walked into the SWAT office only to be summoned into the lieutenant's office. I signed my written reprimand (disciplinary action) paperwork and headed to training. Nothing more was ever said concerning the incident. And SWAT was no longer required to work the Falcons games...

The other time that I opted for disciplinary action was involving a Martin Luther King Day demonstration at the State Capitol building. It was the tradition of the Ku Klux Klan to stage a rally on the steps of the State Capitol to protest the observance of King Day. I'm a person who supports the right and idea of free speech. I have upset a great number of friends with my staunch approach to the protection of these particular rights. I have been accused of being afraid, a "sell out," and "simple minded" because I tend to not be moved to excitement by people's offensive, and sometimes incendiary, verbiage. I contend that every person has a right to their beliefs. It doesn't matter if those beliefs are racist, bigoted, prejudiced, or otherwise indifferent. I could care less what preconceived ideas a person may have of me. I could care less what disparaging name or title some fool may want to address me by. Simply put, I don't care what hatred or venom another person carries in their heart. That's not my business, nor my concern. It also isn't my place to regulate another person's emotions or feelings. Where I draw the line at is in discriminatory practices. Especially, institutionalized discrimination. This is when a person takes all that bias and translates it into a tangible impediment for someone. This is where I take issue. Feel what you want about me, but when you fashion to bring harm to me, we have a problem. Whether that harm is by sociological, educational, economical, or any other tangible institutional devise, it's unacceptable in my book.

I had worked several of these Klan rallies over the years and had no problem. Mostly, because in all of the years that I had worked the detail, there were never any counter demonstrators to show up. It was always just a handful of "yahoos" in hoods, shooting their mouths off over a bullhorn for a couple of hours. It would then be over. Within a few hours, everything in the city would be back to normal.

This particular rally was a little different that year. There were a couple of anomalies I just couldn't wrap my head around. The first was all the children in attendance this year. To see small children spewing such hate filled language was off setting, to say the least. The saddest thing was how convicted these kids were to what they had been taught. In that moment, I felt sad for them and even sadder for our country. The other mind-blowing element was the presence and public address that was given by an African American member of the group. He contributed words of encouragement to support recruitment for several initiatives the organization apparently had going on in the metro area. I guessed that he felt he wasn't doing anything too atrocious since he never invoked the name "Martin Luther Koon" at any point during his presentation. That was the mantra for every single reference to the name of the holiday and any reference to the great civil rights leader himself.

The hatred was at a level I hadn't witnessed in any of the previous years. To make matters worse, a large crowd of counter demonstrators showed up... They weren't happy with the rhetoric at all. Naturally, the more counterdemonstrators showed up, the more the Klan made effort to agitate them. Tensions seemed to be building to a tipping point.

I called the sergeant to where I was positioned on the police line that was dividing the two groups. I advised him that I would be leaving my post. When he asked why, I told him that it appeared that these Klansmen were about to get the crap stomped out of them and with a clear conscience, I couldn't arrest anyone for doing so. My ultimatum was that I would stand by and assist any officer that may be attacked by participants on either side. But I absolutely could not place charges on anyone who flattened one of these hooded clowns. He told me to relieve myself at my patrol vehicle and he would follow up with the disciplinary paperwork later in the week. I did, and he did. Fortunately, nothing became of the mutual hostilities between the two groups, as the police line was effective in maintaining the peace.

In retrospect, if I had it to do over again, I would have handled it differently. I would have protected the Klan's first amendment rights at all cost, as I had done in previous years. I'd always carried the belief that every person has a right to house whatever prejudices and bigotry in their heart. So long as it didn't transform into a hate crime or institutionalized discrimination... Also, every US citizen has a constitutional right to freedom of speech. It is the singular time in my career I'm the least proud of to this day. I shamefully allowed my immaturity coupled with my pride, to cloud my better judgment. That would be the only time in my career I would forsake my oath of office.

Afterwards, when controversial or moral compass type situations would occur, there were never any personal feelings or grudges between me and the sarge. He would usually express his understanding of my position but remind me of the need to balance my personal convictions with the oath I had sworn to. Sometimes I would stand my ground, and other times I would be able to see the bigger picture. In fact, the SWAT team was chock full of highly opinionated and critically thinking individuals. That's what made us so successful on our missions. We never held grudges or harsh feelings for one another, but we always shot straight from the hip (SWAT pun intended). In a unit of that nature, people tend to feel free to speak their minds and express their honest feelings on any issue. In a sense, it was our way of always being prepared for death. We never knew when we might answer that one SWAT call that could turn out to be our last. So nobody wanted to carry anything on their chest to the grave with them. No one tiptoed around the SWAT hut. If you had thin skin, this was not the assignment for you. This was truly a group of brave men and women. Their willingness to go into situations where most would shudder at the very thought is highly commendable. I proudly wear my Atlanta Police SWAT tattoo on my left arm... closest to my heart.

CHAPTER – 14

SILVER SHIELDS & F*%# THE POLICE!!!

After several years assigned to the SWAT team, I decided it was time for me to begin my focus on career development. I took and passed the test to become a detective in the Criminal Investigations Division (CID). My cumulative time spent on three detective assignments was about 2 1⁄2 years. Right off the bat, I was assigned to the Youth Squad, which encompassed child abuse investigations among other youth related issues. Being a father of 4 at that time made the investigations of abused children somewhat difficult to stomach. The horrors of physical and sexual abuse were so traumatizing for me as an investigator. I had a very difficult time wrapping my head around what those children must have been experiencing, mostly, on a regular basis. The unit was understaffed as much of the department was, and still is. I was seeing volumes of work on a daily basis. I spent only 6 months in the unit before I requested, and was allowed, to transfer out. No matter how much I was assured by some of the veteran investigators that I would become desensitized enough to be able to function, it just simply never got any easier to me. Through all the tragedy and sorrow that I faced in that unit, the thing that stuck out the most was the fact that I never made an arrest involving a teenage girl's allegation of sexual abuse against a father, or another male fulfilling a father role. Granted, I didn't have that many in comparison to the other types of cases, but not a single one panned out to be true. Every time we would get to the interview phase, the child would invariably admit to the allegation being a result of revenge against the father figure. This was usually based on the fact that the adult refused to allow the child to have her way. It was usually a refusal to give the child money upon request or demand, refusal to allow the child to hang out in the streets or attend an event unsupervised, or things of that nature. At some point, middle school and high school girls became aware of an almost foolproof way to rid themselves of their mother's nuisance boyfriends who were actually making an attempt to parent a child that wasn't his. I probably had only a dozen of these types of cases in my short six months in that assignment, but not a single one of them was sustained against the accused. Being a dad myself, I would always make sure of their innocence before allowing someone off the hook for such an egregious allegation. Especially since the accused would, more times than not, return to that same environment with the accuser...

At any rate, my transfer came through, and I couldn't wait to leave the heart wrenching dredges of the Youth Squad. My transfer request was non-specific. Anywhere in CID was fine with me. It really didn't matter where I ended up. I just didn't want to have to deal with any more hurt and abused babies. So where did I wind up being transferred to? The Homicide unit. Great! The major had been curiously passive upon receiving my transfer request. Based on the stories I had been told, it was clear that she took transfer requests very personally. However, she never showed any type of resentment when I explained to her my reasons for wanting out of the Unit. Perhaps, I should not have been so forthcoming with my real reasons for the request because I still can't help but feel that my transfer to Homicide was made out of spite. To this day, I still believe that she reasoned "If he thinks he's having problems dealing with abused children, wait until he has to deal with DEAD children on a daily basis." I could be wrong, and I certainly hope I am, but I have never been much of a believer in coincidence.

The Homicide unit was aptly called the "Hat Squad" in those days, as a fedora was a standard item of the dress code. Detectives embraced the prestige and elite status of the unit, and everyone conducted themselves as the consummate professionals on calls. The highest respect was always shown to the families of deceased, regardless of the circumstances surrounding the death. It was, perhaps, the unit that matured me more than any other. Behind the precinct walls was a different story. All of these guys and women were professional level jokesters in their own rights. Some of the pranks played on one another will go down in the annals of history on the department. The atmosphere was very similar to SWAT. Both units had a way of decompressing or coping with daily tragedy. Some of the cases could be so traumatic that the means of escapism would seem quite crass and crude to the rest of the world looking in. I feel that I can speak for every Homicide and SWAT officer in the country when I say that the alternative, of internalizing all of that suffering and carnage, would be much uglier. By the way... my very first homicide call was involving a dead baby whose mother rolled over on him during the course of the night.

I spent about a year and 1/2 on Homicide. During that time, it became somewhat unbearable to watch the relationship between the department and the community, become more and more estranged. It seemed that each and every police related incident that garnered media attention, widened the chasm of distrust and disrespect for the department. The void was so vast that I felt a personal responsibility to fill it. My first efforts were to become more involved with the already established, police unions. There was no shortage of unions. There was the Fraternal Order of Police (FOP), the Police Benevolent Association (PBA), the International Brotherhood of Police Officers (IBPO) and the Afro American Patrolmen's League (AAPL). I became more active in the IBPO and the AAPL. The experience was short lived due to my inherent "northern or mid-western exposure." It was hard to muster patience with the unions, considering I'd grown up in the home of the UAW, with local branches of the AFL/CIO. I could not fathom the concept of "right to work" statehood. It seemed to be the most futile means of arbitration imaginable. As a result, the unions didn't accomplish much compared to what I regarded as acceptable. A little something to placate the workforce on occasion seemed to amount to mere tokenism. Not any real strides, in my opinion, at the time... After all, if a representative body doesn't have the ability to even threaten, let alone actually take any work action, what leverage do they really have to bargain with at the negotiation table? Unfortunately, the APD unions are still handicapped by this condition today. Likewise, the workforce still continues to get the short end of the stick. My heart goes out to each and every one of the men and women who make up the rank and file of the Atlanta Police Department. For to this day, they are still very much underappreciated, at best, and unappreciated, at worst, by their very own department and city government. Yet, they still show up every day, prepared to lay down their lives on a moment's notice. I salute them all!!!

> *During the period while I was still on SWAT, I began to sense the futility of the unions. I decided to create an organization of my own. My organization would not suffer to partnership with the department or the city, per se. Instead, we would*

take a more direct approach to improving employee issues as a residual purpose. Our primary purpose would be to eradicate the growing rift between the police department and the citizens who it was sworn to serve and protect.

This was not unchartered territory for me, as I had established a similar organization with similar purpose during my time spent in Germany while in the Army. I sought out leadership for the organization from 3 friends of like minds. Our Co-Chairman would be a very articulate and socially conscience officer named Ed Brown (retired). Our Secretary was to be an equally articulate and studious officer named Chris Dupree. We rounded the team out with a Treasurer who was beloved and held in high regard within the APD. He was an officer of conscience level thinking named Gary Porter (retired). Once established, we named the organization, the Silver Shields. One of the proudest moments in my career was when we received our corporation certificate from the State of Georgia. As we saw it, there were two primary issues facing the department. First, there was the inequity and disparity in the treatment of Black officers versus White. There was a very obvious and blatant racial component attached to almost every situation concerning disciplinary action issued to officers of different races. The second area of concern was the disconnect between the community and the officers. Particularly, the Black officers...

This phenomenon became crystal clear to me on the first domestic dispute case that I'd responded to as a new officer.

As soon as the older Black woman opened the door and saw me standing on her porch, she told me she didn't need me. I asked if she had called the police, as a way of confirming that I was at the correct address. She told me I was at the correct address and that she did, in fact, call the police. "However, I specifically told that dispatcher not to send me no damn black officer out here" she said. "I specifically told her a-- that I wanted a white officer. So you can go on back to whatever it was you were doing. I'll wait" said the woman. I was flabbergasted. After speaking with several other officers, Black and White, I learned this was a regular occurrence in the African American community. When I enquired as to the reason, there was no further explanation. "That's just the way some folks are" I was told.

I'd never lived in the south. But from my studies of the Civil Rights movement and Jim Crow, I suspected these attitudes were the lingering residue of how Black officers were viewed during that period. I would further deduce that a lot of these sentiments were probably somewhat justified based on how Black officers were utilized during that period. Based on what I've seen in contemporary law enforcement, I can only imagine how heavy handed some Black officers must have been in the Black communities. Even today, some Black officers tend to be unnecessarily brutal with people of color. It's their way of demonstrating to their White coworkers and supervisors that they're not showing favoritism or sparing the rod when it comes to policing their "own" people. I had seen firsthand how this mentality easily results in Black officers subjecting Black citizens to worse treatment than they'd ever suf-

fered at the hands of the most racist, White officer. It conjures up images of the old plantation when a slave would be promoted to the position of overseer and permitted to ride horse back over his fellow slaves. The Black overseer would oftentimes subject the other slaves to more inhumane treatment then the cruelest White overseer. This was his way of demonstrating to the master, his worthiness of his newfound station in plantation life. The most disturbing fact is that most Black officers who fall into this category, haven't a clue as to their shortcoming.

The bottom line was, whatever the reason, more than likely, we Black officers had been primarily responsible for the deteriorated relationship in the community. Therefore, it was our responsibility to take the first step in repairing or mending ties.

So now that we had identified the two biggest problems facing officers, we needed to set a plan in place. Our goal was to provide a different and more homogeneous face for the community on a grass roots level. Our work place was the community itself. Wherever issues arose that concerned the community, we provided a more enfranchised face of law enforcement. When the citizens of a certain community felt the department was being indifferent in its efforts to solve a homicide of a young girl on her way to school, we organized workshops and symposiums to educate the protesters on their rights and the laws pertaining to peaceful demonstration. We then, participated in the march with the community. This placed me in a very precarious position. I was participating in an action that was bringing into question the practices of the very Homicide unit I was currently assigned to. Nevertheless, I felt the concern was legitimate, even from my inside perspective. We conducted several presentations and workshops in troubled neighborhoods to mentor youth on different aspects of young adulthood. We provided Rights of Passage programs for several at risk children. Our mission statement read as follows:

"We want to reclaim our neighborhoods and restore them to their original peace. We want to reclaim our children from the violence that plagues their existence and ours. We want to teach them to take full responsibility for every facet of their lives from this day on. We want to teach them to extol the virtues of spirituality, morality, and education in exchange for materialism, immorality and self perpetuated violence."

The organization began to gain support from officers on the department of every persuasion. After all, we took on issues of fair treatment within the department as well. A lot of the issues we challenged weren't of racial concern, but of a socio-economic nature. Plainly put, patrol level or line officers tended to be treated as "crap" by the chain of command. As I stated before, they were totally unappreciated and treated with absolute indifference.

Silver Shields would take up the mantle on many concerns of this nature.

One of those challenges came at a time before I left the SWAT team. It was in the form of a mayoral meeting between Mayor Bill Campbell and representatives of various APD worksites and unions.

Freak-Nic was quickly approaching that year, and there was growing concern throughout the ranks that we would again be stiffed on our overtime pay for the excessive hours we would be required to work for the event. In previous years, the city had always promised overtime pay for working excessive hours during the Freak-Nic weekend. However, the finance department would always find some last second loophole to circumvent actually paying out the promised funds. This happened on a consistent yearly basis. This year, we would get assurances up front before the actual event. We demanded a meeting with the mayor several months in advance of Freak-Nic weekend. He continually refused to meet with us. He would either come up with last second excuses and then set a reschedule, or flat out refuse to meet. Silver Shields set out on a course of action that would force the meeting with the mayor. We decided to orchestrate the city's first work action, at least in our cumulative careers. We first created small blue leaflets that gave instructions on the intended "Blue Flu." A "Blue Flu" is simply a police mass sickout. It can last a day, a week, or however long it takes to get the desired terms met in arbitration. In our case, its primary purpose was to simply get the mayor to even engage in arbitration with the department's representatives. The leaflets contained information as to the date(s) and time the Blue Flu was to go into effect. Of course, they coincided with Freak-Nic weekend. After crafting the leaflets, we then set out to hand deliver them into the hands of every patrol officer and detective in the department. This was accomplished by visiting every shift change in every Zone and investigative worksite within a couple weeks. By the end of 2 weeks of distribution, the vast majority of officers were aware of the intended action and on board. It began to appear that for the first time in my history on the department, the officers were going to actually stand united on an issue that concerned everyone. In previous years, when such efforts were attempted, there would always be someone who would "sell out" the effort. It would result in the "ringleader" being publicly retaliated against by the department. This would, in turn, frighten off the remaining supporters; and the "rebellion", so to speak, would be successfully routed. The maltreatment would continue as usual.

This time, there was enough identifiable conviction and cohesion within the rank and file that the mayor's advisors were able to convince him that it would be in his best interest to stop putting us off and give audience to our concerns. We were successful in forcing his hand to meet with us. We considered this an important victory of the Silver Shields organization. The meeting was set. It was to convene in the mayor's conference room to limit the number of representatives to a manageable few. He agreed to give a minimum of 2 hours, or even more if necessary. There was representation from every police Union, including the IBPO Local President, Marc Lawson (RIP) and the IBPO National President, Chip Warren. I mention their names because of their professionalism and fearlessness in guiding the meeting to a fruitful resolution. Most worksites within the department had a representative in attendance. At the very least, there was representation from every SOS unit. SOS was the most taxed Section for all large details occurring within the city. I was in attendance with Eddie and Gary, representing both the Silver Shields and the SWAT team. The pri-

mary topics up for discussion were pay and equipment. Some of the outlying issues were concerning the pension and other general working conditions. The two pressing pay issues were the past due Super Bowl overtime pay, which the city was attempting to renege on. There was also the impending Freak-Nic overtime pay.

The meeting started off slowly with the customary courtesies and back and forth. As every issue was brought to the mayor's attention, they were met with his insistent denial of any knowledge of them. Whenever he was requested to voice a resolution for anything, he adeptly sidestepped or avoided the issue. He was in full "politician" mode - promise nothing and deny knowledge of everything. I stood and watched the frustration grow from the officers and representatives in the room until I could take no more. I took the floor. I told the mayor that since he was apparently unaware of anything going on within his police department, and therefore have no resolutions to the concerns being stressed, I would help him out. I went on to provide several short-range and long-term solutions to the issues in question. He tried to doubletalk the issues, and I would pull him back on point by insisting that he provide a direct response to my proposals. The more he continued to evade the question, the harder I pressed and maintained my insistence. He suggested that I move on to my next question, but I insisted that we would be there all night if need be. I wanted an intelligible, layman's response to my propositions. After going back and forth for several minutes, he acquiesced. I was able to move on to what I felt was a more paramount issue.

In the mean time, the IBPO National President, Chip Warren, brought up a concern that he personally had with the mayor. He related how in the previous week, while in a heated meeting with the mayor and other city departments Union reps., the mayor grew angered with Chip for even bringing up the issue of a "Blue Flu." In that meeting, Chip informed the mayor that there was a major movement going on within APD to create a Blue Flu event. The mayor misinterpreted Chip's warning as being a threat that he (Chip) was making effort to enact the work action. The mayor took it personally and became enraged. The mayor then shouted at Chip and said, "F--k You! You can't turn these guys out!"

The mayor stood firm on his proposition that he had never uttered the words, "f--k the police, or anything of that nature." Chip contended that he never said the mayor said "f--k the police." Rather, he insisted that the mayor had said, "F--k YOU (Chip), you can't turn them out because they never stick together for anything." The mayor vehemently denied saying even that, and challenged anyone in the room who had any knowledge of the alleged conversation to speak up. After a standoff of several minutes and several attempts of the mayor to move the meeting along to other concerns, IBPO Local President, Marc Lawson threatened to shut the meeting down if this issue of disrespect by the mayor toward his own police force couldn't be resolved. Marc and Chip knew something that no one else in the room knew besides the mayor. There was indeed a third, independent witness to the alleged statement standing in the room with us. He was the President of the Fire Department's Local union, and he had also been in at-

tendance at the meeting with the mayor the previous week. After a little pressure and some masterful goading by Marc, the Fire rep confirmed Chip's assertions. "Yes, the mayor did say it," he confirmed. The room erupted with angry officers as the mayor threw up his hands and walked out.

We were able to convince the mayor to return to the meeting as there were several more problems that needed his attention. We wanted the agreed upon time to voice them. When the mayor returned to the room, he continued to stand in denial of having made the remarks. We all agreed to disagree in the interest of continuing the meeting.

It was my turn to have the floor to voice my final concern.

The Street Sweep / Zero Tolerance detail was still in full swing from the time I was on the TAC squad. When I brought up the issue of the Street Sweep / Zero Tolerance detail, the mayor had a bewildered look on his face. Perhaps it was the way I phrased it. "Mr. Mayor, I don't know if you're aware of it, but your police department is operating as a modern day GESTAPO" I said. In all fairness, not only did he have a look of confusion on his face, but so did everyone else in attendance, save, the Silver Shields members. I went on to explain to him the concerns with the tactics being utilized by the Street Sweep/Zero Tolerance detail and how it was in blatant violation of people's constitutional rights. I went on to explain in detail how fingerprints, photographs, and vital statistical information were being compiled to create a police file or record on individuals who had never committed no crime, been accused of committing a crime, or even suspected of committing a crime. We were creating files on people whose only crime was being poor and living in a lower income section of the city. I added the fact that this detail was being enforced on the south side of town, particularly the Housing Projects. I then took it a step further and explained to him how his police department was in fact, operating under two sets of rules. I asked him "sir, are you aware that laws and ordinances are being implemented in two very different fashions, depending on the side of town? On the north side and in more affluent areas in the city, the laws are being used for protection; while on the south side and lower income areas, the laws are used for enforcement." The last thing I said was "now sir, I know you said that you cannot provide immediate relief for the vast majority of concerns expressed here today, but this issue can be resolved with a single phone call. I'm asking that you pick up the phone tonight and instruct the chief of police to cease and desist with this so-called Zero Tolerance detail."

A few days after the meeting, I got a visit from someone who said he'd been privy to a conversation the mayor had with the chief later on that night after the meeting. The officer said the mayor questioned the chief as to who exactly I was. The chief informed him that I was his lead Counter Sniper on the SWAT team. The chief then asked the mayor if I needed to be "dealt" with for some reason. The mayor replied "no," but that I had been in attendance at the meeting he had with APD earlier in the evening, and I just seemed to be very passionate about certain things concerning police operations. The chief again inquired as to whether I had "gotten out of line" in the meeting, and the mayor assured him that I hadn't, but again, that I was very "passionate" about the purpose of law enforcement in the community.

I never received any reprimand through official or unofficial channels.

It was clear the mayor had gotten a genuine sense of our concerns, and more importantly, our seriousness and conviction to bring about change. He could tell that we were literally at the end of our rope. We received back pay that was due to us from the recent Super Bowl. We also received overtime pay for Freak-Nic worked that year. Most importantly, the Street Sweep / Zero Tolerance was cancelled and dismantled after having been in practice for several years. Mayor Campbell did not commit to being able to address every concern voiced in that meeting. But I have to say that he was pretty forthcoming about the things he felt he could address immediately, and he showed reasonability toward the things that he couldn't fix overnight. All in all, I have to commend him for his honest efforts to rectify the few things that he could. The gains made that day were not everything that those in attendance set out for. But the mayor did keep his word, and the things that he did commit to fixing, he did.

Almost immediately after starting up Silver Shields, we began to circulate a bi-weekly newsletter to officers that took interest in the things we were doing on the department and within the communities. The newsletter was intended to be educational and informational, but unfortunately it would lead to our premature demise. Because I was assigned to a fairly high profile Unit, and because I tended to shy away from the spotlight, we decided that our Co- Chairman would be the face of the organization. Eddie would handle all of the public speaking and be the spokesperson for the organization. I would scribe the majority of our newsletters. Each board member would fashion at least one newsletter dealing with an issue they championed as well. Everything was to be voted on democratically, but Eddie would be the orator of our collective decisions. We took on all issues head-on. Leadership of some of the Unions, as well as some of the more veteran officers/supervisors, tried to reel us in or ask us to tone down our message. We refused to compromise. We were only lifting up the skirt of the department and allowing the truth to speak for itself. We saw no need or cause to shy away from our efforts. Policy was being rewritten as a result of our efforts, and we were proud to be instrumental in assisting some officers in receiving fair treatment in disciplinary cases.

By this time, I was practicing Orthodox Islam, as was Eddie.

Eddie came under attack by a supervisor for displaying the Star and Crescent on his uniform breast pocket. The tiny pendant fit well into the criteria established by SOP regarding uniform adornment. It was no larger or any more conspicuous than the Star David or Crucifixes that adorned many officers' uniforms. Eddie's sergeant ordered him to remove the pin because it represented what she considered to be a "hate group." She based her position on the assumption that the symbol represented the Nation of Islam (NOI), which the department unofficially considered to be a hate group tantamount to the Klan. This was based on an infamous shootout that the department had with some NOI members back in the 60's or 70's. What she didn't know was that Eddie and I were both adherents to Orthodox Islam. Not the NOI or any radical Islamic jihadist group that was on the horizon. We were simple adherents to a religion that espoused the same peace and community as any of the other major religions. Eddie refused to remove the pendant, and the supervisor relieved him of duty and initiated disciplinary action against him. I was sure she would be overruled as the case travelled up the chain of command, but she wasn't. It reached the office of the chief of police. When it appeared that the chief was intent on sustaining the charges, I took pen to paper in an impromptu, out of cycle, special edition newsletter. The newsletter made it clear the Silver Shields were prepared to pursue this issue to the U.S. Supreme Court if necessary. There was no mixing of words in what would be my most sobering newsletter to date. It was entitled, "Muslim Officers In The Lion's Den." Within weeks, the SOP was rewritten and no longer could ANY religious ornaments be displayed on the uniform. The underlying message – "We hate and/or fear your religion so much, that we're willing to forsake our own religion just to deny you the right to practice or observe yours."

Copy That!!!

Because he was the official face of the organization, Eddie began to receive less than desirable treatment as he began to be transferred from one assignment to the next. It had been a long-standing practice on the department to transfer whoever is perceived as being a problem employee. I too, have fallen into that cycle on several occasions within my career on APD and during my time spent in the Army. After a while, you get used to it. But you never stop speaking out against whatever injustices come to your attention... That's just the way it is. On most departments, so many people are so concerned about choice assignments or career advancement, if YOU don't speak out, literally, no one else will. Besides, I could hardly consider myself as being my father's son if I didn't.

On another occasion, Chris Dupree, Silver Shields Secretary, was singled out by his supervisor for disciplinary action.

The charges were obviously frivolous and gave the appearance that he was being targeted simply because he was a board member of the Silver Shields. One evening I received a call at home that Chris was about to report to his major's office to have disciplinary charges presented to him. Within 40 minutes, I was standing alongside him in the airport major's office as his peer-representative. The major insisted Chris could only have union representation or peer representation, but not both. I looked at the union rep and advised him that he should pack up his briefcase. The major then interjected that by policy, the union rep trumps my right to be in the meeting. I informed him that he may as well proceed because I had no intention of excusing myself from the process. He then "ordered" me to leave his office. I informed him that with all due respect, the office we were in was technically property of the City of Atlanta. I said that as long as I was a city employee, I had just as much right to the office space as he did. Needless to say, he looked at me very strangely and countered by standing to his feet and threatening to have me removed. I retorted by standing to my feet with the question of who he would get to do the job? Surely not the SWAT team... I had trained most of the members on the team and still had a couple of tactics up my sleeve that I never shared with anyone. I assured him there was no doubt that APD's most elite unit would reign victorious over me in the end, but I wouldn't want to be the first 5 or 6 to come through the door to make it happen. At this point, everybody in the room looked at me strangely, including Chris. I guess Chris heard something in my voice or saw something in my eyes, so he asked me to excuse myself so he could just “get it over with.” “They're gonna do what they wanna do anyway" he acquiesced. After a few moments of self-deliberation, I assured Chris that if at any time he felt the union rep wasn't doing an adequate job in representing him, I would be right outside the door as an alternative. In the tradition of Malcolm-vs-Martin, the major struck a fair negotiation with the union rep.

It began to seem that every officer who served as a board member of the Silver Shields had targets for maltreatment situated squarely upon their foreheads.

The more Eddie became harassed, the more militant he seemed to grow in his opinions and views. Now don't get me wrong, 9 times out of 10, when I walk into a room, I'm by far the most militant person on deck. If it's a racial issue, then so be it. It doesn't matter if it's socio- economical, geo-political, sexual orientation, or if its gender or age motivated. As far as I'm concerned, discrimination is discrimination, and I have a humanistic obligation to speak out against it. However, as proud as I am of my heritage and culture and race, I have never held a view of Black superiority. In fact, my greatest efforts have always been in removing the sheath of self-hatred and perceived inferiority from the hearts and eyes of African Americans. Instead of complaining about the remnants of slavery (which still exists today), I try to facilitate people of every persuasion in taking a course of action to eradicate the lingering vestiges. It starts with a self-analysis and if necessary, a recalibration of purpose in life. After that... roll up your sleeves and start fighting!

Eddie published a newsletter that contained what I felt bore a Black Nationalistic slant with a hint of racism. He had just fashioned an exceptional piece of work with an exclusive interview with Imam Jamil Al-Amin, aka H. Rap Brown. There was a heavy concentration of

Muslims in the West End area. The majority of Muslims were Nationalistic in their views, but there was also a faction of Orthodox Muslims. We often sought out guidance and mentoring from some of the Imams to feed our fairly newfound religious aspirations. On occasion, Eddie and I would see Imam Al-Amin in the area and engage him in conversation about the religion. Naturally, it took him a while to trust our sincerity, considering the fact that we were law enforcement. If you know anything about the history of the Student Nonviolent Coordinating Committee (SNCC) or the Black Panther Party, then you could understand his circumspection. Eddie and I certainly did, and we made sure he knew we didn't take it personally. One day, Eddie simply approached him for an interview to gain insight on the struggle of the 60's. He advised Eddie to come to his storefront in the next day or so. It resulted in a powerful interview that captured the liking of all our members and subscribers to the newsletter. Within a few days of the interview, the Imam was arrested on charges of shooting and killing a Fulton County Sheriff's deputy and wounding another.

After the arrest, Eddie followed up with another newsletter that I felt reached over a line that I was not comfortable with. My concern was that this latest newsletter would place the Silver Shields in a racist light. The letters had shades of Black superiority laden with a tone of White demonization. I called a meeting with Eddie, Chris, and Gary and expressed my concerns with the direction such rhetoric would inevitably take the organization. I was outvoted on the motion that we do a retraction. I, therefore, tendered my resignation and made one request of the officers. I asked that any one of them accompany me on a visit to the Secretary of State's office to make the change in organizational officers. I made it clear that since the organization was incorporated in my name, I would gladly transfer the paperwork into either one of their names. My position was that I did not want my name attached to any organization or business that held out views that even hinted at being racist. No one agreed to accompany me downtown, so I officially dissolved the organization.

Silver Shields was no more... Shortly after that, I was transferred to the Narcotics unit.

I had to have an emergency medical procedure performed right before the Olympics. My Homicide chain of command viewed this as some sort of attempt on my part to avoid having to work the mandatory long Olympic shifts. As a form of retaliation, I was transferred to the notoriously dysfunctional Narcotics unit. It was where all detectives went when they pissed off the command. As much as I hated the thought of working in that squad, I was determined I would make the best of it and find some way to sublimate this atrocity into a platform to improve the quality of life for the city's residents.

CHAPTER – 15

SHADY PRACTICES

As stated in an earlier chapter, Narcotics was my least desirable crime to work. I'd had enough exposure to narcotics enforcement in the military and also during the time I spent on the TAC squad to realize that it was nothing more than an exercise in futility. Based on recent changes in the law regarding the legalization of marijuana, I guess I wasn't too far off base in my deductions. But, it was my new assignment. Like it or not... The only thing for me to do was to figure out a way to make the most of my new job. It was actually the first time in my career that policing actually felt like a "job."

It had only been a year or so since I had taken custody of my youngest son.

His mom and I had divorced about 3 years prior but came to a juncture where we both decided it would be in my son's best interest if he came to live with me. She was a terrific mom and still is. It was just that my son had reached the ripe old age of 8 and was beginning to test the waters with his mom. Once we sat down with his school counselor and a couple of teachers, he cited being separated from his dad as the reason for his disruptiveness in school. He was a very bright child and always maintained superior grades, but he was just acting out his inability to cope with the broken family situation. The required course of action was clear and not even up for debate. I took primary custody of him the next week and single parented him until his sophomore year in high school, at which time I remarried. He continued to live with me until he graduated high school and left for college at Savannah State University. The entire time he was with me, he maintained a 4.0 GPA. It started out when he was in middle school. I would bribe him with money for each "A" he brought home. Once he reached high school, he pulled me aside and explained that the bribes were no longer necessary. He said he'd been on the principal's list and in the honors club for so long, that it would be too embarrassing to fall off at this point. At this point, it had become a matter of pride and self-expectation. It was one of several moments I still cherish as being one of the proudest moments of my life. When he graduated, he headed down to Savannah State University on an academic scholarship after turning down an athletic scholarship for basketball. After his first year, he applied and received a scholarship to Georgia State University, where he finished up his undergraduate degree in Commercial Real Estate. He went on to earn his MBA from the University of Georgia, Athens. He held the distinction of being the first undergraduate, as well as the first African American to be awarded a Jr. Broker's position with a major commercial real estate broker in the Buckhead section of Atlanta. Another proud moment was when he called to let me know that I didn't have to worry. He said that he was well aware of what this new position represented and what inherent responsibility he had in taking the job. He told me he understood that he had to make a stellar enough impression, or he would, in effect, be closing the door on any other African Americans that might have otherwise come after him. He assured me that he would do more than decimate any stereotypes. He said he would cause them to question themselves as to why their doors had ever been closed to people of color prior to his employment. Needless to say, this was another of the many proud moments that he and my other children would provide me with.

I had been assigned to the Day Watch on SWAT when I first took custody of Khalfani. This was great, as it enabled me to provide sufficient oversight of his activities in the evening times after school. We continued in this fashion until I was promoted to detective and assigned to the Youth Squad, where I spent a short 6 months on the Evening Watch. After that, I was transferred to Homicide and assigned to the Day Watch.

My transfer to the Narcotics unit would be when my luck would run out.

My first week on the new job, I asked to meet with the unit commander, a lieutenant. I filled him in on my domestic situation and asked if it was possible for me to be provided with a Day Watch assignment. Regular Evening Watch hours were bad enough for my situation, but this Evening Watch consisted of what was considered a "power shift." Instead of working the traditional 3:00 p.m. to 11:00 p.m. hours, we worked from 4:00 p.m. to 12:00 a.m. Depending on what was going on with our caseload, we sometimes worked from 5:00 p.m. to 1:00 a.m. or 6:00 p.m. to 2:00 a.m. This meant that my 14-year-old son would spend his entire day unattended.

The lieutenant was aghast. To suggest that he was insulted by my audacity would be an understatement. He quickly brought to my attention that his standing policy is that any newly assigned detective desiring to go to Day Watch first had to "pay their dues" on the Evening Watch. He stated that there was a long line of folks wanting to go to Day Watch, and I had a lot of nerve to request that shift after being in the unit for only a week. Furthermore, there was an absolute need for every person assigned to the Evening Watch, and he couldn't spare a single detective. PAY MY DUES??? Now I was insulted. I advised him that I had been on the department for 13 years, compared to the average 3 to 5 years of the other Narcotics investigators. I had started my career and spent several years in what was undeniably the roughest Zone in the city at that time. Additionally, I had worked for 8 years on SWAT; going through doors that would make the most macho officers faint of heart. I asked him, "What other dues are you talking about, lieutenant?" He settled down and said that I had a valid point, but his rule still stood, and he was not obliged to change them for anyone. He simply could not afford to spare a single person on the Evening Watch. "Just do a good job for me over here, and we'll revisit your request down the road." "Copy that, L.T." I said. I left out of his office feeling it was going to be fantastic working for another closed minded commander.

After the first night, I had a long talk with Khalfani and made it clear that he was going to have to step up in the evening times while I was at work. He would be responsible for his chores, homework, dinner, and bedtime. I would not be there to provide instruction, but he could always reach me on the new cell phone I purchased for him earlier that day. I told him I would try to find my way onto the Day Watch. But in the mean time, we would make the best of things.

It was only 2 weeks into the job when I identified what I felt were hazardous conditions for me and other newly assigned detectives. I was assigned to a team of 4 detectives, and we operated out of 2 vehicles. Two detectives per vehicle... I was partnered up with a Mike Pippens (retired), who had been a close friend of mine in my academy class. He was a real stand up guy and a heck of a cop. He was also US Army prior service and in the National Guard. The other 2 team members were equally impressive detectives. Phillip "Duke" Ellington had spent a short stint with SWAT during my time on the team and was a jokester of epic proportions. Anthony "AJ" Rawlings (retired) was the voice of reason of the quartet. He had more time on the department than the rest of us and was very level headed in his approach to everything. I felt we had a pretty good crew. We were assigned two different geographical areas of operation. Both areas were in my old Zone 1, but on opposite ends. Naturally, I couldn't do any undercover work in the Herndon Homes area, but I was fairly unknown in the Hollywood road area. Mike had also been a Zone 1 officer, and Duke actually lived in Zone 1. You can begin to see the madness in how we were arbitrarily assigned areas to work. There was absolutely no consideration given to previous assignment histories. The most novice supervisor should have been able to see the recklessness and disregard for our safety by placing us in an area where we were well known.

There were basically two types of vehicles being utilized by the unit. Unmarked police cars, which everyone in the communities knew were police vehicles. These were utilized primarily for basic work or as take down vehicles on raids. No one dared to use them for actual undercover work or surveillance. The rest of the fleet was made up of confiscated or forfeiture vehicles. The standing rule was to give a newly confiscated vehicle adequate time to "cool off" before turning it back out into the streets. Then, it was never to be utilized in the area from which it was seized. This was for obvious reasons. Unbeknownst to us, our team had been issued a vehicle that had been seized from Herndon Homes fairly recently. We were given the impression that it had been in police custody for some extended period of time and was safe to utilize in the area. It was later revealed that another team attempted to turn the vehicle out prior to our arrival in the unit. That resulted with the vehicle being shot at in Herndon

Homes. We were not happy campers when we saw how people broke and ran with every corner we turned in the Herndon Homes area. We may just as well have had a police blue light rack mounted to the roof of the tricked out SUV. Not to mention that Mike and I had met the assignment to Zone 1 with heavy protest because of our previous assignments in the area. It seemed that we were, inadvertently, being set up to be seriously injured or even killed.

Coupled along with the vehicle situation was a standing policy to make a certain amount of arrests. We were given daily instructions on what the target number was for that given day. We were not allowed to go home until we hit the magic number every night. This, of course, didn't sit well with me. I voiced my concerns to my sergeant. A couple of weeks later, the sergeant approached our team and advised that the lieutenant was requesting a memo addressing why we hadn't made any arrests over the course of the 3 ½ weeks we'd been assigned to the unit.

GLADLY!!!

I took pen to paper and explained that for the first couple of weeks, my team had been assigned unmarked vehicles due to a shortage of undercover vehicles. I explained that we were, therefore, unable to make any buys or affect any arrests from surveillance operations. However we had not been just sitting around doing nothing. We had borrowed a marked patrol car from SOS and had come to work in uniform to make a few traffic cases. We also served as a takedown team on arrests made by other teams. I then wrote that when we finally did receive an undercover vehicle, it was unsafe to operate in our assigned area. Then I stated that we had been given confirmation that we would receive a better vehicle within the next few days, and we would then be able to bring in some cases. Since the door was opened, I decided to address the most egregious of our concerns.

I then directed the memo to the issue of required arrest cases. I expressed how I stood in opposition to the fact that the unit had a required quota system. I wrote that I would not be adhering to a quota system of any shape, form, or fashion. Lastly, I stated that the memo was to serve as a formal request for any quota requirement in the future to be provided to me in writing.

After that memo was tendered, my team was the only team in the entire Narcotics unit that was not held to a quota. Other detectives inquired how we got out of having to turn in a set number of arrests every night. My response was always the same... "It's no different from grade school. You should try bringing in an apple for the lieutenant every day." What I wanted to say was that they should grow a backbone and stand up for what's right. But at this point in my career, I was convinced that although the average officer knew right from wrong, for whatever reason, they simply refused to hold the Thin Blue Line accountable. By then, I was resolved to fight the battles alone. It wasn't something I had any control over. My father was deeply seeded in me, and I only knew how to fight. I had learned, through my father's experience, what happens when you bend over in the presence of less scrupulous people. The same way that foreman physically put his foot on my father; I swore to never let another man literally or figuratively place his foot on me. There would never be any bend in my back.

A couple months into working, we started to hear rumors of another team that was engaged in some rather unscrupulous practices. We were told that a team of 4 White detectives would utilize a technique called "Knock and Talk" in a fashion that raised concerns. "Knock and Talk" refers to knocking on the door of a residence and engaging the occupants in a conversation that leads to requesting their permission to conduct a warrantless search of the premises. Otherwise known as a "consent search." We were told that this team was targeting the homes of older and elderly Black women for drug searches. They would appear at an older woman's front door, donned in extremely intimidating tactical raid gear. They would give the impression that the occupant had no choice other than to consent to the search or face charges of obstruction. They would also suggest that if they weren't allowed entry, they would secure a warrant and come back to ransack the home searching for drugs. They would commonly use the concocted excuse that the woman's son or grandson had been selling drugs out of her home. Often times, the women wouldn't even have a son or grandson, but that wouldn't stop them from making entry anyway.

I couldn't believe what we were being told, so our team decided to verify the allegation. We monitored the rogue team's radio traffic and listened for key indications that would perhaps tip their hand. Late into the night, we finally got a hit. When we heard them ask dispatch to hold them out on a routine Knock and Talk, we immediately proceeded to their given location. They had been there for only a couple of minutes by the time we arrived, but they had already begun their search of the premises. They were visibly shocked to see us when we stepped onto the porch area. Primarily, because word of my memo had gotten around the unit... That, coupled with my surmounting reputation on the department as being a trouble making, snitching militant... I pulled the team leader aside and advised him that my team was there to provide additional security for his team. I asked if the woman had given consent for the ongoing search. He said that she had. I then asked if she had also been instructed on her right to withdraw her consent at any time during the search. Again, he said she had. "Ok. Great!" I said. Then I made eye contact and summoned for her to join us in our conversation. I asked the elderly woman in front of the detective, "Ma'am, did any one of these officers ask for your permission to search your house?" She said they had. I asked "Ma'am, did you give them permission to search your house?" She said she had, but only because they indicated that she didn't have a choice, and that she would go to jail if she refused. At this point, my blood was beginning to boil. I could imagine my own mother being subjected to this type of treatment at the hands of Detroit Police. The idea that anyone would be subjected to this type of treatment by the very people who are supposed to be protecting them was downright sickening to me. I went on to ask if she had been advised by anyone that she had a legal right to take back her consent at any time she wanted. She said that she had not been so advised. I asked her one last question with the detective still standing there. "Ma'am, do you want to take back your consent to this search at this time?" I asked. "What do you mean? What will happen?" she asked. "Well, ma'am, if you take back your consent, by law, we have to stop searching and leave your house" I assured her. I could clearly see in her face the fear of going to jail if she didn't cooperate with the search. So I attempted to put her at ease one more time and reiterated that she would not be facing criminal charge for asking us to leave. She said "well in that case, yes, I would like to take back my consent, and I want you all to leave my house." Once she uttered those words, the other members of my team dispersed to the other rooms in the house to advise the other detectives that the consent had been rescinded, and it was time to vacate the premises. We hung around until we were sure the other team was gone, and then we headed back to our assigned area. We all knew we would have a large bulls-eye on our backs the rest of the time we were assigned to the unit. That was of no real concern since we had no intentions of working with anyone outside of our team anyway. We just didn't trust the integrity or agendas of anyone outside of our circle.

When we returned to the precinct at the end of shift, we were ushered into a room by one of the sergeants. We were asked about what transpired earlier. We gave our side of the story. After hearing what we had to say, we were each given a copy of disciplinary charges. We were all charged with endangering the lives of the other officers. The working theory was that our team had placed the other team in a dangerous situation by encouraging the homeowner to retract her consent. Technically, once her consent was rescinded, she would have been within her legal rights to grab her gun and defend herself against any further intrusion on our part. That was their idea of our team having endangered the rouge team. Nothing ever came of the charges. My guess is that when the case reached OPS, the Narcotics unit was most likely advised on how big a can of worms the case would open. The rogue officers were never addressed and allowed to continue their unethical and unconstitutional practices. Of course, many years later, the department suffered a scandal of international proportions involving an eerily similar incident that involved the Narcotics unit and the shooting death of an elderly Black woman (Ms. Kathryn Johnston) on the City's northwest side... Zone 1.

My major concern for Khalfani at this time was his growing popularity. He'd earned the position of starting point guard on the middle school's basketball team. This alone attracted an inordinate amount of friends and groupies of both genders. He was starting to develop an entourage at school, as well as in the neighborhood. I had done my best to instill leadership qualities in him. When I noticed how he was quickly amassing a following, I challenged him to a test of his leadership appeal. He was in complete denial of his natural leadership abilities. I challenged him to wear his pants legs hiked up just a little. Just enough to reveal the two different color socks he was to wear for a week... I told him to just observe what happens and report back to me the following week. He was totally astounded the next week when half of the students in his school were now wearing slightly hiked up pants legs with mixed matched socks. Of course, that experiment was followed up with a lecture on the burden of leadership and its inherent responsibilities. Many years later, his phone call to me after being hired at the real estate firm would serve as confirmation that the lesson of this day had indeed been learned.

My biggest concern was with the girls at school and in the community. Up until that point, I was able to keep a pretty good handle on his social activities. All of his friends, male and female, had to undergo somewhat of an interview process with me. For the guys, if they were what I considered to be knuckleheads, he couldn't hang out with them. I would offer my services as a mentor, but until I saw some change in their behavior, they were strictly off limits to Khalfani. The same rules applied for the girls, but I added an extra criteria. If they wanted to hang out with him, they had to maintain at least a 3.0 GPA. And even that was only under the condition that he could be allowed to tutor them up to a 3.5 GPA. I was determined that my son would beat the statistics and the odds that every young male of color faces in contemporary America. I would be damned if I was going to see all the effort I'd poured into raising him be circumvented and succumbed to peer pressure or the penal system; even worse, incarceration or death.

After 2 months on the Evening Watch, I decided to put former chief, Eldrin Bell's, most famous statement to the test. He'd always been known for his eloquently stated caution to supervisors to "inspect what you expect." So I decided to arrive home early one night as a cautionary signal to Khalfani that I could show up at any time. Therefore, he needed to be certain to always abide by the set rules. I arrived home around 8:00 p.m. 9:00 p.m. passed. 10:00 p.m. passed. Around 10:30 p.m., I heard his key in the front door lock. I sat quietly perched on the living room couch. When he opened the door and saw me sitting there, I thought he would have a heart attack. I'd never before seen his eyes grow so large, as he began to tremble in the archway of the door. I asked how long he had been keeping these hours. He said he started coming home late for the past month or so. I had a long discussion with him about my concerns with his behavior. I expressed to him that I was very disappointed in his choices and deception. In the next breath, I apologized to him for being an absentee parent. I gave him my word that I would figure out some way to be there for him in the evenings after school. After a few days of several more requests, the lieutenant wasn't going to budge on his position concerning transferring me to the Day Watch. He made it very clear that my domestic issues were just that... MY domestic issues. I even wrote a couple of memos to the next two levels in the chain of command. I wrote the major as well as the deputy chief. Finally I wrote the chief of police, herself. I was solidly rejected on every level. There was to be no assistance with my single parenting issues. Part of me was not surprised. After all, I had amassed a pretty full resume of "bucking the system" in my short 13 years on the department. And this was, after all, the same chief that I had openly challenged during my Silver Shields period. Not to mention all the other hell I had been raising since my first week on the department. However, whatever my transgressions, my son would not be made to pay the price. As far as I was concerned, there was not even a choice in the matter. There was only one route to take. The day after receiving my final rejection letter from the chief, I responded to her by putting in my request for a voluntary demotion back to patrol. I then got in contact with the SOS chain of command to ensure I would have a home with the SWAT team once I was reassigned to uniform patrol (Field Operations). It had taken 11 years to earn a gold shield, but nothing was more important than the welfare of my child.

After 2 ½ months of the Evening Watch presumably not being able to function without me, I was demoted back to uniform on the very next personnel order – 2 weeks later.

I was on my way back home to my beloved SWAT team...

CHAPTER – 16

SWAT – PART DEUX

When I was reassigned to SWAT, I was met with opened arms. I was ecstatic to be back aboard, and my teammates seemed happy to have me back. There had been very few changes to occur in the 2 years of my absence. One major change was the addition of a new unit commander. During my tenure on the Team, we had already experienced 5 changes of command. This was now the sixth commander that I would work for, over a period of 10 years. SWAT is a job that's not for everyone. It takes a special mindset to be able to go through doors on a daily basis. The only certainty to a SWAT call is that no matter how much you've planned your entry, you can be certain there is no certainty as to what awaits you on the other side of that door. The nature of policing causes a person to develop an unquenchable need to always be in control. That's the nature and premise of the overall function of law enforcement. To bring peace to a chaotic situation... This requires the officer to maintain control of him or herself as he or she tactically addresses and brings control to the situation and all persons involved. Hence the term "Peace Officers." When you're on a SWAT team, you proceed with the premise that you train for the worse-case scenario but with the understanding that every situation involves at least one unpredictable and uncontrollable factor – the suspect. It takes a lot for a cop to relinquish that kind of control. But when you're assigned to a SWAT team, you have to heavily rely upon and trust in your teammates. I honestly think some of the commanders who passed through SWAT were discouraged to find that however elite and prestigious the assignment was; the job itself was anything but glamorous. A couple of the command assignments to the team were clearly politically expedient at the time. Whatever the reason, there was a high turnover in SWAT command.

However prestigious or elite the SWAT team may have been... However courageous or heroic the acts of the SWAT team... However valuable the daily sacrifice or contribution... Some of its members would never be viewed beyond the color of their skin in mainstream society.

Such was my personal lesson in racial profiling...

> *One day, after a long and exhaustive day of SWAT training, I stopped by the grocery store in my community on the way home. I was still wearing my SWAT training uniform, which consisted of a shirt clearly affixed with the APD emblem and City seal. The shirt also had in bold wording, "Atlanta Police SWAT." I was wearing black BDU trousers, and my metal badge was clearly displayed, clipped on to my belt. I was carrying my pistol in a fully exposed, standard police issue duty holster. I was in the store for no more than 15 minutes. As I was in the checkout line, I noticed a group of Cobb County police officers forming outside in the front of the market. I saw them looking at me, but didn't give it any real thought. There didn't appear to be any sort of emergency unfolding in the store. I paid for my groceries and exited the store with me 2 bags of food. As soon as I reached the outside of the door, I was ordered to the ground and surrounded by the officers. At this point, my badge and SWAT tee shirt were in full view. They actually confiscated my ID card and contacted APD for verification of employment. Only after getting confirmation did they*

allow me to stand to my feet. After they were certain I was actually who I presented myself to be they made an attempt to justify their actions. They informed me their actions were based on the fact that they received a call of a robbery in progress, and I could have been impersonating an officer. They admitted to having witnessed me having a cordial and pleasant exchange with the cashier as I paid for my items. They even witnessed her returning my change for the $50 bill I had given her, which they saw me take from my own pocket. The sergeant went on to even admit that I seemed unusually calm and unconcerned about the forming police posse as I exited the store. All these things were significant, in light of the fact that the caller was a customer in the store and had described me perfectly. She even described me down to the details of my SWAT tee shirt and the APD badge clipped to my belt. It would seem that the dispatcher would have informed them of the greater possibility I was an actual sworn officer, but apparently, that didn't happen. I challenged them on whether or not they felt an actual robber would follow through with the robbery once the robber spotted the police forming outside? Also, would an actual robber have paid for the groceries with his own money that they witnessed coming from my own pocket? Lastly, would an actual robber be wearing a fully exposed departmental issue police style holster? Which, by the way, the weapon was never removed from the holster the entire time of the so called robbery. Not to mention all of the clearly marked SWAT gear and shinny badge I was wearing. The bottom line was, there was no justification for such an extreme response to a situation which spoke for itself. Indeed, the customer and the responding officers were operating solely on the tunnel vi-

sion of seeing a Black man with a gun. Never mind the fact that the State of Georgia was even then an "open carry" state. It was pure and simple. Even dressed in a clearly marked and authorized APD SWAT training uniform, in an open carry state, for all the times I had put my life on the line to serve and protect the citizens of Atlanta... In this very moment, I was still nothing more than a "Black Male With A Gun!!!"

When I left SWAT the first time, I was concerned I hadn't made a significant lasting contribution to the teams' legacy. My father always taught me to leave a thing or a place in better condition than when I received it. In his opinion, the only motivation for acquiring anything in life is to lend to its improvement. Every assignment I received in the military and within the APD was an opportunity for me to improve something. At the time of my first transfer from SWAT, I had contributed to the selection of the new flight suit uniforms and the design of the new SWAT shoulder patch. I had also created our first computerized shooting records database. The database was designed to maintain a more detailed record of all shooting training as well as tracking shots fired on an actual SWAT call. Its purpose was to provide a more detailed account of an officer's shooting training for courtroom testimony and open records requests.

I resumed my duties as lead counter-sniper and team counter-sniper trainer. That was somewhat to the dismay of a couple of the other counter-snipers. My desire was to take the counter-snipers to the next level with our training. I acquired an almanac and scheduled the majority of training for the most inclement weather possible. The looks that some of the guys would give me when I announced certain training days was hysterical. Some would question if I had not heard the weather forecast of below freezing temperatures or gale type winds. Eyes would really roll when I would schedule on an expected snow day, especially if it was an off day. Dismayed, and to some degree pissed off, the shooters would invariably display their commitment and dedication by showing up for the training anyway. They were a group of real troopers. My shooting partner was the second female ever to be assigned to APD SWAT. Dolly Johnson (Sgt., retired) was one of the best shooters I ever came across. She was calm and collected behind the Leopold scope. She and I had attended the State's Counter-Sniper and Advanced Counter-Sniper courses together. Dolly was the only female in the class and, we were the only two attendees from APD. There were officers representing law enforcement agencies from all over Georgia. You could almost see the other teams sizing us up. Since we represented the largest agency in the state, we were the ones that everyone would seek to outdo. This was simply to earn bragging rights that the high and mighty APD "ain't all it's cracked up to be." Dolly and I would have something to say about that. At the end of the course, the individual and overall scores were added up. I would graduate holding the individual shooting record for the State. Dolly and I would also set a record for the "partners" shooting category. If looks could kill. To see some of the most narcissistic shooters in the state be undone by, of all things, a woman, was priceless.

Even though Dolly and I were shooting partners, we partnered up with someone else for regular patrol. My partner was officer Darren Rush (RIP). Rush was the type of guy that everyone instantly loved. Really! You didn't like this guy. If you knew him, you loved this dude. He had the most debonair ways without even trying. He was also the most high-strung person I had ever met. He would give anyone the shirt off of his back. Literally. It was just who he was. He was also a top notch cop and SWAT officer. He was a part of the entry team, so we seldom worked together on actual calls. We did, however, train together a lot due to the fact that I was also one of the primary pistol shooting instructors and a tactics instructor. My partner and I tended to hang out mostly with another team that included the first female to ever work APD SWAT, Deborah Sousa (SPO, retired). Her partner was the one and only Kirk Butler. That's right, the same Kirk Butler that befriended me back in my police academy days. It was a tremendous privilege to work with the both of them. They both enjoyed somewhat legendary status within the department. After working with the both of them for 10 years, I can honestly say their reputations were much deserved. They were the team the SWAT command relied upon the most. Not only were they two of the most veteran members on the team, they were two of the most skilled. There wasn't any aspect of the job they couldn't speak on. They both eventually became certified in EOD and became the team's lead Bomb Technicians.

Rush had been somewhat of a 3rd wheel on the Butler/Sousa team until I was transferred back into the unit. He and I were assigned as partners, and our relationship grew to a level tantamount to brothers. However, for all the love that had grown between us, it wouldn't last for very long.

A year or so after my return, Butler and I began to notice a change in my partner. He seemed to always be distracted and somewhat disconnected from whatever was going on around him. Even on SWAT calls. Kirk and I were two of his closest friends, although there were a couple of people assigned to other areas on the department who Rush was closer to. He'd recently gotten married to a beautiful and talented Parole/Probation officer named Paula (RIP). They appeared to be a couple made in paradise. Whenever Kirk and I would inquire about Rush's preoccupation, he would dismiss it as "nothing to be concerned about." Kirk and I figured that it was simply a case of being a newlywed. Rush seemed to be preoccupied with something that was making him sad and despondent. The most happy-go-lucky person I'd ever known was now in an apparent spiral of depression. Things got to a point where he would regularly miss training. And when he was there, his scores were barely passable. With our growing concern for our friend, Kirk and I decided to take a more direct approach and pressed him for answers. We assured him we would wholeheartedly assist him with whatever he was dealing with, but he needed to let us in. The harder we pressed, the more withdrawn he became. When things grew to a level of him becoming a hazard to himself and the team, we decided to take a "tough love" approach to the situation. We sat him down and told him we had come to one of the most difficult decisions of our careers. We told him we were going to recommend him for assistance from the departments' psychologist and recommend that he be temporarily assigned to another SOS unit until he was cleared to come back to SWAT. His behavior had become apparent to the entire team, including the supervisory staff. Kirk and I felt that if the chain of command didn't care enough about our friend to demand that he receive help, we would love him enough to do what we knew, or felt we knew, was in his best interest. He broke down, and the three of us cried together for several long minutes. He said that he was mad at us but understood that we were only acting out of love. He explained how he felt he was starting to get himself together, and he just needed a little more time to get some things straightened out. We bluntly asserted that his disposition was deteriorating at a rapid pace. We asked if he would rather that we take no action and he or another teammate ends up getting killed on our next SWAT call. We reassured him that even though he felt he was improving, he was, in fact, getting worse. He said he trusted our opinion and observation, but he was still reluctant to fill us in on what was going on, other than that it was domestic related.

I had spent a career looking corrupt and rogue officers in the face as I gave them up to Internal Affairs or to a commander, but this was totally different. As Kirk and I approached the lieutenant to recommend a course of action for our dear brother, my gut wrenched at the thought of taking away something we both knew he loved so much. Even though we knew it was only temporary, we had a hard time getting the words out to the commander. We knew that once we put the commander on notice, we couldn't take it back. And in turn, the lieutenant had no other choice than to act accordingly, per departmental regulations. Within 24 hours, Rush was transferred to the Hit and Run Unit until the doctors could make their evaluation to clear him to return to SWAT.

The next few weeks Kirk, Deborah and I visited Rush at his Hit and Run office on a daily basis. He was in the highest spirits we had seen him in for the past several months. He was enjoying his new assignment and joking about, perhaps, never returning to SWAT. We all knew that was a joke. This was one guy who lived and breathed SWAT 24/7. He took the opportunity to let Kirk and I know that he was grateful for the action we had taken. The removal from SWAT had afforded him an opportunity to take a step back and evaluate his situation. He said he and his new wife were working some things out and their relationship was headed back to the stratosphere it once occupied. Kirk and I were really happy that we'd taken a hard line with our little brother, and we reasoned that perhaps, it saved his life.

In fact, it had. But only for a short while...

As a result of losing my partner, I decided to jump in the car with Kirk and Deborah to become their new third wheel until Rush returned. Kirk and I made a habit of being the first to arrive at the precinct in the morning and the last to leave in the evening. We got there early enough to get in a good portion of our workout before the rest of the Team showed up. Once everyone was there, the fairly small quarters grew quite crowded. After our workout, Kirk and I headed next door to the precinct. We'd just sat down in the precinct when our commander, Lieutenant Mike Crowder (retired), emerged from his office. He had a ghostly look on his face and a stunned or blank stare. He walked around in a couple circles as I looked at Kirk to see if he was also observing the peculiar behavior. Finally, he approached our desk and said he had just gotten off the phone with someone over at Hit and Run. If I live to be a thousand years old, I will never forget his next words. "They said that Rush just killed himself" he said. Kirk and I looked at each other and started laughing. SWAT was the most notorious unit for pranks. Similar to homicide, there tends to be a degree of morbidity to the humor of SWAT types as a means of dealing with the aspect of death that's faced on a daily basis. We looked at the commander, and Kirk said "get out of here with that bullsh-t, lieutenant. That sh-t's not funny!" The lieutenant did not break character for a single moment as he said he was not joking. "They think he killed his wife also" the lieutenant added. Kirk and I began to press the lieutenant for details, but he had none at that time. The only thing he knew was that Rush failed to show up for work that morning. After a certain amount of time and failed attempts at contact, the department requires that someone from the employee's unit is sent to the residence to perform a welfare check.

When the Hit and Run officer made entry into Rush's home, along with the local authorities, they found Rush and his wife deceased from apparent gunshot wounds. I have since learned more intimate details concerning Darren and Paula's passing, but I will respectfully refrain from chronicling them in this rendering.

Officer Darren Anthony Rush will forever be remembered as a great man and an even greater human being. Paula's laugh and quick-witted personality will always be sorely missed. They were both truly loving spirits.

Not long after this dark cloud settled over my life, and after a short 2 years of reassignment to SWAT, I was promoted to sergeant and assigned to the Morning Watch in the familiar territory of Zone 5.

CHAPTER – 17

TRANSFER THE PROBLEM

I approached my return to Zone 5 Morning Watch with an invigorated enthusiasm. Not only was this the assignment I had started my career with, but this time around I was in a position of minimal influence. I was aware that on the department, sergeants were often viewed as being nothing more than glorified patrol officers or overpaid babysitters. None of these views of relegation fazed me one bit. The rank of sergeant wasn't a position of high authority by any means, but it was a position of direct influence at the rank and file level. Being a grass roots type of personality, I was elated with the opportunity to make a difference at the level that most directly affected my officers. In addition, this position still afforded me with the opportunity to maintain direct contact with my citizens. Most importantly, even though I was not yet in a position to draft or create policy, I was now in a position to directly impact how policy was implemented or carried out. Baby steps.

Apparently, what were baby steps to me were being interpreted as giant leaps to the Zone chain of command. I was reminded time and time again that I was overreaching. When I was promoted to sergeant, I was assigned with 1 other new sergeant, Marisha "Shep" Shepherd (Capt., active). We shared the Watch with a veteran sergeant and 1 very seasoned lieutenant. In fact, the lieutenant was very close to retirement. The veteran sergeant, Mark Holder (retired), was happy to work with me and Shep, and he spent as much time with us as he could. He attempted to pour as much knowledge about supervising into us as we could take. He was a very patient and considerate co-worker. The only problem was that we were promoted late in the calendar year. Because the Watch had been operating with a supervisory shortage for so long, Mark had accumulated massive amounts of time. The city had a strictly adhered to policy concerning accumulated time. Up to a certain amount of accumulated hours could be carried into the next physical year. Any overage of allowable hours had to be taken by year's end, or it would be lost. Use it, or lose it. I think his words were something to the effect of being happier than a hog in slop to see Shep's and my name appear on the personnel order. He scheduled leave to coincide with our assignment date in the Zone. As a result, Shep and I were on our own for the first 3 weeks as brand new sergeants. The shift commander was of very little value to us because he was from the old school of, "need me if you call me." We never did. On occasion, he would make such a half-hearted effort of providing us with guidance that we pretty much preferred that he hadn't. His disinterest was offsetting, but we made a pact that we would figure it out on our own before either of us would beg a commander to do his job. After all, we had been supervised by some pretty outstanding sergeants over our 15 years on the department, so it wasn't that we didn't know what first line supervision looked like as a final product on the streets. We just had to fill in the blanks and figure out the backroom chores and secrets to good supervision. The administrative aspects that the average officer on the street doesn't usually see... It turned out that Mark was transferred to another Zone not long after we got there. I was sent to the Evening Watch briefly to fill a void on their supervisor roster. That lasted a couple months. However, I was there long enough to lose one of my officers to the hands of a deranged man. Russell 'Rusty" Stalnaker (RIP) was as gentle and compassionate a human being as you would ever meet. He was kind and considerate of everyone inside and outside of the precinct doors. He was in the act of extending a kindness to a deranged individual when he was turned on and shot dead by that same person. He will always be remembered and sorely missed. He was truly one of the good guys.

Shortly afterwards, I was back on the Morning Watch.

As it turned out, things went fairly smooth for our first few months as brand new sergeants. Whatever issues I drew a blank on, Shep would provide needed insight and vice versa. We began to earn the respect of our officers by the way we leaned on their experience in the Zone. Most supervisors tended to be under the impression, for whatever reason, that they're suppose to arrive brand new to their assignment with all the answers. I don't know if it's an ego thing or a fear of being perceived as lacking in knowledge by their employees. Shep's and my approach was somewhat unorthodox in that regard. Our line of thinking supported the idea that the nature of Policing precluded us from being able to adapt a "fake it 'til you make it" attitude. We thought, while we would have been in the process of "faking" it, there was too much room for error that could result in loss of civilian and police life. This wasn't the type of job that you "fake it" in for one second. Neither she nor I had any problem asking an officer how they normally handled a particular situation based on their experience with a particular person, area, or environment. There are no cookie cutter answers in law enforcement, and we knew it. The way I would have handled a situation in Zone 1 Day Watch may not apply for Zone 5 Morning Watch. Heck, even the way I handled things when I was an officer on Zone 5 Morning Watch 15 years ago, may not fly at this time. So we were open, honest and direct with our officers about everything. As a result, they were more than eager to assist us and respected our common sense approach to the Morning Watch mission.

Shep and I attended the Zone 5 staff meetings which occurred every week in the "front office" precinct on Spring Street. Patrol worked out of the main precinct in the CNN building, but the administrative and command staff worked out of their own precinct on Spring St. All precincts were required to have supervisory representation at these weekly meetings. Since there were approximately 7 precincts or worksites in Zone 5, this would make for pretty well attended meetings. Our lieutenant would always attend as well. Week after week, Shep and I would sit and listen to the Day Watch commander's berating of the performance of the Morning Watch. He would go down a written list and criticize each and every misstep occurring on the Morning Watch... in his opinion. Based on the Day Watch commander's complaints, the Zone commander would then issue directives for the Morning Watch to adhere to. The Morning Watch commander would just sit there without ever responding in any way. Week after week, he would never offer any explanation in defense of his Morning Watch officers, his two new sergeants, or even himself for that matter. Dead silence. When we got to work the following night after a meeting, Shep told me I looked like I was about to say something in the meeting the day before. I told her I wasn't sure how many more weeks I could sit there and swallow unwarranted ridicule just because we were the new kids on the block. I later met with the lieutenant and expressed my disappointment with his lack of defense in the staff meetings. Of course, we were making mistakes, considering that Shep and I were basically training ourselves in our new positions. He said he didn't really "give a sh-t" what they said because he was basically one foot out the door anyway. He said he hated working the Watch, and he was only there because he was being punished anyway. His only interest was in auto thefts. Nothing else about policing interested him. I told him I respected his position on things, and I recognized he was way beyond "burnout." I advised him that I, on the other hand, had a long time to spend in my career and had no intention of spending it with someone's foot on my neck.

I continued to hold my tongue in the staff meetings, but wasn't sure for how much longer.

It was during this period that Shep and I had the incident where retraining was recommended for one of our officers. Our recommendation for retraining was not well received by the Zone's chain of command. Our request was for the officer to receive additional training in the areas of report writing, criminal procedure, criminal law, firearms usage, cultural awareness/ sensitivity training, and interpersonal communications. We were basically recommending that he re-cycled through the entire police academy again. Instead of helping the officer, he was transferred to Zone 1, where he cost the department a hefty $80,000 settlement in a lawsuit. Then he was fired. Shep and I had seen this on the horizon and did everything we could to spare the city and the department the embarrassment and the financial burden. Instead, we were treated as though we had crossed the "Thin Blue Line." To this day, I'm still not sure why the request was taken so personally by the Zone commander. For whatever reason, it was very clear that we certainly hadn't found any favor with our fellow supervisors.

After the aforementioned recommendation was submitted, the Day Watch commander went into overdrive with his attacks of the Morning Watch during the staff meetings. For me, it had finally reached its boiling point. I had taken more than my fill.

I was sitting at the conference table next to Shep when the Day Watch lieutenant began his weekly barrage of insults hurled at the Morning Watch lieutenant. This particular morning, they seemed to be especially venomous. I sensed that it was due to Shep's and my recommendation for the officer to be retrained, but the toxin was being directed at the Watch commander. Even he was for the first time visibly affected by the penetrable words precipitating in his direction. Out of my peripheral I could see Shep looking at me and the impatience building in my face. She later joked that she'd never before seen a Black man of my complexion turn beet red. I waited until the portion of the meeting when the floor was opened to all attendee for comments or suggestions. After everyone else had their say, I offered my comments. I addressed the Day Watch commander directly and told him that it was no secret that Shep and I were new to the ranks of supervision. That it was invariable that we were going to make mistakes. I told him that I greatly appreciate him bringing to our attention whatever deficiencies he spotted with our supervising, because we were still in the learning phase. However, I would appreciate it even more if he would pull either or both of us aside and counsel us in private, as opposed to trying to shame us in front of the entire Zone 5 command staff week after week. I told him that all he does is criticize us but never offered to counsel or offer us direction. I added that I resented the fact that he never had any words of admiration for the excellent job the Morning Watch officers provided on a daily basis. There was never any mention during his rants noting the hard work of the men and women of the Morning Watch. Not to mention the fact that they put their lives on the line nightly without hesitation or complaint. Then I opined that by the tone of his ridicule, he clearly has a problem with the Morning Watch staff. I went on to suggest that if he had a problem with me on a professional level, by all means... let's have a conversation and figure things out. However, based on his demeanor towards me since I'd been assigned to the precinct, it felt his problem with me might be of a more personal nature. I went on to tell him, in front of everyone sitting at the table, that if he had a personal problem with me, we could go out behind the precinct and settle it like men. I was cautioned by the Zone commander that I was coming dangerously close to threatening a "superior" officer with bodily harm. I suggested to the major that the lieutenant I was addressing was, in no way, shape or fashion "superior" to me. I further stated that it wasn't a threat, but an invitation. The Zone commander suggested that we all settle down, and he dismissed the meeting.

When questioned about my demeanor later, I explained to another sergeant that I had no tolerance for commanders who disguise their bully tactics as official authority or use the chain of command to cloak their hidden agendas. If someone has a problem with me, they should be honest about it and not try to hide behind their rank.

The next personnel order came out a week later with my name on it... I was headed to Zone 4 Morning Watch...

CHAPTER – 18

THE GOLDEN RULE

In total, I spent just under 6 months in Zone 5 before being transferred. My hope was that I would have better luck in Zone 4. There was no place I could go on the department without seeing familiar faces. Not just people I had served with in the Zone or CID, but people I had trained in the academy. One of SWAT's primary functions was to put recruits through 2 weeks of survival training before they completed the academy. At the end of the 2 weeks, we would offer recommendations to the academy staff if a certain recruit should not be allowed to continue employment. Our recommendations were based on their performance and ability to demonstrate that they could survive on the streets. This training was mandatory for every recruit attending the academy, with no exceptions. I lost count of how many officers I personally had hands-on time with over the 10 or so years. As a result, every officer with 10 or less years on the department knew who I was, even if I didn't remember them. In addition, the academy staff had been telling stories of my academy fitness test accomplishments for the 15 years since I graduated. As a result, it was not uncommon for an officer to start off his or her introduction to me with "so you're Yabuku! Did you really do 700 pushups?" I never got used to that, and it never stopped being embarrassing to me. So when I arrived in Zone 4, half the officers on the Watch already knew who I was from one or the other of these two sources. Unfortunately, there was now the added inquisition of "did you really threaten to kick a lieutenant's a-- in front of your major?"

Zone 4 Morning Watch was a pleasant change from the hostility I felt in Zone 5. The officers were all hard workers and seemed to really want to do a great job. There was an inundation of newly sworn female officers to the watch. Most of the other officers had no more than 7 years on the job. Somehow, this was my first field assignment that didn't quite have the feeling of being a home for me. Up until then, no matter where I worked, I could always find something to give me sense of belonging. Even in the dreaded Narcotics unit, I felt a sense of purpose. Even if it was policing the police... It was still a purpose, and a very important one in my estimation. Here, it felt as though I just didn't fit in. I quickly established a wonderful working relationship with my officers but was uncertain as to where I fit into the supervisory scheme. I knew there would be apprehension toward me by the Zone command staff simply based on the circumstances of my being there. Not to mention, this was the same precinct commander I had come up against during my Silver Shields days with the uniform ornamentation incident. On the other hand, the officers loved the idea of having a supervisor they knew would stand up for them at all costs. I had no idea how rare I had become. In my mind, I wasn't doing anything that some of my best supervisors hadn't done for me at one time or another. I had examples of supervisor courageousness in the personification of Sgt. Clay Sorrow (Lt., retired) and Lt. Richard "Dick" Webber (retired) during my academy days; Sgts. Donald "Don Juan" Cameron (RIP), Melvin Denson (Lt., retired) and Charlie Owens (RIP) during my earlier Zone 5 days; Sgt. Claude Richardson (RIP) and Major Lovett Goss (retired) during my Zone 1 Days; Sgt. Jessie Pitts (retired) and Capt. Harold Goldhagen (retired) during my TAC days; Sgts. William "Bill" Briley (retired) and Travis Harvey (retired) during my SWAT days. I also had 3 constant mentors over my career, of whom I never worked with. However I am eternally grateful that they sought me out to mentor me. They were Sgt. Charlie Horton (retired), Major Johnny Prince (retired) and Deputy Chief W. W. Taylor (retired).

Like a ton of bricks, it occurred to me that I was now standing squarely in the footprints of these law enforcement giants. They had all either retired or passed away, and the mantle had been passed. Similarly to the epiphany of my son when he accepted his first job with the real estate firm, I was acutely aware that the leadership legacy of these examples before me was now lying squarely on my shoulders. Of course, there were other supervisors and officers around the department doing their part in trying to create a better working environment for the officers. There were also others on the department doing whatever they could do to hold their fellow officers accountable for the type and quality of service provided to the citizens of this great city. But if I was to be effective in my efforts, I had to approach every challenge with the attitude that if I didn't do it, it wouldn't get done. Given the shining examples that had gone before me, I was in no position to shrink from my responsibility to be the best supervisor I could possibly be. At whatever cost...

Zone 4 Morning Watch was commanded by a pretty cool lieutenant named Scott Lyle (retired). Scott was originally from the Detroit area also. He had been recently transferred to the Watch after spending about 11 years in OPS/Internal Affairs. I never knew the reasons for his new assignment, and I never asked. He was very comfortable to work with. Even so, I simply could not shake the feeling of being an outsider in my new assignment. The Watch was rounded out with another sergeant named A.C. Martin (retired) and a female sergeant. We all got along pretty well. A.C. was a veteran supervisor with not much time left before retirement. He was a laugh a minute and had a keen eye for upper management BS. He really knew how to read the handwriting on the wall, so to speak. The other sergeant was a friend of mine from back during my SWAT days. She was always a great person and pleasant to be around. We had a few mutual friends within and outside of the department. She was happy to see my arrival on the Watch and volunteered to show me the ropes.

After being on the Watch for a couple of months, I was approached by the 3 newest female officers. They voiced their concerns about how they felt the female sergeant was being extra hard on them. I told them she was just trying to mold them into good officers that and they should be patient with her. I offered to bring to the sergeant's attention their concern in the event that she wasn't aware of how she was projecting herself to them. I had a discussion with the sergeant, and she shared some rather unflattering opinions of the 3 officers. Within a week, I was approached a second time by the officers who said that the mistreatment had intensified. They were considering filing a formal EEOC "hostile work environment" complaint against the sergeant. I went to the lieutenant and shared the officers' concerns and threat. I asked him, based on his experience working OPS, if the officers had a legitimate complaint. He was pretty satisfied that the issue hadn't reached the proportions of an EEOC complaint. A couple of weeks later, the officers approached me again and told me they had retained Union representation, and they were going forward with their complaint, as conditions were continuing to deteriorate with the female sergeant. Apparently, she was now assigning them to three different foot patrols in the highest crime areas of the Zone – by themselves – on the Morning Watch – without restroom or meal breaks. They felt she was, in fact, placing their lives unnecessarily in harm's way. I tended to agree with them. They then blindsided me with a really uncomfortable question. They told me they had heard from several independent sources that the sergeant had made derogatory and disparaging statements about them. They asked if I could confirm these statements as they rattled off what I had been told by the supervisor verbatim. Clearly, they weren't lying about their independent sources. They cautioned me that before I answer, I should know that one of their sources said they had actually witnessed the sergeant telling me these things. Apparently someone was in the precinct and had overheard the entire conversation. This was highly feasible to me since the sergeant and I were both under the impression that we were alone in the office when she shared her opinions of the officers. In that conversation, I'd told the sergeant I appreciated the "heads up." I then went on to remind her that she knew me well enough to know that I would draw my own conclusions of the entire Watch based on my own observations. Even my own words were repeated back to me by these 3 officers... They explained that was the reason they felt comfortable coming to me with their issues. They also said I had established a reputation on the department of standing up for my officers. They asked me again for a confirmation. I suggested that with their preponderance of evidence they didn't need my confirmation. They said the department would never take the word of three rookie officers over the word of a supervisor. Somehow, I knew they were right. I confirmed their allegations and fashioned a memo to the lieutenant. In the memo, I told him the officers had retained Union representation and were going forward with their EEOC complaint against the sergeant. It stated the memo was to serve as official notification of the ongoing situation on the Morning Watch. Once the officers' complaint was filed, the sergeant was immediately transferred to the Day Watch, and we received a new sergeant on the Morning Watch. Sergeant Marc Lawson (retired,

RIP) was a strong willed officer who had a reputation for never backing down. He had been the president of the IBPO Union for many years and had presided over the AAPL Union before that. He was not someone who was afraid of a fight. We had been best of friends for many years. Marc had endured years of maltreatment from the department for his refusal to back off of issues. He and I had spent many hours over the years discussing ways we could affect positive change on the department. We shared countless conversations over breakfast and lunch at Paschal Brothers, the Beautiful and Chanterelles restaurants. I'll never forget the day he announced to me that he was giving me the distinct honor of naming his firstborn son after me. A few years later, he honored me a second time by allowing me to name his second son. Marc was more like family than a co-worker. He was a welcomed addition to the Zone 4 Morning Watch rotation, as it came to be called. Marc's transfer was a result of having a difference with his commander at his previous assignment. It was beginning to appear that Zone 4 Morning Watch was becoming a dumping ground for undesirable supervisors. Marc had also been instrumental, as the IBPO president, in the now infamous "f--k the police" meeting with mayor Bill Campbell years earlier. We had fought a lot of battles together over the years.

As to be expected, a few weeks later, I was called down to OPS to provide a statement concerning the case against the female sergeant. I gave as truthful and as honest of a statement as I could. There is no question it felt uncomfortable making a statement against someone who had been a friend for a number of years. There also was no question that this act was in clear violation of the unofficial "golden line" that exists within every police agency across the nation, if not globally. That intra-agency line that runs between and separates gold and silver badges (supervisors -vs- officers)... The layers of fraternity within the department are inexhaustible. However, the most prevalent fraternity, as I was soon to find out, is the fraternity of the "gold badge." Supervisors are expected to stick together... even to the detriment of the very officers they are charged with leading and providing for.

A week after giving my statement to OPS, I was instructed to report to the major's office. Once there, she advised me that I was being formally charged with disciplinary action. She said she was recommending a 1-day suspension. The charge was, "Appropriate Action Required." She contended that it had been brought to my attention that there was a brewing concern on the Morning Watch, and I had not taken the appropriate action to address or thwart the growing issue. She said I failed to take the appropriate action of reporting the allegations to my chain of command. She said I had also exacerbated the situation by confirming the officers' allegations against the sergeant. She concluded that I had, in fact, brought the information to the officers unsolicited. I assured her that the officers approached me with the information and not the other way around. I told her the information presented to me was so precise that it would have been foolish and incredibly disingenuous for me to have denied the truth. Then I told her I had indeed brought the issues to the attention of the Watch commander, and he advised me that he would handle it. She said that wasn't good enough and that I should have done more. I asked her what more could I have done but to bring the issue to the attention of the female sergeant and the Watch commander. She said I should have never confirmed the allegations, even if it meant lying to OPS. I explained to the major that I alerted the sergeant with my intention to be truthful in my statements to OPS. I had explained to the sergeant that she might get a slap on the wrist for her behavior towards the officers, but if found to be untruthful in my statements to OPS, I would be fired. The department has always had a zero tolerance for untruthfulness in written and verbal statements. Lying speaks directly to an officer's credibility in a court of law. The department has no use for an officer whose testimony will come under scrutiny whenever he or she is on the witness stand.

The major was still obviously unimpressed. She then said something that stuck with me for the remainder of my career. She said "I'm going to give you a day without pay to teach you a lesson in supervision. The lesson is that "gold sticks together." I tried to maintain my decorum when I snapped back "I'm sorry, major, but in my book, right fights for right where ever the chips may fall." She said if I maintained that attitude, I wouldn't get far on the department as a supervisor. I told her that may be true, but at least I'll be able to sleep at night. I was dismissed from her office and apparently the Zone. A few weeks later, I was transferred to Zone 1 Morning Watch.

While in Zone 1, my case came up for appeal with the Civil Service Review Board (CSRB). The CSRB was the only recourse that officers had to fight disciplinary action within the construct of city government. If you couldn't find relief from the CSRB, your only course of action left was to hire an attorney and fight the city through the civil courts. When the CSRB heard my case, they found that the charges against me were unwarranted and improper. They reimbursed me for the day of lost wages, plus interest. They also expunged my OPS record of all charges. The decision relied heavily on supporting testimony from 2 of the 3 officers. 1 was afraid to testify against the major because they were still fairly new on the department and still working for the same major. She at least gave me the courtesy of showing up at the hearing and apologizing to me while we waited in the anteroom. I'm not sure how I responded to her because I zoned out while she was talking. In my mind, I could hear my ex-wife fussing at me about how I was always jeopardizing my own career by standing up for folks that either couldn't or wouldn't stand up for themselves. She would always remind me of my career aspirations to be chief, but how I was basically engaging in an act of career suicide on a daily basis. I think I told the officer something along the lines of how I understood and not to worry. At least, I hope I did. The other saving grace was lieutenant Lyle. When he took the stand, he contended the charges were erroneous. He confirmed that I had indeed notified him of the situation twice. He recounted that I notified him verbally the first time, and in writing the second time. He admitted that he mistakenly deduced that the issues hadn't risen to the level of being a hostile work environment.

The major's case evaporated before her very eyes, and she was not a happy camper. But she could find some solace in the fact that I was, at least, now out of her Zone... and out of her hair.

There was a new personnel order out...

Zone 1, here I come again!!!

CHAPTER – 19

SECOND CHANCES

Before I could actually make it to Zone 1 Morning Watch, a mishap befell me and my 9-year-old daughter. The events would not only delay my arrival to Zone 1, but it facilitated a major change in my life.

Over a period of time, I made the acquaintance of a guy that worked out at the same gym as I did. Greg was a pretty cool guy. He was a few years older than me, but you would never know it. He was in terrific shape and had a younger looking face. He was also from Michigan. More importantly, he was a distributor for a new garment line that made moisture displacement athletic ware. They specialized in under garments for professional sports. While in conversation one day, I asked Greg if he thought his company's undershirts would be functional under police protective vests, or body armor. He said he would be happy to provide a dozen undershirts for me to sample. I told him my intentions were to have the APD SWAT team try them out and if satisfied, they would perhaps provide an endorsement of the product, since the company was a new startup. He thought it was a great idea and agreed to meet me at the gym the next day with the samples.

It was about 4 in the evening, and my wife hadn't made it in from work yet. My daughter and I loaded up in the SUV and headed to the gym. While traveling south on Interstate-75, I experienced a blowout of the front driver's side tire. Fortunately, I was traveling below the speed limit due to the rush hour traffic. I was travelling in the far left lane. When the tire blew, the car made a sharp left veer toward the retaining wall. I attempted to counter steer to avoid hitting the wall, and the right front suspension became over burdened. The vehicle rolled side over side for the entire 5 lanes of Interstate-75. It continued to roll over until it finally rested in the second lane of the Interstate-285 merge. In all, we rolled over 6 lanes without being struck by a single vehicle. Needless to say, the vehicle was flattened, and it still amazes people that she and I both survived. I have always been religious about the fact that the car doesn't shift out of "park" until ALL occupants are securely seat belted in. The seat belt kept my daughter from being ejected from the vehicle but did not offer much protection from the road burn which resulted from the rear passenger window busting out during the rolls. She suffered her right calf being basically scraped off down to the muscle. Fortunately, her injuries were more cosmetic as opposed to being physically debilitating. She had as much reconstructive surgery as she could handle at her young age. But there was still some scaring that she would probably have to carry throughout life. She never seemed to develop a complex as you would expect of a growing young woman. In fact, she went on to play varsity basketball and run track at her high school.

Another stroke of luck was the fact that there was an emergency room nurse traveling in the car directly behind me. I saw her at the resulting lawsuit proceedings, and she commended me on my attempts to avoid hitting other motorists in the wreck. She said it appeared that when the left tire blew, I was going to be able to steer my way out of the entire situation. When she saw the front right tire give under the additional stress, all she could do was watch the vehicle roll for what seemed an eternity. She was also amazed that no other vehicles became involved. Once the vehicle came to its final resting place, she immediately ran to the car to assist. She said she checked my vitals, and there were none. My daughter was of course in shock, as well as in pain, from her injuries. In addition to her calf, she also had a fractured femur and wrist bone. Fortunately, she was asleep when the wreck occurred, and she was awakened by the pain after it was over. Due to her not actually witnessing the wreck unfold, she never developed any form of PTSD. Since I was nonresponsive, all attention was turned to the welfare and stabilization of my daughter. Once the fire department arrived on the scene, all efforts were centered on getting her extricated from the car. Once she became fully cognizant of what was going on, she became frightened and began to scream to the top of her lungs. When I heard the shrieking from the back seat, I rose up from my slouched position and said "don't worry, baby girl. We're going to be alright!" Needless to say, the rescue party was shocked, confounded, and relieved, all at the same time. They then began to divide their rescue efforts between the two of us. Once they identified that I was APD, they went into high gear. A few seconds later, I was out again. When I gained consciousness, I was at Grady Memorial Hospital. I was treated for a fractured collar bone, some broken ribs and a minor hand injury. My worst injury was the trauma to the base of my skull, which affected my long and short-term memory. Once I recovered, I had to immediately go out and purchase a Palm Pilot. It would substitute for my memory until I could make a full recovery. Once I was released from Grady, I spent a couple weeks in Children's hospital with my daughter and wife. We were allowed to sleep in makeshift beds in her room until she was released. During my stay in the hospital, I received a lot of phone calls and visits from coworkers and family. The phone call that stands out the most was the one I received from the chief of police, Beverly Harvard. Considering all the times we stood in opposition of one another on work issues, and considering I had basically called her out in one of the Silver Shields newsletters, I was humbled that she would even pick up a phone to express her well wishes for me and my daughter. To this day, I still hold her in the highest regard for that simple act of compassion.

Without question, the greatest lasting effect of the wreck was not of a physical nature. During my period of lifelessness out on the interstate, I had an experience that I still find difficult to go into detail. It was very much a spiritual awakening for me. Once I was finally able to have sustained consciousness in my daughter's hospital room, I realized that I was no longer in possession of a "religious" identity. My entire orientation was now purely spiritually based. This is not to say that I was at a place of rejecting religion, but rather the contrary. I was now of a heart and mind that embraced all forms of religiosity and belief systems. It seemed I was now able to tune into the pure spirit of whatever a particular religion was espousing. I was no longer confounded or constricted by the dogma of whatever someone was confessing belief in, but I able to connect directly with what pure spirit dwelled within the heart and soul. It was life altering. I also knew I had been given a second chance for a reason. According to the doctors, there was no logical medical reason I should have survived the trauma of that wreck. Even though I had on my seat belt, the trauma to my chest and head should have resulted in permanent death. I had been a devout Muslim for ten years prior to the wreck and a devout Christian my entire life prior to that. I would emerge from the wreck stripped of all religion and truly on a purely Spiritual path. While I embraced the truly spiritual aspects of all belief systems, I would no longer subscribe to or be an adherent of any.

I would arrive to Zone 1 Morning Watch 2 months past due but very much a new man.

My new assignment was a much more laid back environment than my previous one. Of course, Zone 1 was home for me and I had no trouble gaining comfort in familiar surroundings. I recall that I used to fluster my officers because they had no idea of my history in the Zone. They would sometimes try to pull a fast one over on me, as they were accustomed to being able to do with new supervisors. Unbeknownst to them, I was acutely aware of every nook and cranny pertaining to the Bluff, Herndon Homes, and the entire "C" Sector. We quickly developed a great relationship, as it was clear they were going to have to actually work. I took very personal anyone's efforts to shortchange the community of the police services they were due. Once we set the rules, we were great. The vast majority of the officers were of the highest integrity and work ethic. They were hard workers and conscientious people when it came to performing their duties. There were a couple of officers that insisted on attempting to fly below the radar, but I continuously challenged them to keep them on task. On two separate occasions, I recommended that a corruption case be opened on two different officers. Per usual, it was swept under the rug. Because I still had a lot of informants in Zone 1, I was advised of one officer who was seeking sexual favors from the prostitutes in lieu of arrests. In another situation, I was told of an officer who was sexually harassing female students in the area of the Atlanta University Center. When I checked the precinct records, I found that there had been complaints to the precinct, but no one was able to successfully identify the officer in question. My information provided me with the actual name of the officer. I sent a memo up the chain to have the officers placed under surveillance by the Corruption unit.

Both officers were shipped out to the Airport Precinct. When I learned of the transfers, I told my commander that I was flabbergasted. It was far beyond reason why the department would place two individuals who were identified as sexual predators into an environment where their conduct could possibly cause an "international" incident. He agreed, as we both could do nothing more than shake our heads. Years later, one of the officers made international headlines by his rough handling of a female airport customer in the parking lane.

I was on the Morning Watch a short time when a position on the Day Watch opened up. It was good to be in the Zone during the day time. While on the Day Watch, I was assigned as the administrative sergeant. However, I also filled in for the Sector sergeants whenever they were off. I was, for the first time, in a position where I could have some influence on the written policies of the Zone. I was careful not to take this opportunity for granted but still mindful of the necessity to never pass up an opportunity make things better for the troops and the citizens. No matter how minute, it was important to make a contribution.

Zone 1 Day Watch had a lot of officers who I served with in different assignments over the years. Miguel was still in the Zone. Carlos Wicker (retired), who'd been one of my TAC teammates, was assigned to a fairly new strip mall on MLK Jr. Dr. I'd also worked around 2 of the other supervisors in the past. It was a pretty comfortable place to be. I was truly back home.

I had an officer who was consistently leading the Watch in arrests. He seemed like a pretty squared away individual and was always pleasant to be around. I decided to show up on one of his calls, just to observe his magic. When he 26'd on the call, he cancelled all other units responding. I continued anyway because I wanted to observe his community interrelationship skills firsthand. He advised radio he was in the rear of the residence with the caller. As I came around the building I saw him grabbing a guy by the collar. He shouted a couple of expletives at the gentleman and reared back to slap him. He turned and saw me coming and looked like a deer caught in headlights. He immediately released the guy and told him to never return to the area. After the subject left, I explained to the officer that I was not tolerant of that type of policing. And if I witnessed anything like it again, I would bring him up on disciplinary charges. He tried to laugh it off and stated that he knew of my reputation concerning such things and that was why he released the guy as soon as he saw me. He said the guy was a local dope dealer who he'd warned to stay off his Beat. He said he noticed the guy walking through the back yard as he finished handling his call at the house. That's when he jacked him up to run him off. I explained that every officer had their own style of dealing with the criminal element on their beat, and I wasn't attempting to micro manage him. However, I did draw the line on certain conduct. I told him that when we got back to the precinct, I would need him to sign a written counseling form for what I had witnessed. After that, I would routinely spot-check the officer, as well as the rest of the Watch. I never came across any issues for concern. As far as I was concerned, the Watch was ticking like a fine tuned watch.

The officer was already the Watch leader in arrests. After the counseling session, his numbers increased so much that I recommended him for "officer of the month" 2 months in a row. His performance was so stellar that I even nominated him for the department's prestigious "Officer of the Year" award.

A week or so later, I returned from my off days to news that the officer had been arrested at the precinct by the FBI, assisted by the SWAT team. He was accused of involvement in gang activity. It was revealed that he grew up as a member of one of the local gangs. He'd continued to assist in furthering their criminal enterprise by use of his position as an officer.

Talk about a misjudgment of character. I didn't know whether to be humiliated or pissed off.

I wouldn't have long to decide because I was on the next personnel order to ship out to Zone 2 Morning Watch... as the new Morning Watch commander – I had been promoted to lieutenant.

CHAPTER – 20

PAYOLA IN THE VILLAGE

It seemed that my career was beginning to move at a pretty good rate of speed. I'd been promoted off the sergeants' list in the first round of promotions. Only those promoted in the first round would have the required time of 2 years in the rank by the time the next promotional exams rolled around. That meant I would be eligible to take the very next lieutenants test. I did, and I managed to make that list also. I wasn't promoted in the first round from the lieutenants' list, but my number did manage to come up within 3 ½ years after being promoted to sergeant. Making the lieutenant's rank in my 19th year wasn't exactly blazing a trail, but it was still feasible for me to achieve the chief's rank before my 30th year. There were no more promotions. Only appointments between me and my career goal at this point… The ranks of Major and Deputy Chief were the only two hurdles that stood between me and the fulfillment of my lifelong dream.

Being promoted to lieutenant was also a big deal in other ways. With it came a new level of responsibility; but more importantly, a wider field of opportunity.

I was assigned to Zone 2 Morning Watch as the new Watch commander. I had a certain degree of self-confidence because I had been, inadvertently, well groomed by my former Watch commander in Zone 1. This was by virtue of the fact that he was hardly ever at work. When he was there, he was the world's greatest delegator. I didn't mind because I knew I was on the short list to make lieutenant myself, and he was allowing me real on-the-job experience. I even experienced somewhat of a letdown when he would actually show up. It began to feel that when he was there, he was minimizing or stifling my ability to be completely in charge and the opportunity to figure out complex issues on my own. He was very open and generous with direction and guidance, but his approach to everything seemed to be the lazy route or the path of least resistance. By this time in my career, I was totally accustomed to doing things in a way that yielded the greatest results for the greatest amount of people. My personal comfort, career, safety or agenda never factored into that equation. After all, whatever the rank or position, I was in fact, still my father's son.

Zone 2 Morning Watch brought a tremendous feeling of responsibility. This was MY Watch, and I was responsible for every woman and man assigned to the shift. The safety and welfare of my officers was of great importance to me. That surge of patronage was balanced with an equally enhanced sense of guardianship over the community. I laid down my general ground rules in the roll call of my first day. I intended to hold the officers accountable for the quality of service they provide for the citizens of Zone 2. I intended to hold the sergeants accountable for the quality of service they provided my officers, and I expected everyone to hold me accountable for the quality of service I provide to the citizens and to the Watch. I went on to make it clear that no one in the precinct worked for ME. I worked for the sergeants, they for the officers, and we all worked for the citizens of Zone 2 in particular, and the citizens of the city of Atlanta, in general. After that, I announced that I was totally oblivious to Zone 2

Morning Watch operations and would be joining several people as a ride-along over the ensuing weeks to familiarize myself with the lay of the land. The ride-alongs really helped me to establish rapport with the officers and supervisors. They also provided tremendous insight into the personalities that made up the Watch. They were a truly great group of men and women.

I had been assigned the Watch with 1 new sergeant and 3 veteran sergeants. Sergeant Randy Traylor (retired) had been my Field Training Officer (FTO) in Zone 3 during my academy days. He was a fearless cop with a love for the job and the compassion of a saint. He was as White and as country as they came, but he fit in like a first cousin in the housing projects. He had a way with people that had to be witnessed to be believed. In my opinion, he was the epitome of a "good cop." I was more than delighted to see that I would be working with him on the Watch.

Sergeant Butch Cooper (retired) had a reputation that preceded him. I had never worked with him in my career, but was always told that he was a squared away and very knowledgeable sergeant. He was known as having been a hard worker and high arrests person back in his officer days. He impressed me as a mild mannered and naturally inquisitive individual. He was definitely going to be an asset to the Morning Watch team.

Robert "Bob" Renfroe was a very street smart and hard working sergeant. He was somewhat reserved due to a situation that left him feeling as though he didn't have the backing of the department or the city in a recent incident. I was not totally familiar with the incident, but I got the impression that his integrity had been encroached upon in such fashion that it was going to be next to impossible to get him to trust me as the new Watch commander. I really didn't blame him one bit. I have found that officers only truly need the support of their supervisors in areas of "gray." When an officer finds him or herself in a "white" area, the evidence and/or situation speaks for itself, and there is no real need for further defense. In areas of "black," the evidence speaks for itself also, but in an adverse way. When there has been a blatant and intentional violation of the law or policies, the officer suffers at the fate dealt by his or her own hand. It's the areas of "gray" that an officer needs the support of their supervisor. In moments when the intent is clearly honorable, but the act alone gives room for speculation is when it's important that a supervisor has taken the time to learn the character and substance of his officers and stand in their defense. When you take the time to know a person, you have a better handle on the type of things they are most or less likely to do. This isn't an absolute science, as was proven by my officer who was arrested in Zone 1 Day Watch; but it tends to yield a pretty good average. At any rate, there was no doubt in my mind that Bob was a top notch supervisor, and I was determined to assist him in getting back up on his horse.

Sergeant Anthony "Tony" Singh (Lt., active) was my "newbee" sergeant on the shift. He happened to be on vacation when the promotional order went into effect, so he didn't report for duty until a week later. He was a veteran of Zone 2 Day Watch and was known as a "Traffic Nazi." That's someone who leads a Zone or Unit in writing traffic citations. They tend to have the added element of being non-negotiable when it comes to a driver getting out of a ticket. There are Traffic Nazis who are fabled to have written their own mothers tickets. Of course, that's just urban legend... right? When Tony did show up for his first day of work, he explained to me his passion for traffic. I in turn, explained to him my passion for supervisors being available to their officers and to the citizens, as opposed to being tied up on traffic stops. We struck a compromise. He could write a few tickets per night but I would, in the mean time, train him to be my new administrative sergeant. I sensed my current administrative sergeant either had a disdain or a fear of the street. Tony, on the other hand, seemed to hold an acute avoidance for the office. One of many things I swore myself to as a new lieutenant was that I would not fail to develop my sergeants in every aspect of their jobs. I held, and still hold the opinion that a good leader trains his or her next in command to take over their job. Therefore, all sergeants would be thoroughly trained in their administrative duties and in their field functions.

During this process of cross training, I lost two of my senior sergeants. Traylor and Cooper were transferred to other assignments, and they were replaced by two newly promoted sergeants.

Sergeants Alfonso Graham and Michael "Mike" Pulliam (retired). It was my first time meeting Graham, although he had been on the department for at least 12 years. He spent the majority of his previous years assigned to the Airport precinct. Being in that assignment is almost like being employed with another department. It has often been regarded as the department's "black hole." I found Graham to be a highly religious man with strong family values. He would be the moral compass of the entire Watch. Because he has a reserved nature, it took some doing to convince him that it was alright to pull me aside and put a boot to my back side whenever he caught my slipping in judgment or temperament. Eventually, he grew comfortable with his role as the "Pastor" of the Watch. I can honestly say that even though there were times when I'd rather have forgone his advice, he was never found to be in error on any issue in which he provided me with an alternate perspective.

Mike and I had known each other for most of our careers. He came on a couple of academy classes after I did. He'd been one of the people I spoke of in an earlier chapter as someone fighting similar battles as I in other areas within the department. It would be truly an honor and pleasure to finally work in the same assignment as Mike. It would be refreshing to have a second voice, spirit, and backbone to be about the business of trying to better things on the department. In the past, there had been very few times when I didn't feel absolutely alone as I toed the line on some of the more sensitive, but critical issues plaguing the department. It was going to be great to have by my side someone who had spent their career doing whatever necessary to fix problems within the agency. In addition, he was someone as equally committed as I was in making efforts to bridge the relationship between the department and the community. Mike was also an IBPO union official. In fact, he had been instrumental in the meeting with Mayor Bill Campbell years back. His integrity was above reproach in the opinion of anyone who ever worked with him.

So that was the new line up. Basically, a month into the new position, me and my complete supervisory staff, save one, were all newly promoted personnel. This was really going to be fun. This was also at a time when the famed "Buckhead Village" club district was in full swing. Working the Morning Watch meant we were the shift on duty during the hours the night clubs were at full throttle.

Once they were all cross-trained in the administrative position, it was finally time to make permanent assignments for the sergeants.

Singh, as indicated before, was the administrative sergeant. Once he got the hang of things, he actually fell in love with the assignment. He was still permitted to make his few traffic cases; so life was good for Tony.

Mike was assigned as my "Crime Suppression" supervisor. He and a few hand-selected officers were assigned to the Village during peak hours. They would then work crime "hot spots" throughout the Zone for the remainder of the shift.

Graham and Renfroe were my two Sector sergeants. They covered all supervisory responsibilities concerning the beat and regular patrol officers.

Once everyone settled into their new roles, the Watch seemed to be running as smooth as could be expected. The staff did a terrific job in cutting down incidents occurring in the club district of the Village. Calls for service were being handled as idyllic as ever. Whenever I conducted spot checks of the shift, everyone was always where they were supposed to be. A great deal of the beat officers' high performance was due to the relentless and helpful presence of the two Senior Patrol Officers (SPO's) who were seemingly always present and assisting on each and every call. Warren "W.I." Green (retired) and David Stewart (Sgt., active) were the quintessential embodiment of peer leadership. I can honestly say these two officers had an ability to read the pulse of every single officer on the Watch. They knew what conditions enhanced progress on the shift, and what things needed avoidance or would prove to be detrimental to the success of the Watch. Without question, I relied as heavily on my two SPO's as I did my sergeants. We were a great team.

One night in the Village, Mike and I were conducting our routine checks of the clubs' capacities. The district was known for overcrowding conditions in the clubs, as this seemed to be the draw for even more business. The clubs with the largest crowds were the most appealing. This, in turn, led to even more overcrowding. Far be it for me to rain on the parade of barely legal partying young adults; but I had a particular peeve about club overcrowding. To fuel my passion was the fact that in previous months, it was in the national headlines that a club somewhere up north had suffered multiple deaths due to overcrowding after a fire broke out. There had been the report of another the previous year. As Mike and I were standing just inside the entrance to one of the clubs, we were both disgusted. We literally could not negotiate the room due to the overcrowding. We were finally able to locate the manager and asked to inspect his permits and capacity paperwork. He obliged, and we advised that he needed to start thinning out his establishment. We told him we were going to start the Fire Marshall to the location in the mean time. Once the Fire Marshall arrived, we would completely empty the club and then allow reentry based on the legally permitted headcount. We would then monitor the club for the remainder of the night. The manager voiced his concerns with the plan and asked if we could get our major out to the location. I told him absolutely not. I wouldn't think of disturbing the major at 1 o'clock in the morning for something that's within the scope of my own authority to deal with. He began to complain about the loss of revenue the prescribed plan would create. That's when I grew impatient and reminded him that I had every right to shut him down for the night on the spot. I was extending a courtesy and being considerate of his livelihood by allowing the Fire Marshall to come out and provide an official head count. I told him, furthermore, I had a problem with him knowing his club was overcrowded, yet he made no effort to thin it out on his own. I told him that he also knew what would happen to at least a quarter of those kids if a fire or some other emergency broke out; yet he opted to continue to pack them in for the benefit of a few dollars per head. I told him it offended me that he placed a $5 value on the lives of all those children in his club. The more I lectured, the more I talked myself into shutting down the club for the night. So I did just that. Once the Fire Marshall arrived, he went inside to confer with the manager. When he finished, he came back outside and approached Mike and I. He asked if we were aware of the "arrangements" with the club? We said we were not aware of any arrangements. He then explained how there was a standing arrangement between a few of the clubs and the command staff to allow overcrowding. He then suggested we get clearance from our chain of command before taking the proposed action. Mike and I were visibly aghast as we looked at each other. Mike then asked the Fire Marshall if closing the club was going to affect him too severely financially? The Fire Marshall said it wouldn't cause him great financial strain, but that the folks in our chain of command were going to be really pissed off the next day. I then told him the last thing we wanted to do was to have folks mad at him in the morning, so he could go ahead and leave the scene. I then told him that Mike and I were going to shut it down and deal with the consequences in the morning. I indicated to him that I had no intention of gambling with the lives of young folks just so some greedy people could make a few extra bucks.

After closing the club, I apologized to Mike for involving him in what I was certain to be my next transfer. Based on my experiences, I felt it was inevitable that I would be transferred on the very next personnel order. Hopefully, he wouldn't be affected by my actions because he really made a great supervisor in the Village, and had quickly grown to enjoy the assignment.

Days, weeks and months passed without a word from anyone in the department's chain of command. I'm sure I went over every personnel order with a fine tooth comb for at least 6 months after the incident. Not a word.

The rest of the time in the Village ran even smoother. Word spread quickly that the new Morning Watch staff didn't tolerate overcrowding or other permit violations. In short fashion, when any of us arrived on a scene, it meant automatic compliance. Managers would see us approaching their club and start filtering people out as we walked up. We had a great run for exactly 1 year before the department underwent a major reorganization.

Until now, the entire Criminal Investigations Division (CID) had been located in the headquarters building downtown.

The department was about to decentralize every CID Unit except Homicide, Sex Crimes, and Commercial Robberies (Major Crimes Section). Major Crimes would remain centralized in the headquarters building. Every other investigative unit was to be decentralized and equally distributed to the six Zones/Precincts.

CHAPTER – 21

ROLL-OUT

After 1 ¼ years on the Morning Watch, I was tapped to remain in Zone 2 as the commander of the new Zone Investigations unit. There was only one hitch to the new roll out. There had been no precedence for this new structure to go by. Each individual commander was in the position of having to create his or her respective Unit from the ground up. They would all still be accountable to the chain of command at headquarters but merely located in the individual precincts. After 6 months or so, CID command would review how each worksite was set up and functioning. From that, they would decide which best practices to institute across the board and develop a standard operating procedure (SOP) by which all six precincts would abide. Our precinct was happy to learn that some of the best practices adopted by command would come from the model we developed in Zone 2.

When the original "roll out", as it was called, occurred, the 6 Zone investigations commanders were gathered and given the opportunity to select 1 sergeant. There were to be 2 shifts created, with 6 investigators assigned to each shift. Day Watch worked from 8:00 a.m.-4:00 p.m., and Evening Watch worked from 4:00 p.m. to midnight. We would be assigned a second sergeant but would not have a choice in that selection process. We would also have a little input regarding the investigators to be assigned to each precinct. We were given a civilian secretary and 1 civilian office assistant to be utilized at the unit commander's discretion. Without hesitation, I selected Mike

Pulliam as my sergeant. I was also given David Liber (retired) as my second sergeant, and I wasn't disappointed. Dave had been on the department longer than me and was established as a hard worker with an uncanny ability to solve "who done it" type crimes. He was also known for being an officer-friendly supervisor; in that he never asked an officer to do anything he wasn't willing to do himself. Some would call that being soft, but I regard it as being commendable. He would be a great addition to the supervisory line up. I knew some of the investigators slated for my unit, and I held no objections to any of the recognized names. There was no intelligent objection to be made for the names of the investigators I didn't know, so I didn't make any. I did, however, notice a theme with the names which were familiar. They all were folks who had established reputations for being difficult or problematic employees to supervise. That's police code for men and women who tend to not take sh-t from their peers or supervisors. Men and women who cannot be told there is any justification for stepping outside of the law or human decency. People who aren't predisposed to the assumption that the ends always justify the means... This was the unspoken and unofficial definition of a "problematic employee."

Yep! I was being stuck with a bunch of departmental "misfits"... or so they thought. Naturally, I had long established relationships with the investigators I knew through my various assignments on the department. Every one of them had shared the same or similar views as to the true purpose of law enforcement. They had also been committed to uphold their end while assigned to their various Units throughout their careers. So when CID command thought they were setting me up to fail, they were actually vesting me with a cadre of the highest integrity and work ethic. In their attempt to set me up to fail, they in fact, set me up to do anything but fail.

People like Rick "Big-A" Anderson (retired) and Brian "B-Sting" Anderson (retired) were held in almost legendary standing by officers who'd been around in their REDDOG and Narcotics Unit hay day. Rick had established himself as a top notch Burglary investigator with an uncanny ability to charm a confession out of the most hardened burglars. There didn't seem to be a Larceny that B-Sting couldn't solve from nothing more than a grainy surveillance tape or a barely legible forged signature. Thadeaus Dansby (retired) was one of the most meticulous persons you could know. Due to his background as an attorney, his approach to everything was extremely methodical. Most commanders hated having him in their unit because officers like him tended to not bring in a desirable amount of "stats" due to their slow, but thorough progression with case development. All these traits made him the perfect choice to handle Robbery cases. Richard Griffie (Sgt.) was of a similar mode as Dansby. He had a deep southern drawl that caused people to underestimate his intellect and capabilities. He absolutely loved the advantage that always gave him, and he wouldn't hesitate to capitalize on it. He was a very religious person with high moral turpitude. He had no problem letting someone know when they were infringing on his integrity or character. He was my other Robbery guy. James Postell (Sgt.) was someone with whom I had worked opposite shifts when we were both officers back in my early Zone 1 days. He was known for being hard working and fair. He and Big A had been partners in the consolidated Burglary unit, and I saw no need to take a fish out of water. He covered my Evening Watch Burglaries.

I had never before worked with Investigators Jerry Stafford (retired), Bruce Wilson, John Brock (Sgt.), Jacquelyn "Jackie" Gwinn-Villaroel (Sgt.), Maxine "Max" McGrath, Larry Richardson, James Rose or Tracey Davis.

Maxine was assigned to the unit about a week after everyone else. Her supervisors thought it would be a good idea to dump her from her unit while the dust was still stirred by the decentralization. Naturally, my unit would be the location to dump an undesirable. She walked into my office to report on her first day with the defensiveness of a professional football squad. The first words out of her mouth were "I know they called before I got here to tell you that I'm lazy and disgruntled, and they're right. I've been f----d over so much in my career that I'm just passing time until I retire. I'll do my job, but don't expect anything more than that. I am officially "retired on duty."" I just sat there. I looked at her emotionlessly for a few seconds and then calmly asked "Is there anything else I need to know?" She responded that she was done venting. I then made the statement "hello, I'm Lieutenant Khalfani Bakari Yabuku of Zone 2 Investigations. What, may I ask, is your name?" She looked at me as though I was the weirdest thing she'd ever come across in her life. She smirked somewhat uncomfortably and said "Lt., you've known me since I came on the department a couple years after you. You know very well what my name is." Sensing that she hadn't yet gotten the gist, I repeated "hello! I'm Lieutenant Khalfani Bakari Yabuku of Zone 2 Investigations. What, may I ask, is your name?" She stood there more confused than the first time. I said "have a seat, Max." I went on to tell her I had indeed received the proverbial "heads up" call from her former supervisor. I told her the moment I realized the nature of the call, I cut the caller off and explained to him that he had called the wrong number. I told him that I appreciated his concern, but I would be evaluating the performance of her and all my employees based on my personal observation. I told him to have a nice day and abruptly hung up the phone. I then told her not only had I already heard about her bad attitude and laziness – or – refusal to work, but that in certain circles, it was absolutely legendary. I told her as far as I was concerned the first time she and I had ever met was 5 minutes ago when she knocked on my door. She said she'd heard that many times before but the moment she would walk out of the supervisor's office, she would become subjected to prejudicial treatment. I explained to her how I too had been subjected to the hurtful phenomenon of having a supervisor look you in the face and say they're going to give you a fair chance. The moment they walk out of the door, they instantly begin mistreating you based on an opinion they received from someone else. I promised her I had been on the receiving end of that scenario too many times in my career to do that to anyone else. I asked her to trust that I would give her a fair shot, and I expected her to do her job. After a while, I began delegating greater levels of responsibility to Max. By the end of year, she was recognized as the most improved Investigator in the unit. The next year, she flat out won the investigator of the year award for our unit. It was a pleasure and honor to have had the opportunity to work with her.

Jackie Villaroel was someone I'd never worked with before. I was aware of her based on the fact that she was married to an officer I worked with when I supervised Zone 1 Morning Watch. Her husband, David (Lt., active), had been an excellent officer, so I was predisposed to expect great things from Jackie. She didn't let me down. She hit the ground running with an unparalleled ability to tap into human psyche. There was not a person on earth who she couldn't establish a level of rapport with. She seemed to be able to read peoples' spirits, hearts, and minds regardless of the fabrication they may had been trying to pass off as the truth. It was absolutely magical to watch. She was the easy choice for our Assaults investigator. She worked several high profile and national spotlight assault cases from restaurants and nightclubs in Buckhead. She worked cases involving a couple local Rappers and Hip Hop artists. On one particular case, the entertainer thought he had evaded her custody by fleeing the State. Jackie tracked him to a performance he was giving in Miami, Florida. Her efforts in coordinating with local authorities resulted in the FBI pulling the artist off stage during his performance. When he was extradited to Atlanta, the rapper told her "god---n! Detective Villaroel and that Buckhead investigations squad ain't no joke! Y'all come and get a n----r!" A few years later, in a different assignment, I would be given the opportunity to select an Administrative sergeant, and Jackie would be my first and only choice.

Over the ensuing 3 years, several of the original staff were promoted or transferred out of the Investigations unit. They were replaced by equally talented and dedicated investigators in the personages of Violet Burton, Nathan Deaton, Kim Farner, Raymond Layton, Robert "Bob" McFall (Sgt., active) and Matthew Ramarge. They would continue to uphold the high standard and carry on the tradition of excellence the unit became known for.

The accomplishments of the unit are too numerous to name in this volume. Some of the more rewarding cases were those which involved the victimization of people through terroristic or violent type acts, such as violent robbery cases. Cases that revolved around victims being deprived of family heirlooms and other prized possessions tended to bother me also. I had never been a big Property crimes person until I witnessed grown, elderly men weeping because someone had burglarized them for an heirloom that had been passed down for several generations. It would be as though their entire history had been wiped out. That's a horror that I can relate to, simply by virtue of being African American. Or the tears of a widow when a party guest may have slipped into her bedroom during the festivities and helped themselves to the diamond brooch given her by a deceased loved one...

A couple of these cases to reach local and national headlines were the Buckhead antiques burglaries case in 2004-2005 and the Buckhead jewlery robberies case in 2006-2007. The unit brought to successful prosecution, many other local and national headline cases.

As I stated before, we were the unit most emulated for best practices after the initial 6-month evaluation period. The unit went on to receive the highly coveted Buckhead Business Association (BBA) award for "Outstanding Law Enforcement."

It was a great privilege and honor to have worked alongside these women and men. It was definitely one of the most gratifying assignments of my career. I really felt like I had the opportunity to stand side by side and brush shoulders with greatness. I will forever be humbled by the experience.

CHAPTER – 22

TROUBLEMAKER TO TROUBLESHOOTER

After 3 years heading up the Zone 2 Investigations unit, I was given a call from the chief. It seemed he was not satisfied with how things were developing in the department's Fleet Management unit, and he thought I might be a good fit to bring the unit up to par. Fleet management is the unit which handles the acquisition, purchases, and dissemination of all departmental motorized vehicles. From, squad cars to paddy wagons to motorcycles to riding lawn mowers; if it has a motor and 4 wheels, it's inventoried and issued by the Fleet Management unit. The unit also had the added responsibility of administrating the department's Wrecker Services contract. This meant that it was the Fleet unit's job to procure the 6 wrecker/tow truck companies utilized by the department. The unit also set the protocols and managed precisely how the companies would function within their contract with the APD. If there were any towing disputes or complaints by citizens, they ultimately wound up on my desk for resolution. My proxy's signature determined if there was to be a reimbursement of towing fees and the like.

At first, I was a little skeptical of the assignment due to its lack of proximity to the streets and direct connectivity to the community. However, being one who looks for the opportunity in all situations, I realized this would be a unique opportunity to learn a little something about the procurement and fiscal aspect of how the department functions. After all, I would be sitting in the chief's seat one day and was going to need to have at least a cursory knowledge into every dimension of how the department functioned. I had already graduated the State's Executive Development course at GPSTC some years earlier. In this course, participants are divided into teams of 5 or 6 students and required to build a Public Safety Department from the ground up. That includes land and area zoning surveys, building layouts, equipment, personnel, and budgets. A proposal had to be drafted and presented to a mock county commissioner's board. My team won the bonus windfall, which was awarded to the team with the best proposal. So, I was well aware of how a police agency operated... on paper. This assignment would give me the opportunity to learn how things got done in the real world. From this perspective, I was now eagerly looking forward to getting my feet wet and having the opportunity to make a contribution to improving the Fleet Management unit.

It didn't take long to see that this was unit was operating on cruise control. It was staffed with a terrific crew of folks who were dedicated to turning out a consistently good product. However, as usual, good wasn't going to be quite enough to satisfy my need for excellence. I immediately set to work in finding out how things could run more efficiently and more customer friendly. I had 1 sergeant, Dennis Mullen (RIP), and 2 officers, Mike King and Terrence "T" Williams, assigned to the unit. There were also 5 civilian employees – Mr. Karl Wingard was the Sr. Administrative Assistant. Ms. Marian Freeman and Ms. Shea Stills were the Inventory Systems Techs. The unit was completed by Ms. Bertina Clemons and Ms. Mary Pickett, who were my 2 Property Management Techs. Nine people were entrusted with the responsibility to purchase, distribute, maintain and regulate the department's entire 400+ fleet. In addition, the same 9 people were also responsible for the establishment, administration, protocols setting and enforcement of the city's Contract Wrecker Services (CWS). Now this was a challenge I could sink my teeth into.

Sgt. Mullen had the Fleet Management side of the house down to a science. His shop was without a blemish as far I could see on the surface. He was quite frank with me from the very beginning that I had been brought in to clean up the disheveled Contract Wrecker Services side of the house. Naturally, I accepted his polite and diplomatic way of letting me know to stay the heck out of his stew. However, I made it clear that I would be conducting a thorough assessment of every section, including his, within the unit. Dennis had spent the majority of his career in OPS and was well liked and respected department wide. He was a no nonsense kind of guy with a perfectionist disposition. This was my first time working with him in my career. He was somewhat circumspect of my intentions and initially, a little standoffish. He had been assigned other lieutenants to clean up the unit and had bumped heads with most. He had established himself a little reputation of running lieutenants off. Usually, the new lieutenant would expect the unit to be a cakewalk and basically someplace they could retire on duty. Dennis would not tolerate it, and he would effectively convince the chain of command to make a replacement. I was just the "next one" of a long line of failures as far as he was concerned. Once he gleaned my eagerness and sincerity to improve the unit, we got along great. Just as he had intimated, I would have very little to do on the Fleet Management side of things; but I made him teach me everything there was to know about his job anyway. As I explained to him, I could attend the weekly departmental command staff meetings and read from a list he'd prepared for me to report by; or I could learn the job for myself and make my weekly presentations from actual firsthand knowledge. He appreciated my insistence in doing the work but also my sincere desire to make things better in the unit. After all, if the entire unit functions smoothly, it's less of a strain on the unit as a whole.

It very quickly became clear that the Contract Wrecker Services was the area in most need of attention. It was equally clear that the inefficiencies facing CWS were a result of noncompliance of other departmental units in fulfilling their support roles. The other problem was a lack of controls for how each wrecker service operated within the specifications of their contract. Fortunately, I had a topnotch team on that side of the house. They were poised for a change and knew exactly what needed to be fixed. In the past, they could never find the support they needed from their chain of command. Sgt. Mullen did what he could, but the Fleet shop provided more work than he could barely keep up with. He had literally been a 1-man show prior to my arrival. I was able to take some of the pressure off of him once I learned the job, but my attention grew more and more demanding in the CWS shop as time went on. Once I was able to get a clear picture of the issues facing the unit, it was obvious that all that was needed was a definitive plan of action and leadership in implementing that plan. There were so many other variables involved in the successful functioning of the CWS shop. Most of those variables originated in other units throughout the department. The Communications Section was responsible for receiving the calls for wrecker services. They would, in turn, dispatch the officer and appropriate wrecker service to the scene. The Records Section would then receive and process the relevant paperwork and reports. The Property Section was responsible for maintaining the data and records of all vehicles physically located at the towing companies' yards. They also held the responsibility of releasing vehicles to their proper owners.

I directed "T" and Mike to come in early one morning so we could have a private meeting prior to the regularly scheduled unit meeting with everyone. When they showed, I explained to them my intentions with the entire unit, and more specifically, where I intended to take the CWS shop. This was basically their shop, and they had been left to their own devices by previous unit commanders. They had done the best they could, considering they had no cooperation from the support units. I had them to advise me on the minutest details of what they needed to make their shop function optimally. Once that was all figured out, I gave them my word that we would do whatever was necessary to fix things. I cautioned them that I had a habit of not staying in assignments very long, so I strongly suggested we get started right away. Mike had worked with me when I supervised the Zone 5 Morning watch, so he was aware of what exactly it meant when I gave my assurances on an issue. He told "T" "If the LT. says we're gonna fix it... we're gonna fix it." I thanked him for his vote of confidence but cautioned him that our endeavors wouldn't be for the squeamish or faint of heart. Based on the information they provided, it was more than likely that some toes were going to have to be stepped on. I assured both of them that this would not be a concern of theirs. I was prepared to assume full responsibility for my unit. All I needed from them was their expert opinions and advice.

They both explained how they had received no assistance from the other departmental units in holding up their particular functions in the overall effort. In other words, The Property, Communications, and Records units weren't doing what was required of them in a timely manner. This resulted in the Fleet unit's mission failing to be accomplished. Because their piece of the equation was so miniscule, the other units tended to overlook and even disregard doing their part to support the CWS effort. There were times when the other unit commanders advised "T" and Mike that they'd get to something whenever they had the time to get to it. I understood the other unit commanders had a more primary mission as their priority. However, that same little piece of their puzzle was a gigantic portion of my puzzle and played a major role in my unit's success. Frankly, my unit could not accomplish its mission if the other units didn't play their part.

The problem with previous Fleet unit commanders was the matter of "protocol." Of course, this was a concern for me also. How would I encourage the support of the other 3 unit commanders without seeming to be dictating how they run their respective units?

I fashioned a memo to the other unit commanders spelling out the importance of their assistance with the overall mission of Fleet Management. I brought to their attention how paramount their roles were in the departments' success with its wrecker services. I explained how I knew their CWS roles were almost pesky nuances of their daily functions, but they were absolutely paramount to the Fleet Management mission. CRICKETS!!! Not so much as an acknowledgement that they even received my correspondence.

When that memo was met with no success, after a few weeks, I followed up with a second memo. This time I reiterated the points of the first memo but added verbiage to remind them that their efforts contributed greatly to the bottom line revenues generated by the CWS. My veiled threat was to motivate them by way of the city's revenues bottom line. My point was that their lack of support lent to a loss in revenue, and I would have no problem in being honest with the chain of command as to which unit(s) in the overall process dropped the ball.

I also included an invitation for them to attend the newly formed Contract Wrecker Services Consortium.

The Consortium was to be my answer for the disorganization of the wrecker companies themselves. One of the biggest complaints I'd received from the companies was an allegation of disparate treatment from APD. The owners felt that different companies were given preferential treatment regarding the enforcement of the policies and rules governing the CWS. There were other concerns of disorganization and how information was historically disseminated from my office to the owners.

I committed to holding meetings with the owners of all 6 companies on a monthly basis. There would be the dissemination of information concerning laws, policies, rules, and protocols that would be strictly enforced equitably by my office. The Consortium would also serve as a springboard to publicly air grievances the companies had regarding each other and APD. It would also serve as a brainstorming session to develop and adopt best practices for the collective body. It was to be hosted and moderated by me and would be regularly attended by the other 3 APD units critical to CWS.

Three months into the meetings, I was publicly thanked by the owners for putting together an effort of this nature. It had been the first time that all of them had sat together in any environment, let alone a structured one, since being awarded their contracts with the city years previous. It was also the first time any of them had been together in any environment where they weren't at each other's throats. The meetings themselves were coming along great, and a lot was being accomplished. Invitations and reminders went out on a weekly basis.

One of the things I hated most about being a commander was the unannounced or impromptu meetings. I know that in this line of work unexpected things happen and unpredictable emergencies can arise in a moment's notice. I just hated when there was no rational reason a meeting couldn't have been announced in advance, and the only explanation for the short notice was poor planning. The second thing I hated was a non-productive meeting. Those meetings where your basic topic is what you'll be discussing or accomplishing in the next meeting, and nothing ever gets accomplished... I call it "meeting, just for the sake of meeting."

In my initial invitations for the Consortium, I made it clear that every meeting would result in answers and real solutions to issues identified in the previous meeting. Therefore, it was imperative that all stakeholders attended personally. If they could not attend, they were to supply a representative who was invested with their authority to make concrete decisions on behalf of their company or APD unit. The same expectation was held for any peripheral guests in attendance such as any Federal, State, or County entities.

The only remaining issue was the fact that 2 of the 3 APD units needed for the success of CWS were consistently lacking attendance at the meetings. The Communications unit had at least sent representation, but it was someone who couldn't make any commitments. She was the nicest person in the world, but she would consistently digress to having to get back with us the following week after she cleared things with her lieutenant. Unacceptable!

I fired off a third memo to the commanders of the 3 Units and requested their attendance at the next meeting. When that resulted in continued failure, I forwarded a very concerning memo to the deputy chief over the Administrative Services Division (ASD) and the major over the Corporate Services Section (CSS). I then copied the 3 lieutenants, so as not to ambush them or give them the impression that I was going behind their backs. Needless to say, I had 100% participation in my monthly meetings from that point on. I didn't make any friends in the process, but that wasn't unfamiliar territory for me. The meetings continued for the remainder of my time in the unit and ran without a hitch. Much was accomplished to bring the CWS to a more productive and efficient state.

If the other 3 commanders were mad at me for pimping them out to the deputy chief, they would be seething from my next move.

My original memos to the 3 commanders for the support of their respective units had still not been met. Although I now had their attendance and support in the Consortium meetings, their shops were still not cooperating with "T" and Mike as far as the things they needed in order to get their work out in a timely fashion. I met with each commander and asked them personally if they could help me out by directing their employees to adhere to the established timelines and processes. They all gave me their word, and only the Communications unit actually followed through. I think I mentioned in an earlier chapter how much I despise being lied to in my face.

It was time for my father to make another appearance.

I directed “T” to come in early one day. When he arrived, I explained to him that I was going to have him to escort me to the Records unit and the Property unit. I wanted him to personally introduce me to the technicians responsible for processing the work we needed done. We went to each unit. I introduced myself to the technicians and explained to them how detrimental their role was to the CWS mission. I had “T” to explain to them exactly what we needed of them and expressed my sincere appreciation for their assistance in the matter. They were very forthcoming with information that their supervisors had relegated the CWS portion of their jobs as being of the least priority. If they got to it, great! If not, oh well! They agreed to help us out and did just that.

On the way back to our office I told “T” there would be definite backlash for me breaking protocol, but the totality of the fallout would rest squarely on my shoulders. He stated he wasn’t concerned about the consequences of having done the right thing. He then thanked me for “stepping up and finally doing what needed to be done a long time ago.” Before we could get all the way back to our office, I was confronted by one of the lieutenants. He asked if he could have a word with me away from my officer (“T”). I obliged by stepping to the side as I indicated for “T” to stand by. The lieutenant expressed how he was offended that I didn’t give him the opportunity to speak with his own people regarding the requests I had made of him. He said he felt that I had undermined him and circumvented his authority with his own people. He asked that I not do it again in the future; but rather work with him directly with any further concerns. I told him I fully understood and appreciated his concerns. While I was absolutely aware of the ramifications of my actions, I could not offer him an apology. I went on to tell him that I would, in good faith, offer him a guarantee instead. I told him I hated to have to do what I did, but he and the other lieutenant had blatantly blown me off after several cordial requests. I told him not to bother with a denial as that would only result in insulting my intelligence. I told him the guarantee I was willing to make was that "if lack of leadership in your shop, results in my shop being f----d up, I will be paying your shop a visit again!!!" He looked at me somewhat astounded, as did "T". As we continued on to our office I told "T" to never repeat what he'd just witnessed. I was not proud of having spoken to another commander in such a frank manner, in the presence of a lower ranking officer. After that day CWS ran like a finely tuned engine. It continued to do so until I was transferred to my next assignment. I was proud of the fixes made during my short tenure in the Fleet Management unit. I knew my father would be proud of me too. Unfortunately, after my transfer from the unit, "T" advised that my successor let the Consortium meeting fall by the wayside. They were deemed to be too time consuming and tedious to organize on a monthly basis.

Fleet Management was by far the most educational assignment I'd been given up to that point. The success of the unit is based on the dedication of the men and women that make up Fleet Management. They are a truly dedicated bunch of folks who don't mind putting in the necessary effort and work to make the unit a success. They are perhaps some of the most proud, yet humble people I've had the pleasure of working with. I have to make special mention of "T" Williams because he made extra contribution to the overall mission of the unit. He would lend special support and assistance to my efforts on a personal level. I am deeply indebted to his loyalty and service.

After a year in Fleet Management, I was flagged down by the chief's driver on the parking deck of Headquarters. As he rolled down his window, the chief invited me to stick my head into the car. He began letting me know how much he appreciated the improvements I made in the Fleet unit but that it was time to move on to a new home. There were some issues of concern growing in the Fugitive Task Force unit, and he felt I would be the best person to get a handle on things before they grew anymore out of control.

It was in that very moment that it occurred to me that perception is everything. Where other chiefs had seen me as being a problem employee, Chief Richard Pennington (retired) saw me as an asset. It occurred to me that I had gone from being perceived as a "Troublemaker" to being a "Troubleshooter."

CHAPTER – 23

ACCOUNTABILITY OF THE THIN BLUE LINE

When I was first arrived at the Fugitive unit, I was greeted by a staff of investigators and officers, most of whom I'd worked with throughout my career. There were only a few I had no history with. During my 3-month assessment period, I found that it was a well groomed and smoothly running unit. It didn't take a rocket scientist to figure out that most, if not all, previous issues arising from the unit were most likely command level. The Fugitive unit was one of those types of assignments where micromanagement or over-supervision could completely stifle and flat out countermand the mission. It was an assignment that required absolute trust and faith in the officers who made up the Unit. I had worked with so many of the investigators and officers in previous assignments that I had no trouble allowing them to run with the ball. The tactics employed by the Fugitive unit were not totally unlike SWAT tactics. In fact, another of SWAT's many functions was to train the Fugitive and REDDOG units on the execution of high-risk warrants. Even more, quite a few of the investigators and officers in the Fugitive unit had been previously trained by me personally during my SWAT days. Needless to say, with this level of personal history, I had no problem trusting in the unit's ability to safely and effectively do its job. My primary focus was going to be on learning as much as I could in regards to the South East Regional Fugitive Task Force (SERFTF). This was an offsite task force to which 2 of my officers and 2 of my investigators were assigned. The taskforce was headed up by the US Marshall's Service (USMS) and was composed of officers and investigators from most of the local law enforcement agencies. Their leads could take them anywhere in the US, as their efforts tied in to every US Marshal's Fugitive Task force in the country. It was not uncommon for theses 4 officers to be outside of the state on a regular basis. As far as the day-to-day operations concerning city of Atlanta fugitive warrants, these 4 were pretty much unavailable. APD, being the largest agency in the SE region, provided more personnel than the other local agencies. This basically left me with 11 investigators assigned to day-to-day fugitive apprehension operations. The unit was further divided by cursory assignments to the FBI's Atlanta Metropolitan Major Offenders (AMMO) task force. This task force did not require my guys to be assigned offsite, but it worked within the overall mission of the APD Fugitive unit located in the police headquarters building. Both task forces were a tremendous asset in providing manpower and technological support whenever requested. However, at the same time, maneuvering through the technicalities of the two Memorandums Of Understanding (MOU) was a potential political landmine. The MOU's basically outlined the roles and responsibilities of the APD entity and whatever agency it was combining resources with. The MOU's went into great detail as to the expectations of all parties, as well as specifically how things were to be facilitated. The MOUs laid out in clear language, the Who, What, Where, Why, When and How's of the Task Forces operations. Basically, I was for the first time, faced with having to divide my dedication. In the past, I had always been totally dedicated to my mission within the APD. Now I would have to split those loyalties with the SERFTF and the AMMO task force. But it wasn't a real issue because the overall mission of all entities was to remove the most menacing of the criminal element from the reach of mainstream society.

Another responsibility inherent in the unit was its involvement with the local news segment, Atlanta's Most Wanted. Many of our fugitives that proved unusually evasive were often featured on this news segment. This proved to be exceptionally beneficial to several difficult apprehensions. My real issue was going to be in delegating the responsibility of one of my sergeants to appear on camera. Although Fugitive Unit commanders had traditionally filled this role, I was not comfortable with the literal limelight of the studio cameras. I had always been more comfortable behind the scenes getting results. My sergeants were a little resistant to the idea but acquiesced once they understood my request wasn't negotiable.

The only issue facing the Fugitive unit concerning the Task Forces was the apparent disconnect with a couple of the investigators assigned to the SERFTF. They had grown so accustomed to operating outside of their APD jurisdiction that they tended to lose sight of the overall APD mission. The officers in the APD Fugitive unit began to feel that the APD investigators assigned to the SERFTF had come under the impression they no longer worked for APD and were therefore unaccountable to APD policy, procedures, and even supervision. Since the chief had previously mentioned this as one of his concerns, I took the time to make a few personal observations to confirm the concerns of the APD Investigators and the chief. I met with the 4 officers and their APD supervisor. The meeting served as a reminder to them all of their overall APD mission and the fact that their police authority derived from their status as APD employees. The fact that all members of both Task Forces are deputized by the USMS and FBI served to skew their understanding of which agency actually employed them... The issue was easily resolved in this singular meeting; then we were back to business. I did get some feedback from the other Investigators that the 2 who were singled out were somewhat embarrassed and unappreciative of my approach, but they apparently got over it because they quickly became the 2 most productive investigators in the unit.

The unit went on to enjoy a clear-up (arrest or resolution) rate of 99.28 % for the year. We received special recognition and accolades in the year-end command staff meeting.

The Fugitive unit employees were some of the hardest working and dedicated folks I had the pleasure of working with. I didn't work with them for a long period of time, but they displayed the upmost selflessness and devotion to making the streets of Atlanta safe for its law abiding citizens and visitors.

Sgt. Craig Schmidt was from the Detroit area and a really dedicated supervisor. Sgt. Mike Lewis (Lt.) had been assigned to Narcotics the same time as I and had been a counterpart on the REDDOG Team during my SWAT years. He was well established as a go-getter and relentless pursuer of criminals. Both of these two supervisors made my year in the unit easier. They were never short on advice and direction. They also had no problem with supporting me and trusting in my leadership. They were great to work with. I cannot express enough the unparalleled dedication of the investigators of the Fugitive unit. These guys would make whatever sacrifice to bring Atlanta's most wanted to justice. It didn't matter if it meant sitting on a location for days at a time or coming in to work in the wee hours of the morning to catch someone while they slumbered in what they thought was the comfort of their safe house bed. They were always safe and tactically sound. I was always proud to stand before the executive command staff and present the fruits of their work. The manner in which they brought to fruition some of their cases that had been cold for many years was nothing less than miraculous and truly a sight to behold.

My hat is off to the hardworking and brilliance of the APD Fugitive unit. I want to thank each and every member for their dedication and service. Investigators Stanley Williams (RIP), A. Abercrombie, J. Bilak, D. Buckles, A. Filiberty, T. Gilliard, R. Gordon, M. Gardner, J. Postell (Sgt.), S. Schreckengost, F. Watson, N. Joyner, T. Munson, K. Pope and W. Riggins. Along with my Office Assistant, Ms. Charmin Muse, this was a team to be reckoned with. I am greatly humbled to have had the opportunity to work with them.

However, as wonderful as it all was, it was time to move on. There had recently been a department wide application process for the position of Assistant Commander (Captain, equivalent), and I had applied and interviewed for the position.

After 6 months of waiting and being passed over several times, the appointment had finally come through. I was to be the new Assistant Zone Commander (AZC) of the Zone 2 Precinct. This was a paramount step in my career. I would finally be in a position to affect and even write policy at the Section (Zone/Precinct) level. I still had quite a ways to go before I was structuring and implementing policy citywide, but this was a gigantic step in that direction. I was absolutely humbled by the opportunity.

I was in Zone 2 for such a short period of time that I literally did not have time to unpack my boxes. Within a couple weeks, the order came out that I was being transferred as the AZC of Zone 4. I was equally comfortable in either assignment. In both cases, I had worked previously with both precinct commanders. Majors Robert

Browning (retired) and Moses "Moe" Perdue (retired) had both been my sergeants on the SWAT team at one time. They understood my philosophy regarding law enforcement and vice versa. We all shared the same sentiments on more issues than not, and I had always enjoyed a mutually respectable and friendly relationship with both of them. Robert was Major of Zone 2, while Moe was Major of Zone 4.

Once I reported to Zone 4, the chief explained that I was expected to hit the ground running. Zone 4 was making a serious bid for leading the city in highest crime rate. For whatever reason, it seemed the criminal element in Zone 4 had grown exponentially over the previous few years. Major Perdue had been quite successful in beating down the rate for the couple of years he manned the helm, but it had been a serious uphill battle. Each year he would barely squeak under the wire by showing a reduction in crime by his year's end report. Once I got there, I saw why. He was severely understaffed and under equipped to handle the task at hand. The department had a policy of distributing personnel, vehicles, and other equipment on an equal portions basis. This was to eliminate and calm the expressed outrage of the other Zone commanders, should any one precinct be given more than the others. It was outrageous to see such logic, but that was the way business had been conducted since time immemorial. This left Moses in a position of trying to keep up with elevating crime rates with no additional resources than what he had when crime was consistently low. Simply crazy... But it fit quite comfortably within the age-old expectation of "doing more with less." In this regard, Moses was definitely upholding his namesake. I was amazed at the things he was able to accomplish with virtually no relief or substantive assistance from downtown.

It was a smooth transition to settle in at Zone 4. A few of the officers I had worked with when I was a sergeant on the Morning Watch were now assigned to the Day Watch. Marisha "Shep" Shepherd, who had been a sergeant with me on Zone 5 Morning Watch, was now lieutenant of Zone 4 Day Watch. Seeing her was a sight for sore eyes. Also, the Morning Watch lieutenant, Timothy Algeo, had been an officer of mines and Shep when we were on Zone 5 Morning Watch together. It was great to see so many familiar faces. There were a few issues of contention I looked forward to working out, but nothing major. From my assessment, it seemed the greatest issue facing the Zone was its relationship with the community. This was an area that by now I had developed some degree of expertise in. I looked forward to attending community meetings to get a better perspective on the problem.

One of the problems, which quickly surfaced, was the way the community felt it was treated by officers while on call. This perception of being dismissed by the Zone 4 staff even spilled over into how citizens felt they were treated at the precinct itself when seeking assistance. In a couple meetings, I was apprised that there were poor response times to 911 calls and other similar complaints. I also discovered that many of the officers felt they had received unfair or inequitable treatment from a few of the lieutenants and sergeants. I allowed myself the customary 3-month assessment period and kept meticulous notes based on personal observation. By the end of the assessment period, I had compiled a pretty lengthy to-do list. I shared my observations with Moe and told him that if he would concern himself with issues springing up from Headquarters, I would focus on getting his precinct cleaned up in short order. Based on my observations, the only thing really needed was a revamping of our community relations approach.

The one thing I did not expect was the tremendous amount of pushback I would receive from the Watch and unit lieutenants. There were 3 Watch commanders, an Investigations unit commander, and a Discretionary (Crime Suppression) unit commander. Five commanders in total.

The AZC position was a fairly new position created by the chief of police. The position itself served in the capacity of a captain, but holders of the position still carried the rank insignia and title of lieutenant (Unit commander). The title of Assistant Commander (AC) was understood to infer the vested authority of the abolished captain's rank. In other words, you were an assistant to a Section Commander (Major). Therefore, the Assistant Commander's position was not limited to the 6 Precincts, but to Sections departmental wide. There was a pay increase attached to the position. This, the added responsibility, and additional authority of the position itself were to set it apart from the unit level rank of lieutenant. All this did was create animosity among the lieutenants towards AZC's and ASC's. Invariably, most departmental lieutenants had a difficult time adjusting to the fact that they were now taking orders from someone wearing the same rank insignia and carrying the same general title of "Lieutenant." Being prior military service, I understood the ranking structure and had no problem with it. The problem was that the overwhelming number of lieutenants on the department had never served in the military and had the added burden of inflated egos. It was a truly difficult time for all the departments AZC's and ASC's. My situation was no different.

Be that as it may, it was time to have a sit down with the lieutenants who made up my command staff. It was time to develop and initiate some new ideas pertaining to how we interacted with the citizens we were sworn to serve and protect. We also needed to give some attention to how our officers were treated within the walls of the precinct itself.

I shared with them how I'd spent my entire childhood growing up in the inner-city of Detroit. I also shared with then how I'd spent the vast majority of my adulthood policing the inner-city streets of Atlanta. I talked about how I'd always assumed the position of not caring what prejudices or bigoted ideas another person had; but that I'd always been more concerned about discriminatory acts or practices. My position has always been... Think what you want about me, but treat me fairly. I explained to them how this attitude had carried into police management. I cautioned them to leave their personal ideologies at home. I told them, "You are entitled to your opinions, feelings, and preconceived notions about my sergeants, officers and the citizens of the community. I would go on to say "I can't, nor do I desire to, control that. In fact, you have every right to your biases, whatever they may be. But for at least 8 hours of the day, I do have control over your conduct. And for those 8 hours, you WILL conduct yourself as though you respect and have as much compassion for our sergeants, officers and citizens, as you do for your own mothers." I made it clear that I expected them to hold their sergeants and officers accountable to the same standard. Each lieutenant was to closely monitor officer/citizen encounters and address issues as they arose. No more automatically taking the officer's version of every situation and summarily dismissing the citizen's complaint without objective investigation. I believed in supporting my officers as much as anyone.

My record spoke for itself on that issue. But I had absolutely no tolerance for the mistreatment and relegation of citizens in such matters. I explained to them my theory on supporting officers in areas of white, gray and black. I would not join them in supporting any officer who blatantly and wantonly violated the rights of citizens or had knowingly broken any criminal laws. I made it exceedingly clear that there was a clear level of accountability associated with the Thin Blue Line, and I expected each of them to toe the Thin Blue Line with the greatest integrity.

Another standing rule that was established in this first meeting was that no victim of a crime was to ever leave our precinct feeling as though it was their fault for being victimized; or indeed, feeling as though they had been victimized a second time by the police. It was commonplace for citizens to leave a police precinct feeling they had been in error for even lodging a complaint. This was not a problem that was indigenous solely to Zone 4. Lazy officers all over the department would virtually antagonize victims of crime in the hopes of discouraging them from filing a report. The primary purpose was to avoid paperwork on behalf of the lazy officer. However, there was oftentimes a more ominous motivation. There were cases when officers were instructed by their supervisors and command staff to discourage reporting for the sake of reducing the reported crime numbers. I explained to the commanders how I knew this was a national phenomenon and growing trend, but we would not be participating in such practices. I then added that we also would not be engaging in any quota requirements of our officers. I gave them assurances that Moe had been apprised of everything I would be discussing with them and was on board with everything discussed in this meeting. My bottom line was for the commanders to treat the supervisors with dignity and compassion, for the supervisors to treat the officers with the same respect, and for the officers to pass that treatment down to the citizens.

The last thing I shared with them was the fact that we as Commanders, could do a lot better job of letting our employees know how much we appreciate them. I explained how this could go a long way in influencing how our officers interact with the community. A lot of an officer's attitude that she or he passes on to citizens originates and festers from how they're treated by their supervisors. The theory of transference of emotions is very real. So is the classic cycle of abuse. I broke down my theory on the subject in what I hoped would be more relevant language. I explained how it had been my experience that most people can tolerate a job where they're being paid at their worth, but underappreciated or unappreciated for the job they do. Tolerable, is also being underpaid for your worth, but at least shown appreciation for the job you do. However, no one has a tolerance for being underpaid for their worth, and at the same time underappreciated for the job they do. In this regard, our employees are no different from any other employed person in the world. These less than ideal conditions are bound to develop feelings of spite and resentfulness that is bound to be passed on in the officers' interactions with the public. It was incumbent upon all of the commanders to set the tone of interpersonal relations within the Zone/Precinct. Everyone left that meeting knowing beyond a doubt that very few things bothered me more than a non-compassionate and inconsiderate cop... At any level.

The Zone began to see improvements both inside and outside of the precinct, and I was quite satisfied with the direction we were headed. The year flew by faster than any in my career, I believe. I was originally met with skepticism in all the community meetings, but we were quickly gaining the confidence and trust of community leaders as time went on. The simple formula seemed to be pretty basic. Explain to people what you can't do within the realm of the constitution, laws, and departmental authority. Next, let them know exactly what you can do within those same parameters. Lastly, do exactly what you promised in the precise timeframe that you promised. The issue prior to my appointment as AZC was that while Moe was downtown at headquarters handling the Zones' business, his AZC had become overwhelmed and was not following through with promises that Moe had made in the community meetings. The way I saw it, my job was to ensure that every one of his guarantees were fulfilled. Oftentimes, that meant certain liberties had to be taken. But in keeping with my own criteria of constitutionality, morality, legality, and safety, I was comfortable with thinking outside of the proverbial box. Departmental customs, traditions and practices had never proven to be a hindrance to me in my entire career, so I saw no reason to allow outdated or antiquated mechanisms and mindsets to stand in my way now.

It turned out that Moe and I were a pretty good team, but that was about to change. In fact, the entire department was about to change. The election of a new mayor would usher in a new chief of police as well.

CHAPTER – 24

TWO STEPS BACKWARD

The day after the new mayor named his interim chief of police, I received a call to report to the chief's office. Once there, I was greeted by Interim chief George Turner and assistant chief Peter Andresen (retired). I was asked to take a seat. It was then explained to me why I had been summoned. The chief explained to me that I was being appointed to the position of major and would be assigned the Zone 4 Precinct. He explained how he was satisfied with the work that Major Perdue and I had done and wanted to keep me in position to continue the trajectory the Zone was on. Moe was being transferred to head up OPS. OPS was a highly coveted assignment and reported directly to the chief of police. It was definitely one of the most prestigious and powerful assignments a major could have on any department. He spoke quite explicitly in his conveyance that my number 1 priority was to continue to mend the relationship between the community and the department. He iterated that there was still an expectation of crime reduction, but that was secondary to getting the community leaders on board with the police department. His last point was quite poignant. He said the entire command staff was on a probationary period due to his interim status, and it would be conducive for all of our futures if were to hit the ground running and staking our claim. The bottom line was that my appointment was logically tied directly to whether or not he landed the permanent job of chief of police. I indicated that I understood the terms of my appointment, and I appreciated the opportunity.

As promised, I did indeed hit the ground with a renewed sense of determination to make the chief look good in the eyes of the mayor. Naturally, the objective was to accomplish this by continuing to do the things that seemed, at this point, to already be working. I would also incorporate some new strategies to take the Zone's accomplishments to an even higher level. Although I was advised that crime would be secondary, I knew in my heart of hearts that come the following month, and every subsequent month, I would be expected to show a decrease in crime numbers. As things stood, Zone 4 was the only Zone in the city to start the year off with an elevated crime rate. Every other Zone was starting the year off with their crime either at an even rate, or down. I was up by 7% compared to the same week in the previous year. My plan was to show a monthly decrease in crime of at least 1% for the first 7 months of the year. Based on that theory, I should be able to end the year with at least a 6-10% decrease, and that would put me pretty much at the Zone's traditional year-end numbers. If I was given the support I needed from downtown to implement some of the plans and programs that I was sure my staff and I could come up with, we could even bring the year to an end with an even greater crime reduction than in previous years. At any rate, a 7% deficit wouldn't be too hard to come back from. There had been Zones in the recent past that had overcome greater numbers in the beginning of the year. I knew I had a hard working and bright team of commanders, and I was sure we could collectively beat these numbers down. I for one, was definitely looking forward to the challenge.

Later that week I was informed that all the majors, new and old, were being allowed to select 1 person from anywhere on the department to add to their staff. We were told that we would have the chance to select the one person who we felt would make the greatest contribution to our success. We were instructed to submit the names of our top 3 choices. There would be a sincere effort to assign us our first choice, but we were guaranteed to get at least one of the 3 submitted. For me, the choice wasn't even a choice. I listed the same name for all three slots: 1) Sgt. Jacquelyn Gwinn-Villaroel 2) Sgt. Jacquelyn Gwinn-Villaroel 3) Sgt. Jacquelyn Gwinn- Villaroel.

Jackie had worked with me in Zone 2 Investigations and was my most consistent top performer. She was smart, hard working, conscientious, considerate and extremely loyal to the vision we both shared. She shared the same approach to policing. Together, we had helped a lot of people in our old assignment. I had noticed in the personnel order that she had just been promoted to sergeant. I submitted her name to the chief's office but didn't really expect it to come to fruition due to the fact that she had just been promoted. Usually, only senior supervisors were allowed to serve as assistants to majors and above. When more junior sergeants were given these positions, it generally created dissention among the rank. However, the notification did indicate that we could select "anyone." There was no question in my mind as to who I would be able to trust absolutely with covering my back and furthering the agenda of building a strong and enduring relationship with the Zone 4 community.

Within a day or so, Jackie reported to my office. I was elated to see her and felt reassured that things were definitely looking up for Zone 4. Unfortunately, some of the other folks were not as happy for her arrival as I was.

The inherent problem with being a commander's assistant, regardless of the level, is that the assistant will invariably hold a lower rank than almost 100% of the people he or she is involved most directly with. For instance, the assistant to the chief holds the rank of lieutenant, or even sergeant. Their primary function is to convey the chief's wishes and orders to the deputy chiefs (DC). Often times, the DC would take opposition to being made to feel as though they're being given orders by someone they outrank by 4 or 5 levels. It's basically an ego thing, but very real, nevertheless. The same goes for pretty much every command position down the chain. At almost every level, the commander's assistant carries the rank of sergeant. As I said, unfortunately, my command staff would suffer the same issues with Jackie.

To make matters worse, Jackie tended to have a very cut and dry or matter of fact type personality, which she had developed over time on the department. Being a so-called double minority (Black, female) is challenge enough without adding the fact that she was now a supervisor. Now she could be considered a triple minority. Not unlike a lot of other Black female officers who came before her in agencies all over the country, if not the world. She had to adopt a no-nonsense attitude and approach to her work to be taken seriously by her male peers and counterparts. It doesn't require a degree in American history or US civics to understand and appreciate everything that women of every ethnicity have endured, as they continue to break through more areas of traditionally male dominated workforces and vocations. So Jackie tended to keep things very professional and direct. She had a knack for getting things done. She approached everything with a relentlessness and perfectionism that was inexhaustible. She'd worked very closely with me in Zone 2 Investigations, so she was keenly aware of my style, expectations and motivations. We both identified with and shared the same perfectionist and public servant mentality.

The other issue was the perception that she was coming in and taking over things beyond the scope of her authority. Some of the lieutenants and sergeants didn't like the fact that she had been invested with the authority to take action and address issues on my behalf without my prior knowledge. Because I had been very hands-on as the AZC, they didn't understand how I could turn over the reins to this newcomer sergeant. The rest of the staff felt they had a pretty good handle on my expectations as they grew to know me over the previous year. They just couldn't wrap their heads around the fact that Jackie seemed to be calling shots without even advising me in advance of her actions. She was met daily with the question "does the major know you're asking us to do this," or "don't you think you should check with the major before signing that form on his behalf?" In my first meeting after her arrival, I explained to the staff that I trusted her to look at a situation and know instantly how I would respond to or approach it. This was the level of intuitiveness we had honed in our 3 ½ years together in Zone 2. She had basically filled this same role for me as an investigator during that period. That was the reason I had no hesitation in requesting her for this job. I never had to question her moral position on any subject because she was an ordained minister. I never had any reservation as to whether or not she would do the professional, legal and ethical thing in any situation. She had my absolute confidence, and she never let me or Zone 2 Investigations down. I was certain she wouldn't start now.

My first meeting with the command staff as the new Zone commander wasn't much different from any other staff meeting over the previous year. I reiterated how we were going to approach the new year as a team, just as we had done in the previous year. I took the time to reemphasize my basic marching orders. My marching order for the year 2010 was set in stone: First, do it legally/constitutionally. Second, do it morally. And third, do it safely. After applying these criteria... do you!!! I went on to say “only on rare occasion must an assignment be done or completed in a particularly specific way or fashion. The vast majority of times, things can be done in the employee's own way, utilizing their own initiative and ingenuity. Besides that, the last thing I need is a staff full of "mini-me's".” I added “how am I to learn anything new if my entire staff is emulating me at every turn. I already know how "I" would do something. Impress and surprise me by doing something I would have never thought of. That way, we all grow from the experience and we all take credit in our success!”

After my little speech, I adjourned the meeting and we all set off to work.

The crime would not be a gargantuan issue, but it still required tending to. I had Jackie to set out right away to establish an initial meet and greet with all Zone 4 city council members, community leaders and Neighborhood Planning Unit (NPU) presidents. I had been directly involved with all of these leaders before over the course of the previous year. But I wanted to glean what their current needs were, as well as to share with them some of my short and long range goals as the new precinct commander. My objective was to fully engage the entire Zone 4 community from day one and stay engaged for however long my tenure was to be in this assignment.

As the months rolled by, the crime rate showed a steady monthly decrease of at least 1%. By April, my crime was down by 3%, which meant it was now up by only 4%. The plans that the command staff was coming up with were being quite effective. I hoped there would be an additional push once we stood up 2 new mini precincts and staffed a third. The opening of the West End mini precinct had been a pet project of Councilwoman Cleta Winslow. She was fiercely dedicated to staffing a precinct in the area to cut down on the crime in one of Atlanta's most prominently historical communities. Councilman C.T. Martin took special interest in the revitalization of the mini precinct in the Martin Luther King Jr. Drive corridor. The chief himself, was passionate about standing up full service staffing in the already functioning Greenbriar mall mini precinct. The Greenbriar precinct was already functioning as the home for the Zone 4 Discretionary unit, but now it was to be staffed by a supplement of patrol officers around the clock.

At the same time all this is going on, I was attending as many community meetings as humanly possible. I really took pleasure in interacting with the members of the community. I developed a significant level of rapport with the entire cross section of the Zone. From residents of the most impoverished areas in the Zone, to the most affluent citizens in the Zone, to the business owners who didn't even live within the city limits... It was quite an experience to have the expressed support of people of all walks of life. As I stated before, I never promised anything I knew I couldn't deliver on. But the things I did promise, I made sure I always delivered. Jackie was instrumental in making sure all of my promises were met. She knew better than anyone that I always held myself to a 24 hour standard for making good on fulfilling community requests. I believed that there were very few things which couldn't be accomplished in 24 hours if a person has a genuine intent to do so. The one thing I absolutely would not do was develop a reputation as being one of those Zone commanders who promised everything just to appease someone, and delivered nothing. Of course, it took some doing to meet my own requirement sometimes, but with Jackie's assistance, we always delivered. Oftentimes, we would have things accomplished within a few hours of the request being forwarded to me or her. It was always our goal to leave the office everyday with an empty In-Box. After a while, Jackie began to receive accolades from the community for her professionalism and dedication to problem-solve. Before long, she was established as the bolt that was holding together the Zone 4 machine, and all of her original doubters in the command staff confessed their newfound admiration for her work. I couldn't resist reminding them that I had told them so.

A few months into the assignment, I had to add one more thing to Jackie's growing list of responsibilities. All of my life, accomplishment has always taken a greater priority in my life than even eating. It's always been more important to feel a since of accomplishment at the end of EVERY day than a sense of having a literally full stomach. There would be times when I would get home and realize I had completely forgotten to eat that entire day. Therefore, I had to assign Jackie the task of reminding me to eat on a daily basis. Crazy, right?

Everything was going as planned. I was gaining more and more trust and support from the community, and crime was dwindling downward on a monthly basis. In fact, things were going a little too good for my luck.

At about 2:00 a.m. one April morning, I received a call at home from my Morning Watch commander, Lieutenant Scott Kreher. He was on the scene of a residential burglary and was requesting my presence on the scene. This, of course, was a highly unusual request. Zone commanders aren't usually awoken from their sleep to respond to routine burglaries. This is something that falls well within the pre-vue of the Watch or Shift commander. Scott quickly announced to me that the mayor was present on the scene and was personally requesting my presence. When I asked Scott what specifically was going on, he told me that the victim in this case was a personal friend of the mayor's. The victim's wife and children were in the upstairs portion of the home when the burglars broke into the basement area in the rear of the house. The wife fled the scene with the children and called her husband. He, in turn, called the mayor. 911 was called only after the mayor arrived on the scene, which was well after the burglars had already fled the location. Once the responding officer arrived, the mayor automatically advised the officer to call the major (me) out to the scene. Scott then said that the officer naturally advised his chain of command of the mayor's request. The sergeant responded and notified Scott of what was going on. Scott then proceeded directly to the scene. Scott said once he arrived, he basically announced to the mayor that he would be assisting him. So far, everything that Scott was telling me was proper protocol based on our SOP's. Scott said the mayor rejected his assistance and demanded that he call me to the scene. After a few failed attempts to reach me on the cellular phone, Scott notified the chief of police of the situation, since it involved the mayor. Again... per SOP. The chief then advised Scott to try contacting me at my home phone. It was then that he was able to reach me. The entire time that Scott was relating the story to me, I could hear who sounded like the newly elected mayor in the background audibly upset. I asked Scott to put the mayor on the phone with me. Once on the phone with the mayor, it was clear that he was highly upset with the situation. I told him I was getting dressed as we spoke and would be on my way to his location. I asked if he could fill me in on what was going on in the mean time. The mayor said he had attended many community meetings where citizens had complained about the treatment they'd received from the officers in Zone 4. He said he now understood what their concerns were because he felt that my officers had treated him with less than sufficient service. I asked if he could be more specific about my officers' conduct on the scene. I asked if they had been insubordinate, discourteous, or unprofessional in some other manner. He said it wasn't anything like that. He went on to say that my officers had treated him like he wasn't the mayor of "this d--n city!" "For instance," he said, "I told this officer to call you out here. Instead, I get lieutenant Kreher out here." He said he hadn't asked for a lieutenant, but he had requested the Zone major to respond to the call. I apologized for the fact that he felt slighted by my officers and advised him again that I was on the way to the scene and would get everything straightened out once I arrived. I was dressed in 10 minutes, and I lived 30 minutes from the location, but I was in route. It was obvious to me that the new mayor wasn't familiar with the department's Chain of Command policy. If he was familiar with it, he would have understood that the officer would have been in violation of SOP had he contacted me directly. SOP was clear on the fact that such notifications must ascend up the chain of command without skipping any levels. Therefore, the officer was required to notify his sergeant, the sergeant then notifies the lieutenant, and he then is required to notify the major, and so on up the chain. At this point, it appeared that my officers had done everything by the book and had done nothing wrong. The only issue that I could see at this point was that the mayor's ego may have been bruised because things didn't go exactly as he had dictated, even though the objective had been obtained. I was, in fact, on my way to the scene just as the mayor had requested (demanded).

15 minutes into my 30-minute drive on the interstate, I received a second call from Scott advising me that I could go back home because the scene was clear. The homeowners didn't feel comfortable staying in the house for the night, so they went somewhere else for the remainder of the night. The mayor had left the scene. The ID technicians had already processed the scene and were gone. The officers had finished their report and had also left to resume their patrols. He added that I was welcome to continue, but I would be there by myself looking at nothing. He then told me the mayor said that he would take the matter up with the chief in the morning. I turned around and headed back home to get what little more rest was possible before getting back up to face what was sure to be a Chinese fire drill when I got to the precinct in the morning.

I arrived at the precinct at my usual time of 9:00 a.m. and was told by my secretary that the deputy chief had been calling me all morning. He wanted me to call him as soon as I got in. Before I could get into my office to call him, she advised that he was holding again on line 3. "Good morning, chief" I said as I picked up the phone. "Good morning, Khalfani" he responded. He asked, "What happened out there last night? The mayor's really pissed" he said. "So is the chief" he added. He said that in fact, if my officers had been discourteous to the mayor on a call, then he too was pissed. I told him I hadn't had time to gather the facts, but preliminarily, based on what I could tell from last night, the mayor was overreacting to the situation. I told him I would conduct a thorough investigation into what occurred and would get back to him within a few days. The DC then began shouting into the phone "write those motherf---ers up! They knew what they were doing! They were purposely being defiant to the new mayor! They probably supported his opponent in the election, so they're just trying to show disrespect to the mayor! They hate the fact that a "brother" is the new mayor! Write those motherf---ers up!" I told him I doubted that color had anything to do with it, considering that one of the officers accused was Black. The White officer was the most senior officer in the entire Zone. He was retired military and was the most squared away officer under my command. I had never seen, nor heard of him conducting himself with less than the most upright military bearing. I advised the DC again that I would conduct an investigation and provide a written response to the concerns. I asked him to explain to me what charges the mayor was seeking against my officers. He said he didn't know, but they were going to be charged with something because the mayor and chief wanted it. Over the following days, the DC continued to call me several times throughout the day to see what progress my AZC and I had made with the investigation. Because of all the people who needed to be interviewed, the audio tapes that needed to be obtained from communications and follow-up reports from the Zone Investigations Unit, it took longer than a few days to pull together my findings. Once I did, I had my AZC compile the results in an interoffice memorandum.

I was in attendance at one of the churches in the Cascade community. The church hosted a rededication luncheon every year in April. The precinct commander was always expected as one of the honored guests. I had attended in Moe's stead the previous year, so I was looking forward to attending as the actual Zone commander this year. During the service, I got a call from the chief requesting to meet with me, my AZC and my Investigations commander. He was to be accompanied by the Assistant Chief (AC) and the Deputy Chief. When

I advised him of my participation with the ongoing church program, he suggested that we meet at the church in the basement or some other private area. Obviously, he was under great pressure to bring this situation to closure to even entertain such drastic measures. Of course, his suggestion wasn't actually a suggestion. It was an order. I notified my commanders to report to the church, and we awaited the chiefs' arrival.

We all sat around a table in the basement of the church, and the chief asked where we were at with the burglary case. I had my Investigations commander fill the chiefs in on where we stood with the investigation. We were basically at a dead end. We had plenty of evidence, but we lacked cooperation from the victims in identifying the suspects. The victim had given a fight party at his home the week before the break-in. The house had been wired for video from top to bottom, and all of the guests had been captured on video during the party. There was fairly good footage of the break-in, and the investigator was able to less than positively identify one of the party guests as being one of the burglars. To add to the evidence, the suspect was seen clearly directing the other suspects to the location of everything. It was abundantly clear that the main suspect had prior knowledge of the residence. The investigator contacted the victim for a second interview to show him the comparison footage. He'd hoped the victim would then be able to supply him with the name of the main suspect. When the investigator showed the footage to the victim, the victim clearly reacted as though he recognized the burglar in the video, but claimed otherwise. My investigator tried to convince the victim to cooperate, but the victim refused to assist with the investigation any further. He pretended to be appalled that my investigator would accuse his own friends of burglarizing him.

The victim's actions raised suspicion with the investigator, so he ran a criminal background check on the victim. The results were not too surprising. The victim had a criminal record. Further investigation revealed that in the previous year, the victim had led police on a multi- jurisdictional vehicle chase and fought with officers once he was stopped.

There in the basement of the church, the chief became visibly upset and yelled at my Investigations commander "what the hell does him having a record have to do with him being the victim of a burglary?" He said "you're basically saying that we're not going to investigate the case because the victim has a criminal record?" The commander attempted to explain that the victim's criminality gave credence to the fact that he refused to cooperate with the investigation. The victim clearly didn't want to pursue a case against an acquaintance, and that's alright. All we wanted was the victim's agreement to drop the case so we could stop spending resources on a case that was obviously solved. Then our investigator could go back to handling other cases piling up on his desk. All we were asking was that the victim stop blowing smoke up our skirts and allow us to get back to real work. The case was solved as much as it possibly could be without the victim's cooperation. The chief gave an order to continue to find other avenues to solve the case, and all three chiefs left in a huff.

Once the chiefs left, the Investigations commander told me the investigator had done a little more digging and found out that the victim and the mayor's friendship extended over many years. The victim had in fact, been one of the mayor's biggest campaign contributors.

Everything was starting make sense!

Later on at the precinct, the DC stopped in to find out where I was at concerning charges against my two officers. I advised him that I had completed my investigation and had prepared a memo of my findings. I gave him a copy. When he read that I was recommending no disciplinary action, he became upset and asked me to explain my position. I told him I had spoken to the mayor the night of the incident. I had asked the mayor directly, if my officers had broken any work rules or violated any SOP's. The mayor himself could not provide any offences committed by my officers. The subsequent investigation had shown that my officers had conducted themselves within the departmental policies. In fact, had my officers done things in the exact fashion requested by the mayor, they would have then been in violation of our Chain of Command SOP. I then went on to suggest that if the chief, assistant chief or even the DC himself could explain to the mayor our Chain of Command SOP, perhaps he would understand why the officers made notification the way they did; and that they weren't just blowing him off. The DC exploded "THE MAYOR IS THE F---ING CHAIN OF COMMAND!!!"

It was clearly time for my father to make an appearance.

I instinctively barked back "the bottom line is this chief... I not only can't, but I won't place charges on my officers undeservingly." I went on to remind the DC that the entire department had just recovered from 6 months of imposed furlough days. I brought to his attention that in the past year, my officers had been set up at least 2 times for ambushes by suspects while on patrol. I told him they continued to work in conditions where they are underpaid, under staffed, under equipped and underappreciated. Yet, they still showed up for work every day and they still continued to reduce MY crime numbers every month. I told him since the department had done nothing to earn their dedication, I had to believe that they're working their a--es off for me personally. How could I then turn around and repay their dedication by "f---ing" them over, especially when they hadn't done anything wrong. I told him "I WILL NOT send the message to my troops that Major Yabuku will f--k over you, even when you do things the right way." Again, I told him "no sir! Not only CAN I NOT do that, but I WILL NOT do that to my officers!"

Sensing my passion, the chief's demeanor did a 180 and he began to chuckle. He said "ok, Khalfani! Man! You haven't changed one bit..." or something along those lines.

3 months later I was summoned to the chief's office to be reassigned. That's the departments' way of saying "demoted" back to lieutenant. The meeting consisted of the chief and the assistant chief. The chief explained that I was being reassigned because of my high crime rate. It was 7 months into the year and mine's was still the only precinct whose crime was up. He added that the city Chief Operating Officer (COO) had been monitoring calls for service citywide, and Zone 4 consistently had more calls for service than the other Zones. When allowed to speak, I brought to his attention that my crime was only up by 1%. That based on my current trend, the rate should be even he next month, and down by at least 1% the following month. As far as calls for service, that went hand in hand with the crime rate. I also mentioned the fact that I had no additional personnel or equipment as promised when I was given the job. He advised me that the decision was coming from over his head, and the matter was out of his hands. When he realized he had inadvertently revealed that the mayor was running the department and not him, he tried to back track and assert that this was still ultimately his decision. Too late. He said he wanted to send a message to the other majors on the de-

partment that if they didn't do what was needed, they too would find themselves in my shoes. This was perhaps the only thing that disturbed me about the entire meeting. The Chief himself had been spared this exact fate by his predecessor, Chief Pennington. When the chief was Major of Zone 1, he was unable to get his crime down for a couple years before Chief Pennington removed him from Zone 1. Two years versus my 7 months. Furthermore, Chief Pennington didn't demote him when he removed him from the Zone. Instead, he created the Night Commander's position for him because every other major's position on the department was satisfactorily filled at the time. That's right, he had been spared demotion at all cost, but he had not seen fit to do the same for me. In all honesty, I still couldn't bring myself to be completely disappointed in the chief. I knew the orders had come from over his head. I completely anticipated this would happen. I knew the chief was still in the "interim" status, and if he wanted to be named the permanent chief, he was going to have jump through a lot of hoops. There were two other finalists in the search for chief, so his appointment wasn't anywhere near being a guarantee. I honestly and truly understood all the politics involved in what was happening. I also understood that at the rate my crime was descending, this had to happen now. If he waited another month, my crime would be even and the following month it would be down. That would nullify their supposed justification for giving me the axe. It had to happen now, or never. I got it.

The Chief told me I was to be transferred to command the School Detective unit downtown. I was to keep my head down and not make any waves. After things blew over, I would be re-appointed to the major's position. In the mean time, there were some real issues going on with the School Detective unit, and he needed me to fix it.

I told him I understood his position, and I appreciated him giving me the opportunity to command Zone 4. I shook both of their hands and was excused from the room.

I left out of his office with my head held high, but I was completely and utterly devastated inside. I was proud of myself for making such a big sacrifice for two officers who had been sacrificing for me, the department, and the city for so many years. At least in the case of one of them... The other was a rookie who had only been on for a short while.

We all think we know ourselves enough to predict how we'll respond in any given situation. That is to say that we have an idea of how we hope we'll react, or what sacrifice we hope we would make for our beliefs or passions. For me, it was no longer a theory. I no longer had to imagine how I would handle such a situation. The truth is, we never really know how we'll respond until we're actually faced with extreme adversity in real life. That's the point where theory is put to the test in a very real way. I was proud to find that within me resided the true warrior I had always believed myself to be. I had always believed that I had enough of my father in me to always stand on the truth and do what was right, regardless of the consequence. I no longer had to imagine. This was very real. In fact, it was surreal.

The most devastating thing was, of course, the derailment of obtaining my ultimate goal on the department. This demotion had set me back and removed me that much further from my objective of becoming Chief. I had been motivated more than ever when I was appointed to major. The ability to create and implement policy on the Zone level was the highlight of my career. Along with the officers I worked with, I had actually contributed to reshaping departmental/community relations in those short 7 months. I had been instrumental in the development of a more conducive working environment for the officers by influencing how they were treated by their supervisors. In all, Zone 4 was on its way to being a model Zone for every other precinct to emulate. Once I'd made Chief, I would be able to implement best practices and spread these types of accomplishments citywide. There would be a very real and very feasible likelihood that I would be able to successfully mend the generations old disconnect and chasm that existed between the police department and certain communities of Atlanta. Specifically, the Black communities...

But that was no longer to happen. I was not to accomplish what I had set out for more than 26 years prior. A society where the community and the police department worked together in mutual trust, respect, and commonality was not to be obtained by my hand. My naysayers would have their way after all, and at long last, my lifelong dream would be curtailed, but not extinguished. Now I was convinced more than ever of what needed to be fixed within the walls of police headquarters. I was down, but not out. At least... not yet!

CHAPTER – 25

EDUCATION OVER INCARCERATION

I took a much-needed 3 weeks off after the demotion. I not only needed time to wrap my head around the idea of having my goal postponed, but I needed to visit my daughter, Tamyka in Texas. She was suffering a setback with her 7-year battle with Multiple Sclerosis (MS).

When I finally did arrive at the School Detectives unit (SDU), I knew it was going to be one of the greatest challenges of my career. The chief hadn't lied... Things were ugly in this unit. The greatest problem plaguing the unit was the absolute absence of cooperation between the APD side of the house and the Atlanta Public Schools (APS) side of things. I learned that this relationship, or lack thereof, had been developing/deteriorating over a period of several years. Based on all accounts, the rift started with the appointment of the current APS Safety and Security director. The SDU staff was quick to fill me in on all the issues and problems that stood between APD and APS. In their estimation, every single shortcoming in the relationship was singlehandedly the fault of the APS security director. Of course, this seemed unfathomable to me, but I resolved that I would keep an open mind to the idea that anything is possible. If what they said turned out to be true, it would be the first time I'd witnessed or experienced such an extreme case of one sidedness. I explained to my staff that while I appreciated their concerns, it was imperative that I conduct an objective 3-month assessment of the situation and reserve any conclusive opinions until that time.

When I met with the APS security director for the first time, she was equally frustrated and accusatory of the SDU. In her opinion, she had received absolutely zero assistance from the 2 or 3 previous SDU commanders. She felt there was no trust or respect between the two entities, and basically, her life had been made a living hell at the hands of the SDU. As did the SDU officers, she also wanted immediate remedies to the disastrous conditions. I explained to her that I had worked with almost every officer and both sergeants in prior assignments over the years. If the things she was sharing with me about them were true, it would be a side that I had never witnessed in all the years I'd known them. That being said, I would still conduct my customary 3-month assessment with impartiality and objectivity.

At the end of the initial 3 months, it was obvious that neither party was completely at fault in the existing feud between the SDU and APS. In fact, I found no intentional malice on the part of either party. Based on my opinion, almost every issue was a result of poor, lack of, or flat out miscommunication. For me, that was actually a good thing. I was happy to find no obvious existence of any real intention to sabotage the relationship between the two. The real issue was that both sides mistakenly believed the other despised their existence. Let me explain. The biggest struggle was in the fight for ultimate control over the School Resource Officer (SRO) program. There was no independently standing program for SRO's. APD did not have an SRO Unit, so the positions had to be filled by off duty APD officers. However, the SRO program itself fell under the prevue of APS because of its obvious function within the school system. This meant that the APS security director was responsible for hiring and providing salaries for the off duty officers who staffed the schools in the APS district. The supervision and administration of the officers was the responsibility of APD SDU supervisors. This was due to the fact that even when an APD officer is working an off duty job of any nature, he or she is still accountable to the work rules and regulations of APD. Therefore, they are still held accountable to APD supervision. You can clearly see how easy it is for the waters to become murky in a situation such as this. Both sides hold the belief that they hold the trump card and that the other side essentially works for them. The previous SDU commanders held the opinion that, off duty or not, these were still APD officers, and therefore, ultimately under their control. The APS director took the position that as long as she was the one doing the hiring and paying of the salaries, she ultimately had the last say in their utilization. It was the ultimate power struggle, and I was positioned to be the mediator. It was my responsibility, as explained by the chief, to be the needle upon which the two were to be balanced. There was no doubt in my mind that balance, if not harmony, could be obtained. I saw no intentional or conscious effort on either side to undermine the other. Like I said, there was a serious communication problem, but that had always been my forte. Throughout my career, I had always been sought out by my peers to hear arguments and render an opinion on the facts. 9 times out of 10, both parties would be expressing the exact same sentiments but failing miserably at getting their point across. More times than not, it boiled down to misinterpretation of message or intentions. This situation was no different.

I met with my two sergeants and explained that we were going to cultivate a new relationship with the director. I understood they held out the opinion that the only way to deal with her was with an iron fist, as the previous SDU commanders had resorted to. I assured them that I would be able to reason with the director by way of mutual respect. No underhanded or veiled pretenses, but authentic willingness to work with her on issues facing our mutual mission – the safety and welfare of the students and faculty of the APS district. I then had pretty much the same conversation with the director.

Another thing I noticed during the assessment period was the disturbing proliferation of the criminalization of youth in the school resource system. There was almost no effort whatsoever to resolve conflict with means other than incarceration. Children were being criminally charged for being children, in many cases. There was definitely an element of the student population that merited being jailed. I had not the slightest problem in removing dangerous, predatory offenders from the environment. I took issue with arrests being made in situations where a child is obviously acting out in a fashion that doesn't necessarily warrant an arrest. When I saw that instances of typical adolescent misconduct were routinely being classified as criminal behavior, it struck a chord in me. The idea of children being given criminal records for the exact same things my generation was paddled or slapped on the wrist for was unacceptable to me. I know times have changed since we were children, but a child is still a child. That never changes.

I have the greatest respect and admiration for the teaching profession. I have a special respect for those who teach in some of the country's more challenged or troubled areas. However, I was tremendously disappointed and appalled at the way some of the educators would seek to remedy the slightest of infractions with incarceration. Some of the teachers would literally seek to have a resource officer lock up a child for merely disrupting a classroom. I get the fact that classroom disruptions adversely affect every student in that environment, but come on. In a lot of cases, the teacher would understandably be at their wits end with a particular student.

Or a teacher may honestly perceive the student's actions to be physically threatening toward her or him. I get that also. However, the initial action should not always be incarceration in each and every case. Some teachers had gotten to the point of depending on law enforcement for absolutely every problem that sprung up. It was as if they had given up. It was heartbreaking for me to witness.

I was scheduled to address all 200 SRO's in the annual orientation meetings held before the onset of the new school year. I would have the opportunity to convey my intentions to turn around this apparent systematic mass incarceration of youth and other initiatives developed with the members of the SDU. The meeting went off without a hitch. The only real issue was that many officers new to the SRO program were under the impression that they answered to APS because that's where their check was being cut. They were reminded that there would be no APS check if they didn't have APD employment. Therefore, their adherence to APD policies superseded a teacher demanding they arrest a child for shooting spitballs in the classroom, even though, technically, based on Georgia law, spitballs can be classified as a form of criminal assault. Most of the officers shared my sentiments and were relieved to hear my position on how we would be proceeding. They had never liked the idea of being required to make an arrest based simply on a teacher's demands. But that had been expected of them in the past. Either that, or face the possibility of being terminated from the job. They had been caught between a rock and a hard place for quite some time. I was happy to announce that this was all about to change.

Next, I sent out the announcement that I would be personally meeting with as many principals as possible. I arranged the first meeting with the school described as being the most troubled and holding the highest crime rate in the school district. The meeting was to consist of the school's principals and security staff, including hall monitors. When I got to the part about not locking up students carte blanche, many of them began to squirm in their seats. Some of them vocalized their concern for the safety of the faculty and other students. I reiterated that I was not referring to clear criminal behavior, but rather, that behavior that each and every one of us had possibly engaged in when we were that age. That behavior, that if we had been incarcerated for, we would not be qualified to hold the employment we presently enjoyed. I implored them to remember that the primary objective of the school system is to educate, not incarcerate. I challenged them to come up with new and different ideas of ways to engage and mentor the students rather than criminalizing them at the epidemic rate currently facing the nation. At the end of the meeting, I got a sense of a renewed motivation with most of the attendees. Of course, there will always be your standard "lock them all up and let God sort them out" advocates, but I was satisfied they at least knew what the position of the new SDU command was on the subject. It would no longer be as simple as a teacher sticking his or her head out into the hallway and yelling "come lock him up!!!"

The school year went as well as could be expected. There wasn't anything exceptional to occur. There were no major incidences or setbacks. It was time to renew the APD/APS Memorandum Of Understanding (MOU), but there wasn't anything significant to the traditional back and forth with any contract development. Things seemed to be leveling out between the APD and APS working relationship, and compromise and trust seemed to be becoming more and more commonplace. Pretty much every problem facing me at this point, were all personal in nature.

After 13 years of marriage, I woke up to my first day as a divorcee for the third time on July 1st, 2011. My loving and cherished firstborn, Tamyka, lost her 7 years battle with Muscular Sclerosis the very next month on August 1st, 2011. To make matters worse, the city's new pension plan was scheduled to take effect in a couple months in October. The new plan had been stripped of so many benefits that it behooved me to retire prior to its implementation. Otherwise, I would be left with benefits that were detrimental to what I had originally signed up for almost 28 years prior. To top everything off was the looming thought of failing to accomplish what I had originally set out for in my career. Reports from back home of my father's increasing dementia would serve as the proverbial final straw (A year later on November 1st he excused himself from his usual place at the head of the dinner table to retire to his bedroom to take a nap. That would be his final physical rest as he quietly and peacefully slipped away into Ancestorship to join his granddaughter, Tamyka).

I would be cutting my career short by 2 years, but the stars were clearly aligned. The Universe was speaking and reality was at hand.

It had been an honor to work with the men and women who made up the APD SDU, and I felt a degree of disappointment that we would not be able to complete some of the projects we had developed together to make it a more successful unit. All the same, my greatest respect and appreciation is extended for the support and selfless work performed by this cast.

Sgts. Micah Connor and Calvin Tucker were absolutely instrumental in helping me gain my bearing when I was first assigned to the unit. They were extremely patient and informative throughout my time there. Investigators Larry Bacon (RIP), who was an academy classmate of mine, and Richard Williams (RIP) both served more as mentors for me in the SDU. We had a relationship more akin to being brothers than co-workers. Richard and I spent hours poring over philosophies and designing innovative approaches to student mentorship type endeavors. Investigators R. Huffman, T. Austin, D. L. Dixon, H. Nowell, and Patrice Jackson were outstanding cops and individuals. Each and every one of them took a personal interest and a vested stake in the children they watched over in the schools. Officers R. K. Williams, D. Dixon, D. Terrell, L. Bennett, R. Cambridge, and Veronica Campbell were truly dedicated and committed to their jobs as Alarm Response Officers. They provided an excellent service to the unit and department.

I left the department without any fanfare. I refused to engage in the traditional retirement celebrations and the like. I could not bring myself to accept accolades for having simply done my job to earn a paycheck. In my mind, there was nothing exceptional about that. In fact, all things considered, I wasn't feeling like much of a success in any area of my life in that precise moment. I had even planned out the announcement of my retirement in such a way that it wouldn't even be announced in the weekly command staff meeting, as was tradition. I didn't want to be bothered with the disingenuous congratulations and pats on the back by the executive command staff. I simply wanted to fade away in the hopes that I had made a difference in how policing was perceived by the community, as well as how the community was perceived by the average officer.

It had been almost 3 decades since my first day on the job when I'd sat in that sergeant's patrol car, action-less to the atrocity I'd just witnessed. I had spent the following decades making atonement for my original sin of standing mute at a time when I should have at least expressed my outrage at the sergeant's actions. Although I never forgave myself, I only hoped that my refusal to stand quietly in the wings for the rest of my career had in some small measure, made up for my original shortcoming.

I also resolved that I would not give up my quest for Chief of Police. Maybe it didn't happen the way I anticipated or expected, but that didn't mean it still couldn't happen in the future. Sometimes, despite our best-laid plans, the Universe simply has another inconceivable option in the works. My ultimate hope was that through all the years... through all the battles... through all the struggles... through all the hardships and sacrifice, I was somehow able to restore some degree of clarity to the hastily blurring Thin Blue Line.

CONCLUSION

It has always been, and continues to be, my contention that the healing of the open wound that festers between law enforcement and the citizens they serve must start with the police themselves. Further along these lines, it must emanate from the very top of these agencies and disseminate down through the ranks. The prevailing "us against them" culture that usually has origins in the police academy must be completely be decimated and replaced with a more profound notion of citizenship. That is to say, "we're all in this together." After dedicating 35 years of my life to law enforcement, I have every respect for the Thin Blue Line as a concept of fraternalism. I do, however, draw the line when the spirit of the Thin Blue Line is invoked for the distorted or perverted purposes of closing ranks at a time when accountability is the obvious and responsible path to take. While there is absolutely no question as to the honorableness of all the brave men and women who put themselves in harm's way on a daily basis, greater emphasis on the value of compassion and humility needs to be cultivated in the hearts and minds of many of our civic heroes and she-roes. While the same could be expected of the average citizen in our society, I still contend that the healing process MUST start at the steps of every police headquarters around this great nation.

As stated earlier in the text, a great deal of officers' attitudes toward the public are merely reflections of the treatment they receive from their own commanders. A classic cycle of abuse.

Supervisors and managers have no control over officers' pay, but they can have an influence on and contribute to officer's morale and sense of importance to the organization. Case in point – one of the things I despise most in life is when someone treats my existence with indifference. Nothing gets my goat more than to be standing in the doorway of a higher-ranking officer on the phone and he or she doesn't even make eye contact to at least confirm my presence and obvious request for an audience. Clearly, I would not be shadowing your threshold if there did not exist an issue that I, at least, considered of some degree of importance. Whenever an employee would present themselves in my doorway, I would always establish eye contact with them and offer some sort of jester that I would be with them directly. I would then advise whoever I was on the phone with that I would get back with them later and then entertain whatever concerns the officer had. It didn't matter if it was my wife or the chief of police on the line. To have an officer present him/herself to you and personally witness you advising the chief that you have an officer who just presented themselves for your audience, and you'll get back with him/her later has a profound effect on how that officer perceives your estimation of his/her worth to the organization. Consider this: The officer is at your door, and you advise a higher ranking officer that you'll get back with them in 15 minutes. In the big picture, you've done several things. You've indicated to the chief that you value the needs and the time of your employees. You've indicated to the officer that you value his contribution to the organization, while at the same time conveying to him/her that they have 15 minutes to present their case. More than likely, the jester will be reciprocated with a higher level of commitment, dedication, and most importantly, loyalty from that officer. It's the simplest things that go the longest way. Morale is down in police departments nationally. Mostly due to supervisors/commanders constantly missing opportunities to demonstrate to their employees their appreciation for the job they do. Like I said, we can't do anything about pay issues, but the ability to have a positive effect on the work environment is well within the grasp and control of law enforcement leadership.

NAMEASCRIBEAPHOBIA

The condition or phenomena of "Nameascribeaphobia": The fear that commanders acquire regarding affixing their signature to things. Apparently afraid to see their own name in writing. They want the title, pay, and respect the particular position affords; but they apparently scared sh-tless of the responsibility that comes along with the rank. So they play it safe by not affixing their signature to anything that's remotely non-conformance with the status quo, or unorthodox in nature... Regardless of how much it may simply be the RIGHT thing to do.

One of the things that made a strong impression on me as I entered the command level ranks was the power of the “signature.” As a lower ranking officer, I'd held out some hope that there must have been some factor far above my pay grade which explained why commanders refused to give their approval of things that clearly were the solution to long held pervasive dysfunction within the police department. It seemed the more obvious and simple the solution, the more reluctant the commander was to issue an order to remedy the deficit. I mean, just plain ole common sense and human decency would resolve 80% of the issues plaguing the department. I couldn't wait until my first command level staff meeting to have the opportunity to see what mechanism or logical phenomenon was the cause of making the obvious so oblivious. I would finally see that what ties the hands of the upper ranks and keeps them from making seemingly easy decisions to improve our delivery of services to the community and improve the work environment for our hard working officers. After all, after 34 years in law enforcement (at that point in my career), if I hadn't learned anything else, I knew that things are seldom as they appear on the surface. I was extremely saddened to find that there was no torture session taking place. No threat of physical harm to anyone's family or person. Nope! Not so much as a threat of a horse's head in the bed or a fish wrapped in news paper. Not even the slightest indication or threat of reprisals toward any commander in the room. It was simply a case of commanders knowing what was expected of them and an unwillingness to challenge the ethicality, constitutionality, or even borderline criminality of long held departmental systemic practices. I watched issue after issue go around the table. Every issue required no more than the appropriate commander's approval of an action. A mere signature on the god---n paper. No one was willing to take the responsibility of a resulting shortcoming or less than stellar outcome. A bunch of commanders afraid of their own shadows. Insurmountable fear of losing, in a single act, what had taken them an entire career of a--kissing and boot-licking to obtain. With regularity, the only commanders to speak up against some of the questionable, at best, proposals were majors Khirus Williams (retired) and Valerie Dalton (retired). Were it not for them, I truly would have been the lone voice of accountability in almost every command staff meeting. However, with just as much consistency, our contentions would be politely ignored or overruled by the deputy chief. The clearly unethical order would go forth. It seemed that week after week, the three of us would be challenged with another clearly unconstitutional or unethical initiative presented in the name of fighting crime. We would constantly voice or opinion that the ends do not always justify the means. Especially since we're supposed to be the upholders of the law and constitution... We were definitely 3 flies in the ointment.

Of course, it would only be a matter of time before Khirus would also be demoted back down to lieutenant under questionable circumstances. He opted to take early retirement before the demotion became official.

High command spends so much time crucifying officers for making what amounts to honest mistakes that they figure the best way to not fall to scrutiny themselves is to not make a decision in the first place --- at any time --- for any reason --- at any cost! I learned real fast that a commander can actually be about the business of fighting crime and improving the quality of life of the citizens that he's sworn to protect and serve - by a mere signature. A commander can actually put in place processes and mechanisms that serve to improve the working conditions of their officers - by a mere signature. In fact, a whole lot of sh-t can be fixed by simply affixing your name to a god---n piece of paper. Who'd have thunk it???

Throughout my career, and even more so in retirement, people often ask me to sum up my police career. I always have to shamefully admit that I spent 40% of my time policing criminals and 60% of it policing police! While I don't classify my struggle as being one against what is classically defined as "corruption," it was without question, a constant uphill battle against blatant misconduct and systemic, unethical, and unconstitutional practices. I truly felt that if I didn't speak out or step in, no one else would. My tendency to not just speak out, but to take action, caused me numerous setbacks in my career. However, I felt there was more to this job than climbing the ladder, so to speak. To me, it was more important to look back over my career and know that I fought the good fight outside and inside of the precinct walls. Though from the very beginning my primary objective was always to be the chief of police, there was always something more deeply rooted in my spirit which drove me to risk all for the sake of honoring the true and noble purpose of this profession I still love so dearly. I never set out to be the "Accountability Police," but When The Thin Blue Line Begins To Blur... and you're the son of Mamadou and Ruth Yabuku... there really is but one path to take...

Memoirs of an Atlanta Police Commander's struggle to maintain accountability within the APD

ABOUT THE AUTHOR:

Khalfani B. Yabuku is a retired police commander of the Atlanta Police Department (APD) in Atlanta, Georgia. He has almost 35 years of law enforcement experience. He began his career in law enforcement as a Military Police officer in 1977. He later served for a decade as a US Army Reserves Counter-Terrorism Special Agent Supervisor. He joined the APD in 1984 and retired in 2011, after almost 28 years of service. He holds a BA Degree in Criminology and a Masters Degree in Public Administration/Police Management. He is a certified Fitness Instructor, certified Shao-Lin Kung-Fu Instructor and certified Firearms Instructor. He is the Owner/Operator/Chief Instructor of Atlanta based, Triple F Training, LLC (tripleftraining.com) – a company which teaches Fitness, Fighting and Firearms techniques to the law enforcement, military and civilian communities.

79321574R00178

Made in the USA
Columbia, SC
30 October 2017